P9-CPZ-888

BLACK SEA

Constantinople ● Scutari

Mt. Athos

● Troy

egean
Sea

's
boea

ASIA MINOR

Rhodes

SYRIA

Crete

Cyprus

● Baalbek

● Damascus

E A N   S E A

PALESTINE

Jerusalem

Dead Sea

Masada

Alexandria

● Petra

Desert of Tih

EGYPT   Cairo   ● Suez

River Nile

Mt. Sinai ▲

Gulf of Suez

Libyan Desert

EDWARD LEAR
The Life of a Wanderer

EDWARD LEAR

The Life of a Wanderer

by

VIVIEN NOAKES

HOUGHTON MIFFLIN COMPANY

BOSTON

1969

First American Edition 1969   R

Copyright © 1968 by Vivien Noakes
All rights reserved. No part of this work may be
reproduced or transmitted in any form by any
means, electronic or mechanical, including
photocopying and recording, or by any
information storage or retrieval
system, without permission
in writing from the
publisher.

Library of Congress
Catalog Card Number 69-15024

Printed in the United States of America

To
Anya, Jonathan and Benedict

Preface

'I cannot help thinking that my life, letters and diaries would be as interesting as many that are now published' wrote Lear in 1873, shortly before he left for a tour of India with his old servant, Giorgio Kokali, and before going he went through all his papers and letters and sorted them into bundles in case he should not return. He did come back to live another fourteen years, and when he died in San Remo he left these papers, still methodically arranged, to the trusteeship of his literary executor.

Perhaps it was the distance from England, or may be it was Victorian discretion, but most of these carefully preserved documents of Lear's life were then apparently destroyed. Some of the letters were returned to their writers and thirty years of diaries were kept, a few small family heirlooms were sent to his nephew's children in New Zealand—but the rest is lost.

In working on this book I have drawn in particular on the diaries, now in the Houghton Library, Harvard, and the letters Lear wrote to Chichester Fortescue, Lord Carlingford, published as the *Letters* and *Later Letters of Edward Lear* and preserved now in the Somerset Record Office. Of the letters he wrote to his sister Ann covering the years from 1837 to her death in 1861 no trace has been found, though these were still in existence in the 1930s in South Africa. Lear's great-great-niece who owned them had several copies made of which only one now seems to be extant, and it is from this typed copy that I have also extensively drawn.

Even had all his papers been preserved it is doubtful if we would have known a lot more about Lear's childhood, for he hardly ever referred to this desperately unhappy time. However, he did occasionally recall incidents in his diary, and facts about his family are to be found in public records, so that this part of his life has been built up from a mixture of concrete facts and speculation and

7

Preface

there are still doubts about his childhood which will probably never be settled.

For narrative reasons I have not always indicated omissions from the middle of a quotation, and similarly I have occasionally paragraphed text which was originally continuous—I have not, however, altered or distorted the sense by doing this but simply abbreviated a lengthy passage or made it easier to read. There are very few of these modifications and in every case the exact reference has been given so that any student of Lear's writings may examine the original manuscript himself.

'It is queer (and you would say so if you saw me) that I am the man as is making some three or four thousand people laugh in England all at one time', Lear wrote after the publication of *More Nonsense* in 1871, and part of the fascination of Lear is in discovering the tragedy of the humorous, compassionate, much-loved man he was.

Contents

Contents

III. SAN REMO 1869–88

Part I

MR LEAR

CHAPTER ONE

Childhood

1812–28

Edward Lear was born in Holloway on May 12th, 1812. He was the twentieth child of Jeremiah Lear, a London stockbroker, and his wife Ann.

It was the second year of the Regency, an age of exaggerated contrasts, of rich patronage and struggling industrial awakening. The boldness and grace of Nash's London, of the fashionable new houses built around the Regent's Park with their Grecian porticos and ostentatious stucco, contrasted sharply with the cramped poverty of the tenement houses springing up around the textile factories in the industrial towns of the north. There may have been time in more privileged circles for the young ladies to titter over the gallant officers of the militia in their scarlet tunics, and for the young and the ageing to pursue their amours in the fashion set by the Royal court: in under-privileged circles a working day which could last from four in the morning until eight at night left no time for such frivolities.

But England was moving towards another age, a time of agitation and reform, and alongside the picturesque figure of the Regency buck was the dedicated, purposeful middle class evangelist. Thomas Bowdler purified Shakespeare for the family in 1802, and in 1807 William Wilberforce succeeded in abolishing the Slave Trade: a frightening narrow-mindedness on the one hand, and a real sense of moral responsibility on the other, were preparing the way for Victorian England.

Lear seldom spoke of his family, and what little he said was misleading. 'My own [name]', he once told a friend, 'as I think you know is really LØR, but my Danish Grandfather picked off the two

13

dots and pulled out the diagonal line and made the word Lear
(the two dots and the line and the O representing the sound -ea).
If he threw away the line and the dots only he would be called
Mr Lor, which he didn't like'[1]—which is delightful, but quite
untrue.

At the end of the seventeenth century, George Leare, the son of
a butcher from Gillingham in Dorset, came up to London. He was
apprenticed for seven years to a London fruiterer, and in 1692 he
became a member of the Fruiterers' Company, one of the City
livery companies, and a Freeman of the City of London. He never
learnt to write, but within twenty years he had become Renter
Warden of the Company, and was firmly established in the City.
He died in 1745, and was buried in the vault of St Anne's, Westminster: it was a quiet funeral at his own request, with 'only a
hearse and three coaches and twelve branch candles'.

George Leare had at least seven children, and some of them were
apparently connected with a sugar-refining business which the Lear
family established in the middle of the eighteenth century.[2] At this
time refining was immensely profitable, for England had a virtual
monopoly of trade with the West Indies—even sugar for the Continent had to come through British ports—and refiners were opu-
lent and respectable.

In this successful family business we find Edward's grandfather
Henry Lear. The earliest mention of him is in 1744 when he was
married at All Hallows, London Wall, the church of his bride,
Margaret Lester. He was living then in the drab river-side parish of
St Benet's, Paul's Wharf, and working in Thames Street just above
London Bridge. Jeremiah—Edward's father—was born in 1757,
the youngest of six children, and when he was six his father died of
a sudden fever at the home to which the family had moved in
Whitechapel. Margaret Lear carried on the business after her
husband's death, and Jeremiah later joined her as a sugar refiner.

In 1788 he married a young Whitechapel girl, Ann Clark
Skerrett—he was thirty-one and she was nineteen. Family tradition says that they eloped, though this is unlikely as the banns were
called three times; but they were married out at Wanstead in
Essex which was several miles from where either of them lived, and

as nobody from either family was there to witness the ceremony it does look as if they didn't approve of the marriage.[3] We don't know why this was, but it may have been because they came from different social backgrounds—for although Jeremiah's ancestors had been very successful they were undoubtedly 'trade', whilst Ann's family were not.[4]

Her great-great-grandfather—John Grainger, Gentleman—lived in the hamlet of Sunnyside, five miles outside Newcastle; he had six children and the youngest was Ann's great-grandmother.

Sometime after the '45 Rebellion her daughter—Ann's grandmother—Florence Brignall Usher, came south to settle in London, and when she died in 1802 she owned property in the City and in Whitechapel, which must have been where Jeremiah and Ann met. Her eldest daughter, also Florence, married an Edward Skerrett about whom we know nothing, except that he had three daughters of whom Ann was the eldest.

Jeremiah and his wife went to live in Pentonville, and here their first child, a daughter, was born on January 17th, 1790, and christened Ann. In the same year he was admitted to the Fruiterers' Company, and at once became a member of the Livery;[5] by 1797 he was Renter Warden, as George Leare had been nearly a century before, two years later he was elected Master of the Company— and he left the family business to become a stockbroker.[6]

Cobbett, as he travelled round the south of England on his rural rides, came to loathe these pretentious gentlemen who had no roots in England's soil, and who buried the green fields of Middlesex under their sprawling, status-seeking houses. Certainly a broker could become very wealthy, but he could also lose large sums of money, and as Jeremiah was now over forty and had five children to support he was taking a risk. He had some capital, for both his mother and his sister had died and left him money, and he was probably relying on his City contacts to get himself established. He chose his time well, for Stock Exchange business was expanding, and the gentle coffee-house transactions had been replaced by business-like negotiations in Sweeting's Alley; in fact, by 1802 business was so good that the brokers collected amongst themselves to build the London Stock Exchange at Capel Court in Bartholomew

eremiah bought one £50 share in the new Exchange and was
ed to call himself a Proprietor.[7]

.e prospered, and by 1806 was able to follow Cobbett's status-
.kers when he moved his family to Holloway,[8] at this time a
mall village fashionable for wealthy City gentlemen. It was high
and the air was salubrious; it was set amidst fields and woods, and
there was a coach into London every half hour. The elegant
Georgian house stood on the site of an Elizabethan archery range

Bowman's Lodge, where Edward Lear was born

on the corner of the Holloway Road and the Seven Sisters Road, and
was called Bowman's Lodge. From the large first floor drawing-
room there was a fine view south over the countryside towards
London, and one of Edward's earliest memories was of being
wrapped in a blanket and held to the window so that he could see
the illuminations celebrating the victory of Waterloo.

The family increased yearly, but many of them died as babies.
After Ann came three Sarahs, for the Lears persisted in using a

name until one of the children survived, and three Henrys. Then there was Mary, Eleanor, Jane, Olivier, Harriett, Cordelia, Frederick, Florence, Charles, Catherine, Edward, and finally a second Catherine.[9] There were two others, a boy and a girl, but they apparently died unnamed. Perhaps it isn't surprising that when their mother died in 1844 the cause of her death is given as 'general decay'.[10]

It was a large family to support, and they appear to have lived in some style. It is said that they had twelve carriages, and it seems likely that Jeremiah was living to the limit of his income, and even beyond it. But then came the economically unsettled aftermath of the Napoleonic wars, and suddenly in 1816 Jeremiah fell a defaulter in the Stock Exchange.[11] He owed £2,150. 11s. 1d., which was then a considerable amount of money; fortunately this related only to his dealings within the Exchange, and when a friend settled his account for him by paying the creditors 2s. 6d. in the £, Jeremiah was free to resume business. But all this time bills had been coming in, and as he had no income to meet them he soon found himself very deeply in debt.

According to family tradition Jeremiah Lear became bankrupt and was committed to King's Bench Prison where he languished for four years.[12] The house, the furniture and the twelve carriages were sold; the family split up, some of the children going with Mrs Lear to 'horrid New Street' where she could be near her husband. Every day she would visit him taking with her 'a full six-course dinner, with the delicacies of the season'. The girls were put out to work as governesses, and within four months four of them had died from sudden hardships.

This tradition seems to be based on truth, but is a colourful exaggeration. Jeremiah Lear was never bankrupt, nor was he ever in the King's Bench Prison. It is likely that he did serve a short prison sentence for debt, but he kept up his regular attendance at the Livery of the Fruiterers' Company during all this time, so he couldn't have been away for long.[13] Certainly the family left Holloway, but the house wasn't sold: instead it was let furnished to a Jewish family who 'always opened the windows in thunder-storms—for the easier entrance of the Messiah, but to greater spoiling of the furniture',[14] so that brought Jeremiah capital loss

17

ıs temporary gain. Almost certainly they split up, and those
ere old enough apparently had to fend for themselves, but
re are later references to all but one of the girls, four of them
ın't have died, at this stage anyway.

o ease the burden on his mother, Edward was given to Ann to
looked after. He was just four, and from then on—even when
ıey were back at Bowman's Lodge again—Mrs Lear had nothing
more to do with his upbringing. He was a rather ugly, short-
sighted, affectionate little boy, and he was bewildered and hurt by
her unaccountable rejection of him. He understood a little of why
they had had to leave Bowman's Lodge, and he seems to have
blamed the encumberance of house and possessions for his sudden
misery. When he grew up he became terrified of burdening himself in the same way: even the Yonghy-Bonghy-Bò possessed
only 'Two old chairs, and half a candle,—One old jug without a
handle,—' and Mr & Mrs Discobbolos proclaimed:

> We want no knives nor forks nor chairs,
> No tables nor carpets nor household cares,
> From worry of life we've fled—
> Oh! W! X! Y! Z!
> There is no more trouble ahead,
> Sorrow or any such thing— . . .[15]

In fact, Ann seems to have loved him very much and to have
been a kind and rather jolly little woman. She pulled his leg and
indulged him a little, but gave him a strict, maidenly upbringing.
She never married, although at least one man—Sir Claudius
Hunter—proposed to her, but though she loved him she 'did not,
or would not'[16] marry him. Instead she devoted herself to Edward;
she was twenty-two years older than he was, and she became as
nearly a mother to him as she could.

The family wasn't away from Bowman's Lodge for very long.[17]
Jeremiah was able to borrow £1,000 from his bank to help him to
get straight,[18] but when they came home again they lived very
simply and there was never any money to spare. But the house was
theirs once more, and it was here that Edward spent the rest of his
strange and unhappy childhood.

Ann and Jeremiah Lear, Edward's mother and father

It was a disturbing atmosphere for a child. He lived in the same
house as his mother who had probably never wanted him, and his
father whom he practically never saw; there were undoubtedly the
usual stresses which accompany financial trouble, and despite—or
because of—the twenty-one children the marriage doesn't seem to
have been a very happy one. All his life Edward tried to avoid
quarrelsome noise and arguments, and to search instead for gentleness and tranquillity.

When he was about seven the emotional strain began to show
itself in sudden changes of mood with bouts of acute depression
which he called 'the Morbids'. Significantly the first of these came
on after a rare happy evening with his father. 'The earliest of all
the morbidnesses I can recollect must have been somewhere about
1819—when my Father took me to a field near Highgate, where
was a rural performance of gymnastic clowns etc.—& a band. The
music was good—at least it attracted me:—& the sunset & twilight
I remember as yesterday. And I can recollect crying half the night
after all the small gaiety broke up—& also suffering for days at the
memory of the past scene.'[19] He was a sad, lonely little boy grasping onto happiness when it came and savouring every bit of it—

and broken-hearted when it had slipped beyond his grasp again.

But even earlier, when he was only five or six, had come the first attack of epilepsy—'the demon' as he called it. It must have been inherited, for his sister Jane was also an epileptic and he remembered watching her attacks.[20] His own seizures were often violent, and for a child they were terrible and frightening. The illness affected his whole life profoundly: it was a constant threat for sometimes he had several attacks a day, and though they grew fewer as he became older they were no less violent. He had warning before they came on—the aura epileptica—so that he was able to get out of the way, and apparently nobody apart from his family ever realised that he was an epileptic.[21] But this perpetual secrecy forced him into isolation. Even today epilepsy is a lonely disease, and although the idea of 'demoniac possession' can now be laughed at there are still irrational lingerings of shame. In the early nineteenth century it was obscured by ignorance and old wives' tales, and one of these was that attacks could be brought on by masturbation. Lear certainly believed that there could be a connection between the two, and as an adult he constantly blamed the attacks on his lack of will power.[22] The usual threat offered to a little boy was that his penis would drop off and, like the Pobble whose toes disappeared when the scarlet flannel wrapper was taken away, Edward must sometimes have thought that he would be happier without it; the Pobble was given a feminine concoction of 'Lavendar water tinged with pink', and perhaps this was the best solution.

Doctors urged that children suffering from epilepsy should never be allowed to sleep by themselves, and it sounds as if sister Harriett was entrusted with disciplining him, for many years later Lear 'reflected on days long gone—when I was but 8—if so many years old. And this demon oppressed me then "I not knowing" its worry & misery. Every morning in the little study when learning my lessons: all day long: & always in the evening & at night. Nor could I have been more than 6 I think—for I remember whole years before I went to school at 11. The strong will of sister Harriett put a short pause to misery—but very short. How well I remember that evening!—Thus a sorrow so inborn and ingrained so to speak, was evidently part of what I have been born to suffer—& could

20

not have been so far avoided willed I never so much so to do.'[23]

No clinical treatment for epilepsy had yet been discovered, but a careful diet and plenty of exercise certainly helped, and it may have been to relieve the attacks that Ann and Edward went for a holiday to Margate. A belief in the therapeutic value of spa waters was centuries old, but the idea that sea water and sea air could also be salutary was only just becoming fashionable. 'Sea air and Sea Bathing together were nearly infallible, one or the other of them being a match for every Disorder of the Stomach, the Lungs or the Blood,'[24] wrote Jane Austen in 1817, and she summed up the fashionable belief.

The resort was easily reached from London by the Margate hoys, small sailing boats which carried their passengers down the busy Thames and out into the estuary. It couldn't offer the fashionable Pump Rooms and glittering clientele of other resorts, but there was plenty to excite a small boy, and years later Edward reminded Ann of 'the hawk Mr Cox had;—& the colliers disbarking coal at the pier—& the windmills—& the chimney sweep you so cruelly made me walk round and round to be sure he was not smoking—shocking! My imperfect sight in those days—ante-spectacled—formed everything into a horror.'[25]

Ann was concerned about his health and her anxiety was justified, but her single-minded attention to him wasn't a good thing, and he grew up swathed by protective older sisters. Often ill and thrown back on his own resources his imagination became his plaything; but though a more boisterous boyhood would have been much better for him and a more balanced childhood would have made him a happier man, it would also have made him a different one.

It was from Ann that he had all his early tuition, and she probably taught him from one of the popular question and answer guidebooks—*Magnall's Questions*, or *The Child's Guide to Knowledge*—which were 'intended to awaken a spirit of laudable curiosity in young minds'. They certainly succeeded with Lear, for his soundly based but incomplete education left him always anxious to find out more. 'I am almost thanking God that I was never educated,' he wrote when he was forty-seven, 'for it seems to me that 999 of those who are so, expensively and laboriously, have lost all before they arrive at my age—and remain like Swift's Stulbruggs—cut and dry for life, making no use of their earlier-gained treasures: whereas, I seem to be on the threshold of knowledge . . .'[26]

Ann read to him a good deal, tales of classical mythology and stories from the Bible, and while he was still small he discovered the modern poets—and particularly Byron. When Lear was born Wordsworth and Coleridge were still writing, Shelley had just been sent down from Cambridge, Byron had published the first two cantos of *Childe Harold*, and Keats was apprenticed to a surgeon at Edmonton and had hardly yet discovered poetry: by the time Lear was twelve Keats, Shelley and Byron were all dead. Byron's death affected him in an extraordinary way: 'Pale cold moon', he wrote in 1861, 'yet now, as in 1823—ever strangely influencing me. Do you remember the small yard & the passages at —— in 1823 & 1824—when I used to sit there in the cold looking at the stars, &, when I heard that Ld. Byron was dead, stupified & crying.'[27] The poet-idol, the social outcast, the figure-head of Greek independence—it was a mature hero for a boy of eleven, and it's unlikely that he knew that Byron too was an epileptic. Lear's reaction to the news from Missolonghi is like that of the fourteen-year-old Tennyson who lay numbed by the sense of finality, and carved on a sandstone rock the words, 'Byron is dead'.

But the most important part of Ann's tuition was her enjoyment of painting. Jeremiah had owned some good paintings, no doubt in his wealthier years, and he must have encouraged his children's interest, for one of the downstairs rooms at Bowman's Lodge, next to Ann's room and just across the hall from the nursery, was set aside as the painting-room—and to Edward it was the happiest in the house. A little of his early work has survived,[28] and it shows that he was talented in a rather precise way. Ann taught him to paint flowers and butterflies and birds—in fact she taught him one of the social accomplishments as she herself had learnt it.

Lear tells us that when he was eleven he went to school, but nothing at all has survived from this period. At about the same time he began to stay with his sister Sarah who had married in 1822 and was living in Arundel. There is a tradition in the Lear family about

Drawing by Lear's sister, Ann, who gave him his early drawing lessons

Sarah's marriage.[29] One day, Jeremiah Lear was walking in the City when he saw a name-plate inscribed 'Jeremiah Lear'. He was intrigued, and decided to introduce himself to his namesake: the two families came to know each other, and in this Jeremiah Lear's house Sarah met her future husband, Charles Street. The second Lear family lived at Batsworth Park, Lyminster, about three miles south of Arundel. There were three children, and the youngest— George Lear—was articled in 1827 to the solicitors Ellis and Blackmore of Gray's Inn. In the same year this firm took on a young clerk named Charles Dickens, and when he was writing the *Pickwick Papers*, he remembered George as 'the Articled Clerk, who has paid a premium, and is an attorney in prospective, who runs a tailor's bill, receives invitations to parties, knows a family in Gower Street, and another in Tavistock Square, who goes out of town every long vacation to see his father, who keeps live horses innumerable; and who is, in short, the very aristocrat of clerks'.[30] Coming from life with his sisters at Bowman's Lodge, Edward must have felt a little overwhelmed by such a worldly family.

The countryside around Arundel where Sarah lived has changed very little since then, with rounded hills and sudden scurrying

23

streams running into the River Arun, and small stonebuilt villages which lie in the gentleness of the downs. Even as a boy Lear was always unusually aware of his natural surroundings and he loved the wide, peaceful landscape; the tranquillity of the hills must have come as a relief from the unhappy atmosphere at Bowman's Lodge. He was often in Sussex between 1823 and 1829, and some of his happiest memories were of these days. He made a lot of new friends there, and away from home he found another part of his personality, for he discovered that he could make people happy by making them laugh. He understood so well the unhappiness of life that for him making people happy was something positive and real. He was content to be thought a rather lovable oddity, '3 parts crazy—& wholly affectionate',[31] and when he was nineteen he wrote: 'My Sussex friends always say that I can do nothing like other people'.[32] This was particularly true of a family called Drewitt; they lived in Peppering, a tiny village beside the River Arun, and it was for one of the daughters, Eliza Drewitt, that Lear wrote his earliest surviving poems.[33]

The first of these is called 'Ode to a Chinaman':

Who art thou—sweet little China Man?—
Your name I want to know
With your lovely face so pale and wan—
With a high diddle diddledy do.

Your high cheek bones:—your screwed up mouth,
How beautiful they be!—
And your eyes that ogle from north to south,
With a high diddle diddledy dee!

. . . . .

'Good folks'—(& he shook his noddle-ding-dong)—
'It's enough for you to know—
That in spite of my eyebrows—two feet long—
I'm Miss Eliza's beau!!'

The second, which is incomplete, is called 'Miss Maniac'. It is the sad tale of a young girl who is sent away from her father's house after the birth of an illegitimate baby. She has been deserted by the gay young buck who is the father, and as she wanders brooding on the happiness she once knew, her grief destroys her reason and she goes mad. The rhyme is intentionally bathetic and absurd, and with almost every couplet there is a drawing which completes the descent into the ridiculous. It is an immature humour, but it does bring out two characteristics of Lear's nonsense—a combination of humour with real sadness, and an interdependence of words and pictures. It also expresses Lear's belief that happiness is a thing of the past, and the present is incomprehensibly sad.

The poem, 'Peppering Roads', which he wrote for the Drewitts when he was seventeen, is quite different:

> If you wish to see roads in perfection,
> A climax of cart ruts and stones;
> Or if you have the least predilection
> For breaking your neck or your bones;
> If descents and ascents are inviting,
> If your ankles are strangers to sprains,
> If you'd cure a penchant for sliding,
> Then to Peppering go by all means.
>
> Take a coach some dark night in November,
> A party of four within side;
> Ah! I once had that jaunt, I remember,
> And really I pretty near died.
> First across to my neighbour I tumbled,
> Then into the next lady's lap,
> For at every fresh rut we were jumbled,
> And jolted at every new gap.
>
> So that when we had finished our journey,
> The coachman, who opened the door,
> Found us tangled so very top turvy,
> We rolled out in one bundle, all four.
> And then we were so wisped together,
> Legs, dresses, caps, arms blacks and whites
> That some minutes lapsed before ever,
> They got us completely to rights.

Mr Lear

If you go in a gig you are sure to
Get lost in a mist on the hills;
There's a gibbeted thief on a moor, too,
Your mem'ry with murder that fills.
And besides if you ride in what fashion
You will—you are sure to get splashed,
Till you get quite incensed in a passion,
And peppery—like mutton that's hashed.

Or if on some fine frosty morning
You make up your mind for a walk,
Oh! ere such be your project, take warning
For sunbeams will liquefy chalk.
Step by step you get clogged so—for sarten,
With chalk round your shoes like a rope,
For to comfort—and eke Day and Martin,
You might as well walk upon soap.

From one end of the walk to the other,
It's one awful bootjack to feet—
One mighty pedestrial slither
For Christianlike progress unmeet!
Oh! The Peppering Roads! Sure 'tis fit there
Should be some requital at last,
So the inmates you find when you get there
Amply pay you for all you have past.'[34]

He made other, older acquaintances in Sussex, and it was these
who influenced both his immediate and eventual careers.[35]

The grossly uneven distribution of wealth in England at this
time had one particular advantage—the rich had money to spend
on beautiful things. They built themselves magnificent houses and
had their gardens landscaped in the style of Capability Brown,
then they filled their homes with beautiful furniture—and with
pictures. This was a great age of English landscape painting, and
although Constable was largely unrecognised in England, Turner
found both patrons and friends in the rich. One of these was the

One of Lear's sisters, drawn by him in 1832

Earl of Egremont who lived at Petworth, twelve miles north of Arundel. He was famous for the encouragement he gave to artists, and for the splendid paintings he had gathered together at his home. This was before the days of big national collections, and privately owned works of art weren't generally seen by the public, so when Lear first visited Petworth in the 1820s the paintings must have excited him. Perhaps he shared some of the charming enthusiasm of the author of *British Galleries of Art*, writing in 1824: 'To those who have not already seen the princely domain at Petworth, I would fain convey such a notion of it, that, till they set out to visit it for themselves, it may thus dwell in the distance before them, like a bright spot in the land of promise.'

During one of his visits to Sussex Lear was introduced to Lord Egremont, and to the family of another of Turner's patrons, Walter Ramsden Fawkes. In 1826 he met Lord de Tabley who had founded the British Institution for the Encouragement of British Art twenty years before, and had opened his house in Hill Street to the public so that they might share his delight in the paintings he had collected—for patronage was still guided by enthusiasm and was not yet ruled by the value of investment.

In Sussex Lear found himself on the fringe of the painter's world, and during these years his childhood enjoyment of painting matured into an ambition to become a painter. He developed an admiration for Turner which lasted throughout his life,[36] but if he hoped to follow him and become a landscape painter he would need to go to an art school—perhaps the Royal Academy where Turner had studied and where he now occasionally taught—or at least to be financially independent whilst he taught himself how to paint.

If this had been in his mind it was suddenly quite impossible. Jeremiah Lear was now over seventy, and he had decided that it was time to retire. He had found a small house in Gravesend for himself and his wife and one of their daughters, Florence—but he wasn't able to make any provision for Edward whom he probably regarded as Ann's responsibility anyway. She had apparently inherited a small annual income from her grandmother so they weren't destitute, though Edward always spoke melodramatically of being 'thrown out into the world without a penny'. But it did mean that any plans he may have had must be put on one side—at least for the moment—and at fifteen and a half he had to set about earning his own living.

CHAPTER TWO

The Family of Parrots

1828-32

Like the ancient Medes and Persians,
Always by his own exertions
He subsisted on those hills;—
Whiles,—by teaching children spelling,—
Or at times by merely yelling,—
Or at intervals by selling
'Propter's Nicodemus Pills.'[1]

Upper North Place, Grays Inn Road is not a fashionable part of London, and it was here—on the top floor at No. 28—that Ann and Edward found rooms they could afford. Then Edward started looking for work, and he began doing 'uncommon queer shop-sketches—selling them for prices varying from ninepence to four shillings: colouring prints, screens, fans; awhile making morbid disease drawings, for hospitals and certain doctors of physic.'[2] As well as this he visited houses in Cavendish Square and St James's to teach drawing, probably through introductions from his Sussex friends.

In fact, so little has survived from this time in his life that it is almost impossible to know what happened, but sometime between 1828 and 1830 he began to earn his living by drawing birds. There was a vogue then for large, lavishly illustrated books about the new and exotic animals and birds which were being brought back to England by sailors, and naturalists on scientific voyages of discovery. The landed gentry could go further and collect the animals themselves, and occasional wandering zebra and wild hog, or a handful of strutting peacocks were considered very *à la mode*. Private menageries, even on quite a big scale, weren't new; Henry I had formed his own royal collection of animals at Woodstock at the beginning of the twelfth century. This was later transferred to the Tower, and in 1829 the animals were taken over by the newly formed Zoological Society of London and formed the nucleus of the Zoological Gardens which were opened in Regent's Park.

As the system for the classification of animals became established, naturalists turned their interest to the animals in their own countries, especially where there were signs of whole species being exterminated. In 1820 Audubon began on his task of drawing and cataloguing all the birds of North America before they disappeared at the slaughtering hands of the new colonists, and in England Prideaux Selby and Sir William Jardine were at work on *Illustrations of British Ornithology*, a beautiful book which is now almost forgotten. The first volume appeared in 1825 and set the style of lively ornithological draughtsmanship which was followed for the next fifty years: it is a large book full of delightful birds with sweeping tails and impudent expressions, and there is nothing of the stuffed, dead specimens of most earlier books. By the time Lear was sixteen he was working with Selby,[3] in fact he may have been helping him with drawings for the later volumes.

They probably met through the daughter of Turner's patron, Walter Ramsden Fawkes—a Mrs Godfrey Wentworth. Her father had been an amateur zoologist as well as a patron of the arts, and he had known Selby. Lear always spoke with gratitude of Mrs Wentworth's interest in him, and he tells us that through her he was introduced to the Zoological Society in London.[4] Mrs Wentworth may have seen Lear's talent for drawing, and decided that she would help him to get started; perhaps she knew that Selby was looking for a young assistant, or maybe she persuaded him that he could use one. It was a fortunate apprenticeship for it taught Lear to be bold and lively and imaginative in his work, in fact encouraging characteristics which were probably already there.

In 1830 Lear decided to try a book on his own, and on June 16th he was given permission to make drawings from the parrots in the new Zoological Gardens, and at Bruton Street where some of the birds were being housed until the aviary was completed.[5] He

Baudin's Cockatoo, from 'The Family of Parrots'

may already have done some work at the Zoo, for the previous
year a visitors' guide-book, *The Gardens of the Zoological Society
Delineated*, had been published, and the drawing of the Blue and
Yellow Maccaws is signed E.L.[6]

Unlike earlier naturalists, Lear decided to confine himself to
one family, and he chose the parrot. They were fashionable and
exotic birds, and they varied from the brown-feathered Baudin's
Cockatoo to the brilliant Red and Yellow Maccaw. Like Audubon,
Lear never worked from a stuffed bird unless he had to, but unlike

31

Audubon who was working with wild birds, he didn't first kill the animal and draw the gradually decaying carcass; instead he drew the live, moving, screaming bird. Whilst the keeper held it he took measurements of the wing span, the length of the legs, and the size of the beak; then he made quantities of pencil studies and careful colour notes.[7] Sitting in the parrot house he was obviously regarded as something of a curiosity himself, for the visitors came and stared at him and his work, and as a change from drawing birds he would make indignant, Doyle-like sketches of the bonneted ladies and startled gentlemen who peered at him.

When the details of the drawing were worked out Lear transferred it in reverse onto a lithographic plate. In deciding to use lithography he had found a process which was perfectly suited to him. With engraving or wood-engraving, which were the more usual methods of reproduction at this time, the original drawing had to be transferred to the plate or block by a professional engraver and much of the subtlety of drawing could be lost on the way. But with lithography, little extra skill was needed to transfer the drawing beyond the essential one of being able to draw at all, and this meant that Lear could carry out the whole process himself and control exactly what was printed. He took the finished plates to Charles Hullmandel, the lithographic printer in Great Marlborough Street, and in Hullmandel's studio he could look at the pulls as they came off. He made trial runs of heads alone or whole birds to see how they looked, and would alter anything which didn't satisfy him before he drew the final plate. The prints were then coloured by hand, and he employed someone to do this under his supervision.

He called the book *Illustrations of the Family of Psittacidae, or Parrots*, and he planned to publish it for subscribers in fourteen folios. After working hard through the late summer and autumn of 1830 the first two were ready on November 1st. They are quite remarkable for a boy of eighteen, for they were superbly observed and confidently drawn, and they gave him an immediate reputation as an ornithological draughtsman. The next day he was nominated as an Associate of the Linnaean Society,[8] and he seemed to have found work which really suited him.

The Family of Parrots 1828-32

He worked on the parrots throughout 1831, and the drawings spilled over his rooms at Upper North Place. 'Should you come to town I am sorry that I cannot offer you a home pro tempore,' he wrote to an acquaintance in October, 'pro trumpery indeed it would be, if I did make any such offer—for unless you occupied the grate as a seat—I see no probability of your finding any rest consonant with the safety of my Parrots—seeing, that of the six chairs I possess 5 are at present occupied with lithographic prints—the whole of my exalted and delightful tenement in fact overflows with them, & for the last 12 months I have so moved—thought—looked at,—& existed among parrots—that should any transmigration take place at my decease I am sure my soul would be uncomfortable in anything but one of the Psittacidae.'[9]

In order to encourage subscribers he limited the edition to 175 copies, and the plates were destroyed after the printing. The list of subscribers was headed by Mrs Wentworth and seven members of her family, and included Lord Egremont, many leading zoologists, and the Right Hon. Lord Stanley, M.P., who was President of the Zoological Society, from whom he had borrowed several of the birds he had drawn and who later became one of the most important men in Lear's life.

Publishing his own book was a long and costly process, especially as he worked so carefully on each drawing in turn until he was satisfied with them all, and as the year went on he was finding it hard to keep going. 'I have pretty great difficulty in paying my monthly charges,' he wrote in October, 'for to pay colourer and printer monthly I am obstinately prepossessed—since I had rather be at the bottom of the River Thames—than be one week in debt— be it *never* so small. For me—who at the age of 14 & a half was turned out into the world, *literally without a farthing*—& with nought to look to for a living but his own exertions, you may easily suppose this a necessary prejudice—& indeed—the tardy paying of many of my subscribers—renders it but too difficult to procure food—& pay for publishing at once . . . I have just nine and twenty times resolved to give up parrots & all—& should certainly have done so had not my good genius with vast reluctance just 9 and 20 times set me a going again.'[10]

A month later he received an enthusiastic letter from the zoologist William Swainson, who had studied under Audubon whilst he had been in England to publish *The Birds of America.* 'Sir, I received yesterday, with great pleasure the numbers of your beautiful work. To repeat my recorded opinion of it, as a whole, is unnecessary but there are two plates which more especially deserve the highest praise; they are the New Holland Palaeornis, and the red and yellow maccaw. The latter is in my estimation equal to any figure ever painted by Barraband or Audubon, for grace of design, perspective, or anatomical accuracy. I am so particularly pleased with these, that I should feel much gratified by possessing a duplicate copy of each. They will then be framed, as fit companions in my drawing-room to hang by the side of a pair by my friend Audubon.'[11]

But despite all the praise and encouragement, Lear never finished the work, and when the twelfth folio appeared in the following April, it was the last. 'I had originally intended to have

Self portrait of Lear aged 19, October 1831

figured all the Psittacidae,' he wrote to Sir William Jardine, 'but I stopped in time, neither will there be (from me) any letterpress. Their one publication was a speculation which so far as it made me known procured me employment, but in the matter of money occasionally caused loss.'[12] Yet he'd been supplementing his income by working for other people since the middle of 1831, and as this meant that he no longer had to rely only on the *Parrots* for a living it does seem strange that he didn't go on and complete them —and what did he mean by, 'I stopped in time'?

A few weeks after the last folio of the *Parrots* came out Lear had his twentieth birthday.[13] He had grown into a tall, rather ugly, bespectacled young man, and in October 1831 he drew a self-portrait and added, '. . . this is amazingly like; add only—that both my knees are fractured from being run over which has made them peculiarly crooked—that my neck is singularly long— a most elephantine nose—& a disposition to tumble here & there— owing to being half blind and you may very well imagine my tout ensemble.'[14] He felt a youthful gaucheness in society, but he had an unassuming charm and thoughtfulness which had already attracted Mrs Wentworth's attention—all through his early manhood he found that elderly women liked to help and mother him.

He does not seem to have had many young friends in London, though he saw quite a lot of a boyhood companion from Holloway called William Nevill, and of a Sussex friend called Bernard Senior who was working in a solicitor's office with George Lear, the Pickwickian clerk. Edward and Bernard Senior explored London life together, and at some point Lear contracted syphilis.[15]

He still went down to visit Sarah, and staying in Sussex at the end of 1829 he had experimented with writing serious poetry. Some was a pastiche of Byron praising the glories of ancient Greece, and some was more personally his, like this poem written on Bury Hill, one of the east Sussex downs which looks over the Arun valley:

> When the light dies away in a calm summer's eve
> And the sunbeams grow faint and more faint in the west
> How we love to look on till the last trace they leave

Glows alone like a blush upon modesty's breast!
Lonely streak! dearer far than the glories of day
Seems thy beauty, 'mid silence and shadow enshrined,
More bright as its loneliness passes away—
And leaves twilight in desolate grandeur behind!
So when grief has made lonely and blighted our lot,
And her icy cold chain o'er our spirits has cast,
Will not memory oft turn to some thrice hallowed spot,
That shines out like a star among years that are past?
Some dream that will wake in a desolate heart,
Every chord into music that long has been hushed,
Mournful echo!—soon still—for it tolls with a smart,
That the joys which first woke it, are long ago crushed![16]

Here again was the feeling he had when he came home from
visiting the clowns with his father, the realisation that happiness—
which for Lear meant being surrounded contentedly by people he
loved—had slipped into the past. It was a theme to which he
returned frequently in his nonsense—

Often since, in the nights of June,
We sit on the sand and watch the moon;—
She has gone to the great Gromboolian plain,
And we probably never shall meet again!
Oft, in the long still nights of June,
We sit on the rocks and watch the moon;—
She dwells by the streams of the Chankly Bore,
And we probably never shall see her more.[17]

A few weeks later he tried something more lyrical:

From the pale and the deep—
From the dark and bright—
From the violets that sleep
Away from light:
From the lily that flashes
At morn's glad call—
The bee gathers honey
And sweets from all.

The Family of Parrots 1828-32

There are hearts like bees
In a world such as this,
That are given to please
Through sorrow and bliss:
Be the heaven of life
As dark as it will—
Amid pleasure and strife
They are smiling still.

They've a tear for the sad,
But there's balm in their sigh,
And they laugh with the glad
In sunshine and joy:
They give hope to the gloom
Of the mourner's thrall—
Like the bee they find honey
And sweets in all.[18]

At the end of 1831 Edward and Ann moved from Grays Inn Road to more pleasant and convenient rooms at No. 61 Albany Street, which runs down the eastern side of Regent's Park just a few minutes' walk from the zoo. Really he was too old to be living still with a protective older sister, and they didn't always get on well now. She had known how to cope with a small child, but it must have been difficult for her to know how to treat a man of twenty, and although she remained unruffled and kind, Edward found himself getting impatient and irritable with her.

Although the *Parrots* had to come to an end there was plenty of work for Lear to do, and he found himself in demand. He illustrated the *Transactions of the Zoological Society*, *The Zoology of Captain Beechey's Voyage* and *The Zoology of the Voyage of H.M.S. Beagle*,[19] the boat on which Charles Darwin had been employed as naturalist. He did drawings for a series called the Naturalists' Library,[20] and prepared for Professor Bell the lithographs of *Tortoises, Terrapins and Turtles*, which was not published until 1872. He was also working for Dr Gray of the British Museum, and John Gould.

Gould, who was eight years older than Lear, was the son of a

Mr Lear

gardener at Windsor Castle. In 1827 he had been appointed taxidermist to the Zoological Society, and during the next few years he became a self-taught zoologist. In 1830 he was given a collection of a hundred or so Indian bird skins, and when he had stuffed them he decided to publish drawings of the birds. The first folios of Lear's *Parrots* were just appearing, and Gould used the same format for his book, with notes describing the zoological features of each bird. Gould planned and wrote the book himself but he wasn't an artist, and almost all the beautiful drawings associated with his name are

Chelodina Longicollis, lithograph for 'Tortoises, Terrapins and Turtles'

the work of other people. His first book, *A Century of Birds from the Himalayan Mountains* which was published in 1831, was illustrated by his wife Edith, and Lear. But Gould apparently felt that as he had paid Lear for the drawings he could claim them as his own, and there is no mention of Lear's name anywhere—indeed in later books, though he now acknowledged Lear's help in drawings, he would quite happily subscribe plates 'by J. & E.

Tengmalm's Owl, from Gould's 'Birds of Europe'

Gould' even when Lear's signature appeared in the drawing itself.[21]

The book was a great success and was much more rewarding financially than Lear's had been, and it must have been depressing for him to see Gould appropriate his work and make a profit out of it. After this came *A Monograph of the Ramphastidae or Toucans* and a five-volume work called *The Birds of Europe*, and one summer—probably in 1831—Gould took Lear with him to the Continent to visit zoos there and make drawings of some of the birds. They went together to Holland, Switzerland and Germany, and it seems that in Amsterdam Lear committed himself to work for Gould until *The Birds of Europe* was finished—a decision he regretted, for although he worked with him on and off throughout the next six years it wasn't a happy relationship. When Gould died in 1881, Lear remembered: 'He was one I never liked really, for in spite of a certain jollity and bonhommie, he was a harsh and violent man. At the Zoological Society at 33 Bruton Street, at Hullmandels —at Broad Street ever the same, persevering hard working toiler in

his own (ornithological) line,—but ever as unfeeling for those about
him. In this earliest phase of his bird-drawing, he owed everything
to his excellent wife, & to myself,—without whose help in drawing
he had done nothing.'[22]

Nevertheless, he did some very good work for Gould particularly
in *The Birds of Europe*. He was at his best when he was drawing
majestic, unpretty birds like ravens and owls; he endowed them
with sagacious personalities, and it is tempting to wonder if Lear
found a common bond with the birds, for they too were at the mercy
of unscrupulous men.

But then in 1832 Lear was asked to do some work for a different
kind of man—Lord Stanley, heir to the Earl of Derby. At his home
outside Liverpool he had built up a private menagerie that was
famous throughout Europe, and he asked Lear to come and stay at
Knowsley and make drawings of the animals there: it was the most
far-reaching invitation of Lear's life.

CHAPTER THREE

The Knowsley Menagerie

1832–37

Later, in his morning rambles
He perceived the moving brambles—
Something square and white disclose;—
'Twas a First-class Railway-Ticket;
But, on stooping down to pick it
Off the ground,—a pea-green Cricket
Settled on my uncle's Nose.[1]

As his carriage rattled through the gates at Knowsley a new life
was beginning for Lear. At such a moment it would be happy to
think of him coming down the main avenue across the Park and
sweeping round to the foot of the steps leading to the main door:
in fact he was probably brought to the back of the house and shown
straight into the Steward's quarters—for although he had come as
Lord Stanley's guest he had also come as his employee.

The Stanley family had lived at Knowsley since the fourteenth
century when John de Stanley, grandfather of the 1st Earl of
Derby, married Isabel Lathom, who was heiress to vast estates in
the hundred of West Derby in Lancashire. The oldest part of the
house dated from the thirteenth century, but the main body of it
had been built and pulled down and rebuilt ever since then, and
most visitors found it ugly and old-fashioned and rambling. The
12th Earl had planned to rebuild the house completely, but though
he abandoned this idea he did add a vast dining-room which was
entered through a pair of Gothic doors which reached to the ceiling,
about which General Grosvenor is reputed to have asked: 'Pray,
are those doors to be opened for every pat of butter that comes into

41

the room?'[2] But the 12th Earl needed his dining-room, for he was a warm-hearted and compulsive host, and from June until November his table was always laid for forty people—except on Mondays when he invited the Liverpool neighbourhood to come and visit him in turns, and then it could be laid for as many as a hundred guests. His first wife, Lord Stanley's mother, had deserted him for the Duke of Dorset, and after her death in 1797 he married the actress Miss Elizabeth Farran, of whom it was said that she was a lady on the stage and an actress off it. It was he who founded the Derby stakes, and he was immensely proud of his stables at Knowsley.

He was now nearly eighty, but the house was still pervaded with his spirit of welcome. 'Dear old man! his joyous temperament, and his love of society and good cheer made his guests as happy and merry as himself,' Lady Shelley recalled. 'He constantly bantered the young ladies on their good looks, and about their lovers, which, though not always in the refined taste of modern times, so evidently proceeded from a natural *gaieté de coeur* and kindness, that no one could possibly have been offended.'[3]

Knowsley was a meeting place for the whole family, and Lord Derby's children, grandchildren, and great-grandchildren would all arrive for extended visits, which delighted the old man. His exceptionally ugly sister, Lucy, had married the Rev. Geoffrey Hornby, an opportunist who didn't mind about his wife's looks as the marriage gave him the living of Winwick, which was in the gift of the Earls of Derby and carried a stipend of £7,000 a year. Their second daughter had married her cousin, Lord Stanley, and their eldest son had married Lord Stanley's sister, so the families had become very interwoven.

It was through his grandsons that the Earl heard that Lear was in the house, for he began to realise that instead of sitting with him after dinner as they had always done they were slipping away as soon as they politely could; and when he asked them why this was they told him that the young man in the steward's room who had come to draw animals was such good company that they were going down to visit him. If he is such good company, said Lord Derby, then the young man shall come and dine upstairs with us.[4]

Lear had known some of the nobility of Sussex, but we don't

Vitoe Monkey: a drawing for 'Gleanings from the Menagerie at Knowsley Hall'

know if he ever mixed with them socially. In 1831, the year before he went to Knowsley, he confessed that he was 'very little used to company or society',[5] so he must have been rather startled to find himself suddenly flung into it with a reputation for being entertaining. But Lord Derby was a happily spontaneous man who probably wouldn't have worried if Lear tripped up on complicated social etiquette, and it gave him a rare opportunity for learning how to move in the top layer of English society.

Mr Lear

Knowsley at this time was a complete little village, where meat and poultry were home-killed and vegetables and fruit home-grown. In the dairy the cows were milked and the butter churned, and on the estate beer would have been brewed, horses shod and even soap and candles made—and since Lord Derby's invitations to stay extended as well to children, servants and horses, there must sometimes have been literally hundreds of people on the estate.

The day for the family and their guests would start at about 9 a.m., when the house-maid or man-servant would draw back the curtains, stir the fire into life, and set out the jugs of water and the towels for the morning wash. But Lear was always an early riser, and he would have put in two or three hours' work, drawing the animals and birds in the menagerie, before breakfast at 10 a.m. He would have worked through the morning as well, whilst the gentlemen were out shooting and riding, and the ladies talked or read or wrote long letters telling their friends what the other guests wore and did and said, and passing on the scraps of gossip which had been confided to them.

Lord Derby forbade any of his guests to shoot more than five brace of partridge in one morning for he wanted them back in time to ride out with the ladies, and Lear may have joined them for the ride round the park. He certainly joined them for dinner, and he seems to have been as great a success with some of the guests as he had been with the grandsons. 'The Earl of W[ilton] has been here for some days,' he wrote to Ann, 'he is Lord W[estminster's] 2nd son, and married to Lady Mary S[tanley]. He is extremely picturesque if not handsome, and dresses in crimson and a black velvet waistcoat when he looks like a portrait by Vandyke. Miss . . . says and so does Mrs . . . that he is a very bad man, tho he looks so nicely. But what I like about him, is that he always asks me to drink a glass of champagne with him at dinner. I wonder why he does. But I don't much care as I like the champagne. . . . I have asked why on Earth she thinks the Earl of W always asks me to drink champagne, and she began to laugh, and said, because he knows you are a clever artist and sees you always look at him and admire him: and he is a very vain man and this pleases him, and so he asks you to take wine as a reward.'[6] How sad it is that Lear

44

destroyed all the diaries that he kept at Knowsley, for this scrap, which he copied into a letter to Ann, is all that has survived.

But he didn't find all the people so colourful. A great many of them were just very rich and very dull. 'The uniform apathetic tone assumed by lofty society irks me *dreadfully*,' he told a friend, 'nothing I long for half so much as to giggle heartily and to hop on one leg down the great gallery—but I dare not.'⁷

But in the nursery it was another matter. Two of his brothers had families but they were all living in America, and Sarah's two sons were only a few years younger than he was, so this must have been the first time he had lived with small children—and he found in them an exuberant enthusiasm which was the very opposite of dullness.

'There was an old man on whose nose . . .'

He began to amuse them by drawing odd looking birds and animals and people with funny noses, and he made up ridiculous rhymes for them; and then someone asked him if he had seen a book which had been published about ten years before, called *Anecdotes and Adventures of Fifteen Gentlemen*.⁸ It contained illustrated verses like this one:

> There was a sick man of Tobago
> Liv'd long on rice-gruel and sago;
>   But at last, to his bliss,
>   The physician said this—
> 'To a roast leg of mutton you may go.'

Mr Lear

Obviously this kind of rhyme and drawing could be adapted to tell the remarkable stories of all kinds of unusual men and women, and when Lear made up some for the children they were greeted with 'uproarious delight and welcome',[9] a fitting start to his career as a nonsense writer.

But although there was a nursery full of children, and he was meeting 'half the fine people of the day',[10] Lear sometimes felt horribly lonely, and then he would escape from all the busy guests and walk alone through the park. After the unhappiness of his boyhood he found it hard to see so much money being squandered on such a fruitless, superficial existence. In September 1833 his father had died of a heart attack; he was seventy-six, and until a few months before his death he had been coming up to London from Gravesend for the meetings of the Livery of the Fruiterers' Company. So now Mrs Lear was on her own with Florence, who only lived four more years: Cordelia and Catherine died about this time as well. Compared with the harshness of his family's tragedy, life at Knowsley must have seemed unreal.

Lear worked at Knowsley on and off between 1832 and 1837, and over a hundred of the drawings he did then are preserved still in the Library there: some were reproduced in a book called *The Gleanings from the Menagerie at Knowsley Hall* which was privately printed in a small edition in 1846 and soon became valuable. He was not at Knowsley all the time: he was still drawing for Gould, and did most of his work on the Toucans and *The Birds of Europe* during these years.

But it was close, exacting work and Lear's eyes had never been good. Now they were becoming strained and he knew that he couldn't go on for much longer without risking his sight altogether. In 1835 he enrolled at Sass's School of Art in Bloomsbury where they prepared students for the entrance examination to the Royal Academy Schools.[11] Perhaps he hoped to go from there to the Schools, but his financial position hadn't altered and it would have been impossible for him to think of starting on the ten-year course.

Lear couldn't have been at Sass's for more than a few months, but he was obviously unsettled. That summer he went to Ireland.

The Knowsley Menagerie 1832–37

He was travelling with Arthur Stanley, who was later Dean of Westminster and a nephew of the 1st Baron Stanley of Alderley, another branch of the Stanley family with whom Lear had often stayed to give drawing lessons. Arthur Stanley's father had to be in Dublin for a meeting of the British Association, and Lear went over and walked with Arthur through the beautiful Wicklow mountains to Glendalough and the Seven Churches, and he collected a sketch-book full of drawings.

The following summer he spent ten weeks in the Lake District, and by the time he came back he knew that what he wanted to paint was landscape. At the end of October he told Gould: '. . . it is impossible to tell you *how*, & *how enormously* I have enjoyed the whole Autumn. The counties of Cumberland and Westmorland are superb indeed, & tho the weather has been miserable, yet I have

Rydal Water, Westmorland, 1836

contrived to walk pretty well over the whole ground, & to sketch a good deal besides.'[12] But he added, '. . . my eyes are so sadly worse, that no bird under an ostrich shall I soon be able to do.'

And now there was another complication. As a child Lear had had a tendency to bronchitis and asthma, and the time he had spent in the damp northern climate of Lancashire had made this worse. In 1837 his health deteriorated suddenly, and he knew that he must get away to somewhere dry and warm. 'It is a significant fact, and one which testifies to the naturally loveable qualities in Lear's character, that, throughout his life, his best patrons remained his greatest friends', [13] Angus Davidson has said of Lear—and this was never more true than now. Lord Stanley, who had now succeeded to the title as the 13th Earl of Derby, got together with his nephew Robert Hornby, who had become a particular friend of Lear's, and they offered to send him to Rome where he could recover his health and learn to paint. It was a gesture of real, practical friendship, and for Lear it meant an exciting new beginning.

CHAPTER FOUR

Italy

1837–45

Lear left England at the end of July 1837, and Ann travelled with him as far as Brussels where she had decided to stay until the following May. It must have been a sad parting for her as she wasn't to see him again for four years—and then only for snatched visits squeezed into his new and busy life—and for the rest of her life she lived alone.

He didn't hurry on his journey to Rome, for there was a lot to see. He wandered south through Luxembourg and Germany, stopping to draw busy street scenes in Frankfurt and strange medieval castles poised high on granite pinnacles in Bavaria, and it was September before he crossed the Alps into Italy in the gentle autumn weather.

Then he left his baggage in Milan, and taking only a knapsack and sketch book set out on a walking tour of Como and Lugano. Excitedly he explored the lakes—high rock peaks climbing out of the dark blue water and thrown back into echoing reflections 'jiggy jaggy' below, picturesque lakeside villages with huddles of white spires and busy quays, and 'large mummy-like barrels carrying wine drawn by milk white oxen—rows of women with baskets loaded with immense logs, and Capuchin friars in quantities'.[1] The Alps at sunset were perfectly pink, the autumn woods were a blaze of glorious crimson and gold, and on the lake the boats with their red, blue and white sails looked like huge butterflies. It wasn't all so romantic though, for the inns were cold and draughty, and they served 'mutton and goat's flesh, half putrid—and dreadfully sour wine'.[2] But the discomfort was worthwhile, and he arrived back in Milan a fortnight later with a folio full of sketches.

49

Frankfurt-am-Main, August 25th, 1837

The journey from Milan down to Florence took seven days, across the flat Lombardy Plains to Bologna and over the Apennines on the old Roman road. 'The Pass of the Apennines is quite unlike the Alps', he told Ann, 'and as we had a most lovely day, I never enjoyed anything so much. Thick woods of oak are on every side, and the road which is very steep and winding, looks quite over all the enormous flat plain of Lombardy;—and in clear weather,—as far as the Alps. Right and left one sees tops with snow, but one only crosses the lowest part, though oxen were necessary to draw up the carriages. You may imagine how beautiful the road looked, with a string of 8 coaches being so pulled up—and all the passengers walking. So much for the loneliness of mountain passes!—at the places we lunched—32 people—all English, sat down together.'[3]

On the seventh morning they came over the top of the mountains, and Florence lay spread below them in the wide Arno valley. It looked like the paintings by Claude Lorrain that he had seen at Knowsley, and was as beautiful as he had imagined. '. . . the world cannot produce anything prettier than that beautiful city,' he wrote enthusiastically to Ann, '. . . the magnificent bridges (6 close together over the Arno)—& the immense picturesque buildings of the middle ages—the clear lilac mountains all round it— the exquisite walks on every side to hills covered with villages, convents, and cypresses, where you have the whole city beneath you—the bustle of the Grand Duke's court and the fine shops— the endless churches—the Zebra Cathedral of black and white marble—the crowds of towers and steeples—all these make Florence a little Paradise in its way.'[4]

There were reports of cholera in Rome, so he decided to stay in Florence until it was safe to travel again. There was a wealth of things for him to see, '. . . the galleries—the pictures—the statues—the churches—the tombs of Michael Angelo—Dante . . . It is all a hurly-burly of beauty and wonder.'[5] At once he found people he knew in the large English community, and within a day or two he had been asked to give them drawing lessons during his stay.

But by the end of November sharp winds were blowing from the snows of the Apennines, and as Rome was now clear of cholera he decided to continue the journey south. As he was leaving he was introduced to two other artists on their way back there for the winter—one of them was William Theed, who sculpted 'Africa' on the Albert Memorial. They invited him to share their vetturino for the five-day journey, and as they rattled past the endless vineyards and olive trees of Tuscany they told him about the other artists in Rome and the life that they led there. On December 3rd, 1837, they crossed the wild and melancholy waste of the Campagna, and by the evening he had arrived in Rome.

Rome. St Peter's from Arco Oscuro, March 4th, 1840

Lear found rooms in Baboon Street—No. 39 Via del Babbuino—
'close to the church and the Piazza di Spagna—The Academy—the
eating and coffee houses—all the English and all the artists.'[6] There
were painters and sculptors from all over Europe and from America,
and with Theed to look after him and introduce him around he was
soon settling happily into their routine. 'At 8 I go to the Café,

where all the artists breakfast, and have 2 cups of coffee and 2 toasted rolls—for 6½*d*. and then—I either see sights—make calls— draw out of doors—or, if wet—have models indoors till 4. Then most of the artists walk on the Pincian Mount, (a beautiful garden overlooking all Rome, and from which such sunsets are seen!)— and at 5 we dine very capitally at a Trattoria or eating house, immediately after which Sir W. Knighton and I walk to the Academy —whence after 2 hours we return home. This is my present routine but there are such multitudes of things to see in Rome that one does not get settled in a hurry, and bye and bye I shall get more into the way of painting more at home, for I have 2 or 3 water coloured drawings ordered already, *so I shall not starve.*'[7]

But to begin with he spent most of his time just exploring the city. Christmas was coming, and everywhere there was business and bustle. The roads were choked by sleek grey cattle with enormous horns, decorated with ribbons and bells and pulling wobbling carts and waggons behind them, and the pavements were crowded with shoppers and ubiquitous priests, 'white—black—piebald—scarlet— cinnamon—purple: round hats—shovel hats—cocked hats—hoods and caps—cardinals with their 3 footmen (for cardinals *never* walk) —white friars with masks, bishops and Monsignori with lilac and red stockings—and indeed thousands on thousands of every description of religious orders.'[8]

It was quieter away from the centre of the modern city, and for hours on end he explored the ruined greatness of the Palatine Hill, the city of Romulus and the home of the Caesars, or he sat under the gentle warmth of the winter sun, drawing the tumbled, grassy ruins of Emperors' palaces and pagan temples. '. . . if you expected to see a fine collection of splendid antiques all in a bunch, you would be disappointed,' he told Ann; 'you stumble on pillars— temples—circuses—and tombs—all more or less mixed up with modern buildings.

'The arches of Titus and Constantine and Severus are the most perfect things—the Coliseum, and some of the gates—and the Pantheon—and by some lights—the melancholy and grandeur of these huge remains are very awful. But as to the extent of the ruins of Rome—no one who does not see them, can form an idea;

the palaces and baths of the Emperors—some filled up into convents—some covering acres of ground with masses of ancient walls —the long lines of acqueducts and tombs on the desolate and beautiful Campagna,—and (in the enormous palaces of the modern Capital and Vatican) the thousands of busts and statues!—judge how bewildered one's noddle becomes!—for my part, I am taking things very quietly—and like better to poke about over and over again in the Forum, than to hurry with the stream of sight seers all day long.'[9]

There were quantities of English people wintering in Rome, and he found that he knew a great many of them. There were cousins of the Stanleys, and cousins of the cousins; and people like Lady Susan Percy—a niece of the Duke and Duchess of Northumberland who had each brought a copy of his *Parrots* six years before—who at once commissioned work from him and encouraged him as Mrs Wentworth had done then, and Sir William Knighton, whom he had known at Sass's. Amongst the artists he found Richard Wyatt nephew of the Georgian architect, Frederick Thrupp who later sculpted the Wordsworth bust in Westminster Abbey, John Gibson, Penry Williams and Thomas Uwins.

He was invited to grand balls and elaborate soirées, when coroneted carriages would jostle and manoeuvre for room to set down their noble occupants, but he confessed quietly to Ann that 'when I come home at night with my key I often think of Gray's Inn Road, Albany St!'[10] for amidst all the hustle he could still feel as lonely as he had sometimes felt at Knowsley.

But there was something very particular about the atmosphere in Rome which he could never have recaptured in England. Here art was an honourable and even enviable occupation, and painters were hardly looked down on at all—though one couldn't go too far, and they weren't admitted as members of the English Club. The younger artists wandered freely into each other's studios, to talk or to criticise one another's work—no doubt some of them wished they were isolated in England again—and they would share models, the peasants who came into Rome for the winter months wearing their colourful costumes and who would gather at the foot of the Spanish Steps waiting to be hired. But though Hazlitt had accused the English artists in Rome of lounging and loafing, and Haydon despised the dirty habits they acquired, Lear managed to place himself between the bearded Bohemians and the English aristocracy, whose ways he was better able to understand than most of his fellow artists.

But it was outside Rome on the Campagna that he found the beauty and the grandeur that he most wanted to paint. This desolate plain had once been widely populated and the people had cultivated the land for generations, but when the small farms were replaced by large estates the quality of the farming declined and the land became poorer. Then the barbarians came in succeeding waves on the city, destroying the houses and roads, pillaging the crops and the cattle, and leaving behind them a rotting wasteland into which the waters of the seven hills of Rome drained in marshy swamps. For centuries it had been uninhabited, with grotesque pillars and splintered roads and lines of fractured aqueducts forming a weird graveyard of industry. Foxes and tortoises and porcupines wandered freely, and beside the marshes herds of buffalo congregated. But to Lear it was an uninhabited wasteland of beauty, with chunky rock shapes, gnarled olive trees and rhythmical lines of hills disappearing into wide, distant horizons. Sometimes he went further to explore the beauties of Tivoli, or the sullen, silent lake of Nemi near the Pope's summer palace: when the retreating German soldiers burnt and destroyed the treasures in the museum at Nemi in 1944, they left just a few small things untouched, and one of these is a watercolour drawing of the Lake by Lear.

He was feeling well and happy and the winter climate suited him perfectly. But the summer in Rome was dangerous, for when the sun was hot, fever heavy air would steam off the marshes, and then it was unsafe to be within twenty miles of the city; after Easter the coaches and carriages piled with luggage would start to rumble out of the city gates, and Rome became quiet and empty.

At the beginning of May 1838 Lear left with Uwins to spend the summer in the Bay of Naples.

His first impression of Naples itself was appalling, and the whole of their short stay there was an ordeal. It was dirty and crowded and unbelievably noisy, and it seemed to gather to a climax in the Toledo, the main city street. 'If you empty all the streets of all the capitals of Europe into one—then turn in some thousand oxen, sheep, goats, monks—priests—processions—cars—mules— naked children & bare legged mariners—you may form some idea of the Toledo', he told Ann. 'Once I walked up it—but would not again for a great deal, as I was nearly deaf & run over (almost) 20 times before I came out of it. It is a dreadful place,—yet at 8 o'clock people lounge & eat ices at every door—although the noise is like all the thunder in the world.

... 'But at Santa Lucia—the fish market—you become so stunned & bewildered, that you don't know if you are dead or alive; it is like a horrid dream—when all the world is shrieking at you. As you pass, every woman screams out—"will you sit?" "will you drink?" "will you give me something?" "anything" "a grana?"—Signor, Signor, Signor, Water, Water Fish—Meat mussels—oysters—baskets—eggs—roses—apples—cherries?" — while every man steps before you overwhelming you with the most tremendous shouts of—"Come along Sir—come: a boat! a boat! instantly, now, this minute, this minute! to Capri—to Vesuvius— to Sorrento—to wherever you please—a boat, boat boat boat!!!" '11

'*Vedi Napoli e poi muori*', Lear might well have thought.

They stayed only four days in Naples, then they went round the bay to the ancient Roman resort of Pozzuoli. But the sulphurous air began to bother Lear's chest and he started to cough, so they went quickly back to Naples and then climbed into the hills behind the city to search for somewhere cool and peaceful to spend the rest of the summer. They found a tiny village called Capo di Cava perched at the end of a deep valley where the only sound was the early morning singing of the birds. 'Now what do you think I live for?' he asked Ann, 'today, for instance, we had coffee & eggs at 5—at 12, beautiful macaroni soup,—boiled beef & mutton cutlets, strawberries, cherries, & a bottle of wine each—& at supper, macaroni & an omlette, wine & oranges—to which you are to add lodging—& now guess? actually, for 8 carlinos is all this—which is equivalent to 2/8 of our money—daily!!!'12

Lear in 1840

They went for long walks past tiny villages where the peasants gathered under the shade of canopies of vine, and out onto the cliff road leading down to Amalfi with views across to the Gulf of Salerno, or inland through chestnut woods busy with cuckoos and nightingales; and they made expeditions to Paestum to see the Greek temples, and to Pompeii which Lear thought 'alone, worth a journey from England.'[13]

On August 30th they were in Rome again, and he was glad to be back 'for I am beginning to find,—"the rolling stone gathers no moss." '[14] His landlady—'the old hussy'—had decided to double the rent, so he had to look for new rooms and he found some in the Via Felice, close to the Pincian Gardens just a little out of the artists' quarter. The city was even fuller than it had been the previous winter, but for Lear this meant more work and the year rushed round into spring. 'All through the winter (which was a very fine one, though cold) I was over head & ears in employment,' he wrote to Gould. 'Rome was more crammed than it had been

since the days of Titus. People slept in ovens and pigstyes for want
of lodgings so that what with pupils (of which I had numbers) &
friends & drawings indoors and sketchings out of doors the spring
came before one knew where one was. You will lift up your hands
and eyes and legs and possibly fall quite off your chair when I tell
you that I was enabled to send some of my earnings to my mother
& sisters & to put by 100£ besides for the use of the summer!!'[15]

When the summer came he went on foot to join some of the artists
in a mountain village north of the city. With their help he began
oil painting which he had tried unsuccessfully on his own the
previous summer, but he made disappointingly slow progress, and
when he got back to Rome in the autumn he told Gould: 'It takes
a long while to make a painter even with a good artist's education
—but without one—it tries the patience of Job:—it is a great thing
if one does not go backward. Meanwhile I am extremely happy
as the hedgehog said when he rolled himself through a thistle-
bush.'[16]

In fact, these were the most satisfying years of Lear's life, and
with Goethe he could have said: 'The first thing I did in Rome was
to discover myself and to achieve a mood of balance, harmony and
happiness.' He was surrounded by people with whom he could talk
and work; he was painting well, despite his doubts; he had enough
money; and the future was full of time and hope. Just one thing was
missing, and he wrote to Gould: 'I wish to goodness I could get
a wife! You have no idea how sick I am of living alone!!—Please
make a memorandum of any lady under 28 who has a little money
—can live in Rome & knows how to cut pencils and make pud-
dings.'[17] He never thought of women with much passion—no
doubt catching syphilis had increased his diffidence—and his ideal
was a gentle companion who would look after him in a rounded,
contented kind of way. But as a young man he seems hardly to have
considered marriage as a real possibility, partly because he knew
that if he married there would be too much risk of unhappiness.
He would have to break the secret of his epilepsy, and he might
pass the disease on to his children and see his own horror beginning
again in another child; and he could never be sure that his wife
would go on loving him—his mother had stopped loving him once

and he knew that he couldn't go through that kind of despair and hurt again.

In 1841 he decided to spend the summer in England, for it was nearly four years since he had left and he wanted to see Ann again. 'What I shall do *in* England I have no idea,' he wrote to Gould, 'run about upon railroads & eat beefsteaks. I am & have been, as you have justly heard—going on very well—which is more than ever I had a right to expect, in spite of your good opinion of me: I am very glad I took to Landscape—it suits my taste so exactly—& though I am but a mere beginner as yet—still I do hope by study & staying here to make a decent picture before I die. No early education in art—late attention & bad eyes—are all against me—but renewed health & the assistance of more kind friends than any mortal ever had: I hope will prove the heaviest side of the balance.'[18]

He and Ann must have had a long talk about their future that summer. She had kept on the rooms in Southampton Row to which they had moved together in 1835, and she must have been hoping that he would come home and settle down again. But he had written to her, 'Rome is Rome; do not think about the future; let us be thankful that so far all is and has been much better than we could ever have expected.'[19] Better for him perhaps. Ann doesn't seem to have put any pressure on him to stay, but now that she realised he didn't want to live in England again she gave up their last remnant of a home and began on an endless succession of furnished lodgings and visits to friends; when she looked forward her life must have seemed empty and very lonely.

Lear couldn't afford to spend the summer doing nothing, and he decided that he would publish some of his drawings of Rome. In August he went up to stay with Lord Derby, and he took lithographic stones and chalk with him to Knowsley so that he could work on them there. Since the ebullient 12th Earl had died Knowsley was much quieter, and Lear told Gould, 'my life here is monotonous enough—but such as pleases me more than all the gaiety in the world. Dear Lord Derby is surrounded by his children, grand-children, and nephews and nieces and is really happy. He

59

1   2

breakfasts with us after prayers:—then about 12 takes a drive with one of his daughters or his sons and also myself—he takes the greatest interest in all his grounds etc.—He dines in his own room when we lunch—but after our dinner at 7 he sits with us all the evening . . . The lot of things is immense here—birds and beasts etc.—but I am so thoroughly confined by my Lithography as to have little time to see them.'[20]

At the end of September he left Knowsley with Robert Hornby's cousin, Phipps Hornby, for a holiday in Scotland. They went by boat up the west coast and then crossed into the southern Highlands, and Lear recorded the holiday in a series of drawings:

1. P. & L. leave Knowsley—1841.
2. L. & P. dine at the Adelphi and observe a painful letter-writer.
3. P. & L. being hurried insert the remains of their lunch in their boots . . .
22. L.—on ascending the cabin stairs—nearly loses his eye by the abrupt and injudicious promission of a new broom in the hands of a misguided infant.

Views in Rome and its Environs was published in the autumn. It is a superb book of fresh, carefully observed drawings, rhythmically composed and confidently handled. Lear used Claude Lorrain's convention of a bundle of interest on one or both sides of the foreground framing the receding middle and far distance, and every inch has been imagined from the curling fuss of vine

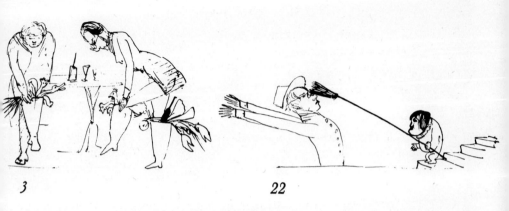

3   22

canopies to the dramatic mountain shapes which go right back in space. Tonally they are most successful, but Lear's lack of formal training sometimes lets him down; the perspective is often very odd and the figures are generally bad, for when he was drawing people his courage seemed to vanish and it is difficult to believe that they are done by the same person who drew the bold and completely successful nonsense figures.

At the end of 1841 he returned to Italy and settled back into the routine of his life there. In the spring of 1842 he visited Sicily, and the following summer he went across central Italy through the Abruzzi to the Adriatic coast, travels which he described in the first volume of *Illustrated Excursions in Italy*.

He was away first for two weeks, travelling on horseback with a friend from Rome called Charles Knight. They left on July 26th, 1843, and went south-east to Frascati and then through Subiaco to Avezzano. It was mountainous but green, and the only people they passed were local peasants gathering in the harvest and tending their sheep.

On the second evening they reached Avezzano near the Lake of Fucino, an ancient Roman playground which has now been drained and divided between the local farmers. They went first to the only inn in the town, 'where three ineffably polite females shewed us into a large, raftered room, of a bewildering aspect, with much furniture, and a great assortment of old clothes, and strewed with articles of female dress, intermixed rather oddly with fowls of all sizes, fluttering about in every direction, over and under two very misshapen beds. All this, added to the walls having a speckly appearance, which to the initiated denotes the presence of certain flat entomological visitors, did not promise much repose; nor did the pensive chirping of an afflicted, one-winged chicken, upon whom one of our landladies lavished the most touching caresses, at all strengthen our admiration of the dormitory we had selected. . . .

'There was no lock to our door. All night long, two or three frantic hens kept tearing round the room, and would by no means be expelled: the afflicted chicken with a broken wing scrambled about the floor without intermission: vermin of two species, (politely called B flats and F sharps,) worried us beyond endurance: a perpetual chorus of pigeons thrilled over our heads, and an accompaniment of pigs resounded below.'[21]

The next morning they went to explore the lake. Knight wanted to see the ruins of the Emissario, but Lear preferred to sit out in the sun soaking in the scenery: 'The plain of Avezzano; the clear blue lake; Alba; the Velino, with its fine peaks, alternately in bright light, or shaded by passing clouds; the far snow-covered mountains beyond Solmona; the bare pass of Forca Carusa; the precipitous crag of Celano,—all these at once, brilliant with the splendour of Italian morning formed a scene not to be slightly gazed at, or lightly forgotten.

'A herd of white goats blinking and sneezing lazily in the early sun; their goatherd piping on a little reed; two or three large falcons soaring above the Lake; the watchful cormorant sitting motionless on its shining surface; and a host of merry flies sporting in the fragrant air,—these were the only signs of life in the very spot where the thrones of Claudius and his Empress were placed on the crowd-blackened hill: a few distant fishing-boats dotted the Lake where, eighteen centuries ago the cries of combat rent the air, and the glitter of contending galleys delighted the Roman multitude.

'The solitary character of the place is most striking; no link between the gay populous past, and the lonely present; no work of any intermediate century breaks its desolate and poetical feeling.

The Lake of Fucino, from 'Illustrated Excursions in Italy'

I could willingly have lingered there for hours, for I can recall no
scene so impressive and beautiful.'[22]

After a fortnight the two men parted, and Lear spent the next
couple of months re-covering the ground more slowly on foot, stopping to draw on the way.

In May 1844 his mother died at Dover, a life-worn widow; she
had had twenty-one children and seen thirteen of them die, and she
had plunged from genteel comfort to the verge of poverty. It is sad
that we know so little about her: all we have is a drawing of a
rounded and rather sympathetic woman. In the letters and diaries
that have survived Lear mentions her probably no more than six
times, and then only to ask Ann how she is or to say that he has
been able to send her money. He never reminisces about her—
either this was too painful, or he had grown to dislike the memory
of her so much that he didn't want to recall her—and we know
nothing about her personality at all. In fairness to her it must be
said that twenty-one children in twenty-four years would sap
the natural affections and sense of responsibility of most women,

and she had the added worry of trying to guide the family through their acute financial troubles. Perhaps if Jeremiah Lear had continued to prosper she would have supervised Edward's upbringing herself, or she may anyway have decided that she had had enough of children—we don't know. Certainly Lear expressed himself strongly on the worries of large families in the second part of Mr & Mrs Discobbolos, when Mr Discobbolos simply climbed down from the 'ancient runcible wall' and blew the whole family into tiny pieces.

Now that Mrs Lear was dead there was nothing to keep Ann in England, and he wrote asking her to come out and join him in Rome, a thing he'd been talking about ever since he first went there. He told her how to travel and where he would meet her, but he was just a little worried that she might let him down. 'I hope you will dress *very nicely*—(although we shall be both in deep mourning)' he said— . . . 'You would have a capital bedroom with a fire place, for I should give you mine—and a sitting room. Your drawback would be the want of society for a few months—(for of course you would not be in the gay world;) but when you consider that the seeing Rome merely is much—and the excursions I shall take you, and perhaps the going home by Switzerland and Milan— I do not think the balance is bad. (Besides you will see *me*!)—do not forget to bring good *warm clothing*, and if you want any handsome, plain shawl or dress in Paris, (not odd looking, my dear old sister!) buy it, and keep it as a present from me. You know that I am very much known here, and live in the "highest respectibility"—and so you *must not* be too dowdy. Do not forget a thick veil—for cold winds. We shall dine at home etc.—and I shall be as much with you as I can considering my great occupation and the quantity of people who come to me.'[23]

But it must all have sounded too overwhelming, and she wrote and told him that she couldn't manage the journey. He was disappointed, but as he was planning to go back to England in the summer he hoped that she would come back with him then. In the meanwhile he decided to spend a few weeks going over some of the Abruzzi he had missed the previous year.

In one village a drunken carabiniere demanded to know who he was, so Lear told him his name and showed him his passport 'which was one from the Foreign Office in 1837, with "Viscount Palmerston" printed thereon in large letters, "Lear" being small, and written. *"Niente vero"*, said the man of war, who seemed happy to be able to cavil, *"voi non siete Lear! siete Palmerstoni!"* "No I am not", said I, "my name's Lear." But the irascible official was not to be so easily checked, though, knowing the power of these worthies, I took care to mollify his anger as much as might be. *"Quel ch'è scritto, scritto è: dunque, ecco qua scritto Palmerstoni:— dunque siete Palmerstoni voi"*. You great fool! I thought; but I made two bows, and said placidly, "take me to the Sott'Intendente, my dear sir, as he knows me very well." *"Peggio"*, said the angry man, *"tu! incommodare l'eccellente Signor Sott Intendente; vien, vien subito: ti tiro in carcere"*.

'Some have greatness thrust upon them. In spite of all expostulations, Viscount Palmerston it was settled I should be. There was nothing to be done, so I was trotted ignominiously all down the High-Street, the carabiniere shouting out at everybody at door and window, *"Ho preso Palmerstoni!"*

'Luckily, Don Francesco Console was taking a walk and met us, whereon followed a scene of apologies to me, and snubbing for the military, who retreated discomforted.'[24]

In the spring of 1845 Lear met a man who became one of his closest life-long friends, a man of sympathetic understanding with whom, in later, sadder years, he could talk. His name was Chichester Fortescue, he was twenty-two—ten years younger than Lear—and he had just come down from Oxford where he had got a first in Classics and won the Chancellor's English Prize. Now he was touring Europe before following his father into a parliamentary career. He was a quiet, self-questioning man who never felt really at home in political life, though under Gladstone he was to become Lord Privy Seal and later President of the Council. He was happier in the less formal company of painters and writers, and he liked Lear at once. And Lear certainly enjoyed his company, for in Fortescue he found his two favourite virtues—sensibility and enthusiasm: Rome was new, the artist's life exciting and the older man splendid company. 'I like very much what I have seen of Lear,' he wrote a few days after they had met, 'he is a good, clever, agreeable man—very friendly and *getonable* with.'[25] They went sketching together on the Campagna, they visited Tivoli, and Fortescue wrote in his diary: 'Lear a delightful companion, full of *nonsense*, puns, riddles, everything in the shape of fun, and *brimming* with intense appreciation of nature as well as history. I don't know when I have met any one to whom I took so great a liking.'[26] Here was another person, like his Sussex friends, with whom Lear could indulge in absurdities and nonsense, and his letters to Fortescue over the next forty years make delightful reading.

In April he left Rome to spend the summer in England. 'Lear came to say goodbye just before dinner—he had gone by diligence to Civita Vecchia,' Fortescue wrote in his diary. 'I have enjoyed his society immensely, and am very sorry he is gone. We seemed to suit each other capitally, and became friends in no time. Among other qualifications, he is one of those men of real feeling it is so delightful to meet in this cold-hearted world.'[27] He had discovered the essence of Lear.

CHAPTER FIVE

A Queen and a Revolution

1845–48

Most of the best-loved children's songs and tales were made up without any idea of publication. Charles Dodgson told the story of *Alice in Wonderland* to three little sisters as he rowed them down the river from Oxford one dreamy afternoon in June, Beatrix Potter wrote *Peter Rabbit* for a small friend who was ill in bed, and Hugh Lofting created *Doctor Dolittle* in the trenches of Flanders for his children at home. And so it was with *A Book of Nonsense*, for it wasn't until 1845 that Lear decided to publish the 'nonsenses' that had so delighted the children at Knowsley.

Many people now find it hard to understand why *A Book of Nonsense* should have been so popular, and they remember that as children they didn't particularly enjoy it. But then today we are used to the benign, kindly personalities of characters like Mole, Winnie the Pooh and Dougal who are so often foolish in the happiest way, whilst a hundred and fifty years ago most writers for small children disliked folly of any kind.

In 1762, Rousseau wrote a book about a boy called Emile, who was brought up by a system of 'natural education'.[1] He was to discover the world by his own experience. He would never be forced to do what he didn't want to do, but too late he would realise that because of his own laziness he had missed what was best. If he wished he could lose his temper—but if he did so he would be treated as though he were ill. The stories he would hear would be about the world around him, for there was no point in telling him tales of fairyland. In England Maria Edgeworth became the great missionary of natural education, though Rousseau's genuine ideas of self-discovery became a little buried at her hands for the situation was always arranged so that the good child made the wise and

67

true decision and was raised to yet higher virtue, whilst the bad
child sank deeper and deeper, becoming an object of pity to the
rest of the visionary world. When Evangelical Christians added
their ideas of virtue and wickedness, the terror of the moral tale
had reached its peak. 'Babies do not want to hear about babies,'
Samuel Johnson had written; 'they like to be told of giants and
castles and of something which can stretch their little minds.' But
what children wanted didn't matter—it was what would do them
the most good that was important, and in the first part of the nineteenth century the realms of giants and castles were shut to all but
a few lucky children.

Of course, it wasn't all so bleak. The terrible tales of the brothers
Grimm appeared in English in 1824, and Hans Andersen's stories
were published in London in 1846, the same year as Lear's nonsense. There was a rich inheritance of nursery rhymes, and
occasional books without a high moral tone slipped through like
The Butterfly's Ball, published in 1807.[2] In 1821 the first known
book of limericks appeared,[3] *The History of Sixteen Wonderful Old
Women*, and in the following year came *Anecdotes and Adventures
of Fifteen Gentlemen*, the book which had inspired Lear.

Some of these early limericks were soon popular in the nursery,
but the books themselves had none of Lear's lasting success. Perhaps there are two reasons why children then enjoyed his book
so much. The first is that his people are so very human. They
aren't righteous, in fact virtue sometimes brought absolutely no
reward:

> There was an old Person of Cadiz,
> Who was always polite to the ladies;
> But in handing his daughter,
> He fell into the water,
> Which drowned that Old Person of Cadiz.

Some of them are vain and others are greedy, and one even runs
away with a thief. Some are sad and some are violent, and a few
are quite shockingly weak willed—and if they haven't the strength
of character to see a thing through, they have instead a handsome
honesty:

A Queen and a Revolution 1845–48

There was a Young Lady of Clare,
Who was sadly pursued by a bear;
When she found she was tired,
She abruptly expired,
That unfortunate Lady of Clare.

Unlike the virtuous heroes of the moral tales they are on the children's side, for Lear still remembered how it had felt to be a child: he wanted to make them happy—society would do its best to make them good. 'My dear child, I'm sure we shall be allowed to laugh in Heaven!'[4] he said to a little girl many years later.

And the other reason is the vitality of the drawings. Children's book illustrations then were generally either rather stilted woodcuts, or elaborate, often very charming, drawings—but the illustrations to the limericks are fresh and clear and almost crude in their simplicity, yet at the same time they are very professional. Running through them all is a sense of movement—the arms are flung

'There was an old man who said 'Hush . . .'

spontaneously back like birds in flight and the legs stride out or stand poised expectantly on tip-toe as if they are going to be spun round like a child's top. There is none of the genteel decorum which was thought so proper but instead, like children, the Old Men and Women are hardly ever still and nobody minds at all.[5]

We don't know why Lear decided to publish the nonsenses at this point, for as always when he came back to England he no longer needed to write letters and it is difficult for us to discover what was going on. Perhaps his friends persuaded him to publish them so that other people's children could share their enjoyment. Possibly he was hoping to make some money to pay towards the expense of coming home.

This was certainly the motive for another book on which he was working in 1845. This was a book about the Abruzzi describing his journeys there the two previous summers, and it was illustrated with large lithographic plates.

In the autumn he was at Knowsley working on the drawings, but there were so many friends to see that he found it difficult to get much done, and before the winter began he came back to London where there were fewer distractions. Ann was living at this time in Richmond, so he took rooms on his own at 27 Duke Street, St James's, and settled down to work. There was a lot for him to do, for he had to write the text of the Abruzzi book and finish the thirty lithographs and forty vignettes, and then he had the long task of writing round asking people if they would like to subscribe. The proofs of the nonsense book had to be checked, and this was published first, on February 10th, 1846.

There were altogether seventy limericks in two volumes selling at 3s. 6d. each, and they were published by Thomas Maclean, who had brought out *Views in Rome* in 1844. It was called *A Book of Nonsense* by Derry down Derry, and on the title page there was a rhyme:

> There was an Old Derry down Derry,
> Who loved to see little folks merry;
> So he made them a book,
> And with laughter they shook
> At the fun of that Derry down Derry.

There was no mention of Lear's name anywhere, although anyone buying a copy of the second volume of *Illustrated Excursions in Italy* later in the year might have guessed the secret, for on the last page there was an unlikely advertisement for *A Book of Nonsense*. Perhaps Lear had decided to use a pen name because he wasn't yet established as a painter and he wanted to become known for one thing at a time, or maybe he was frightened of damaging his emerging reputation by publishing such a light-hearted work. But he was really very proud of it and loathed hearing it attributed to other people, and in the new and enlarged edition which appeared in 1861, almost too late to damage any reputation, his name was printed firmly on the title page.

The first volume of *Illustrated Excursions in Italy* came out in April. It was dedicated to the Earl of Derby and, like his earlier books, was extravagantly illustrated and expensively priced at four guineas. It is a beautiful book, and Lear's enjoyment and excitement in discovering every new sight and sound make it very good reading. And its publication had a worthy outcome—for Lear was summoned by the Queen. Her Majesty had seen the book and so admired it that she wanted Lear to give her lessons in drawing.

The twenty-seven-year old Queen was having a very busy summer. Her fifth child, Princess Helena, had been born on May 25th, and just a month later Peel's administration had toppled. The Whigs, whom she loathed, had returned to power under Lord Russell, and within a few weeks Palmerston, who was the new Foreign Secretary, had created an international crisis by upsetting the arrangement which the Queen herself had made with the French over the marriage of Queen Isabella of Spain.

She had gone down to stay at Osborne, which was then being rebuilt, and it was there that Lear began the course of twelve lessons. The Queen recorded them in her diary:

July 15th, 1846. Osborne. 'Had a drawing lesson from Mr Lear, who sketched before me and teaches remarkably well, in landscape painting in water colours . . .'
July 16th, 1846. Osborne. 'Copied one of Mr Lear's drawings and had my lesson downstairs, with him. He was very pleased with my drawing and very encouraging about it . . .'
July 17th, 1846. Osborne. 'I had another lesson with Mr Lear, who much praised my 2nd copy. Later in the afternoon I went out and saw a beautiful sketch he has done of the new house . . .'
July 18th, 1846. Osborne. 'After luncheon had a drawing lesson, and am, I hope, improving . . .'[6]

Queen Victoria aged about 30

Lear wrote down the details of his stay at Osborne, but all this has disappeared except for one memory which he recalled to Fortescue when he heard of the Prince's death at the end of 1861. 'Prince Albert showed me all the model of the House, (then being built only,) & particularly a Terrace, saying—"This is what I like to think of—because *when we are old*, we shall hope to walk up & down this Terrace with our children grown up into men & women." '[7]

At the end of July Queen Victoria returned to London and the lessons were resumed at Buckingham Palace, and it was probably here that two embarrassing incidents occurred which Lear used to recall.[8] He was accustomed now to mixing with earls and viscounts, but he had no experience of the finer points of Court etiquette—though he did know that he enjoyed standing on the rug in front of the fire warming his coat tails. But each time he took up this position facing the Queen, the attendant Lord-in-Waiting invited him to see something on the far side of the room. The charade was repeated several times and no one explained what was going on, and it was only later that Lear realised that a subject must not stand with his back to the fire in the presence of his monarch.

But Queen Victoria had apparently taken a liking to her drawing master, and she decided to show him some of her bijou treasures which were kept in display cases. Lear was delighted with what he saw, and exclaimed exuberantly: 'Oh! where *did* you get all these beautiful things?' Calmly Her Majesty replied: 'I inherited them, Mr Lear.'

The twelfth and last lesson was on August 6th, and a few days later a second volume of *Illustrated Excursions in Italy* was published. This was a book similar to *Views in Rome and its Environs*, with drawings of places not often seen by tourists, like Sermoneta and Ardea.

By coincidence, in the same year as the publication of *A Book of Nonsense*, the result of Lear's other activities at Knowsley appeared, for Lord Derby decided to reproduce some of his drawings in *The Gleanings from the Menagerie at Knowsley Hall*.

And so it had really been a remarkable year. He had been drawing master to the Queen, and seen the publication of a book of nonsense, a travel book, a volume of landscape drawings and one of natural history illustrations. It was almost a microcosm of his working life, and—characteristically—he made only £100 profit.

Ann still couldn't be persuaded to return with him to Rome. He stayed in England until the beginning of December 1846, then he packed his things and left for Italy.

It was nearly two years since Lear had left Rome, and his friends were delighted to see him. 'Everybody exclaims at my well-looks and says I have come back half as big again as I went,' he told Ann. 'I have hardly time to write, so many people are calling to congratulate me on my return.'⁹

When the first flurry was over he settled down to his routine of painting and walking and dining out, but after his unexpected success in London it all seemed rather tame. And he hadn't been forgotten in England. He had presented to the Queen the drawings that he had done at Osborne and she had had one of them engraved. 'I had nearly forgotten to tell you a piece of honour which has happened to me,' he told Ann within a few sentences of starting a letter to her, 'namely, that one of the Queen's Ladies-in-Waiting who is here, has delivered to me a little print engraved from one of my drawings—of Osborne House,—at Her Majesty's desire. This is one trait of many that have come under my notice that Queen Victoria has a good memory for any little condescension and kindness. I am really quite pleased with my little engraving, and shall have it placed in a good frame as soon as I can get one made;—you need not however, tell the incident to everybody;—for it would look like boasting upon my part, who have done little enough to deserve so gratifying a notice.'[10]

In fact he was rather worried about appearing to do too well, for now he was starting on a busy winter with a lot of work, and he told Ann: 'I have so much more to do than I merit by my actual place in artistic repute, that such success may give rise to complaints from those who are more skilful & yet have little to do.'[11]

But for all this it wasn't going to be an easy year financially. The paintings were small and the journey out with large packets and trunks had been expensive. 'I reckon that I may get £100—or perhaps £120 this year, & that is what I certainly cannot save much out of. You must remember that I work only up to May—& that the summer does not count. Still, that is far cheaper than I could live for in London, where £300 does not seem an overplus.—We must therefore be grateful on account of my publications—whatever trouble they gave me—& (what is done without trouble?)—for through them I laid by a whole £100. And when we consider that eyesight is not of long duration—laying by now is really a necessary duty.'[12]

But he had begun to think that he might settle once more in England. Ten years before, Rome had given him a thrilling introduction to a completely new way of life, but in those years he had matured and changed whilst life amongst the English there had hardly altered. The winter visitors, kind though many of them were, went monotonously on asking the same questions, making the same bright remarks, and what had once seemed so vital now just seemed horribly dull. He had to be realistic though. Living was cheaper in Italy, and so long as there were English people in Rome there was always a sale for his paintings. And though the city might look 'filthier and duller than ever after England',[13] the country around was still beautiful and the climate usually perfect. But that winter was one of the worst of the century: there were long, dark days with pouring rain and so little light that he could hardly see to paint, and this gave way to intense cold and heavy snow which kept him snared indoors and unable to get the exercise he needed to keep off attacks of epilepsy.

In the end the decision of whether or not he should stay was made for him. For many years Italy had been grumbling with discontent. The people wanted a united country but their struggle was going to be a hard one, for they had first to overthrow the autocratic rulers of the existing Italian states who had strong reactionary forces under their command. By the end of 1846 the atmosphere had become so unsettled that many English people decided not to risk spending the winter in Italy, and they went no further than the south coast of France.

But Lear wasn't going to leave before he had to. He wanted to see the rest of Italy whilst it was still possible for travellers to move freely. He hadn't yet been to the north-east coast round Venice or the north-west round La Spezia, nor had he been to the foot of Italy—and as he wanted to revisit Sicily he decided to go south first. Fortescue wrote saying that he would like to join him in Naples in mid-August to walk with him in Calabria, so Lear decided to spend the early summer in Sicily and be back in Naples in time to meet him there. Meanwhile, a friend of a friend in Rome, a man called John Proby, was hoping to go with him on the first part of the tour. Proby had come to Italy to study painting, and during the dreadful winter of 1846–47 he had contracted Roman fever. Now he felt better he wanted to do some walking and drawing, though it is doubtful if he realised how whole-heartedly Lear went about his sketching tours.

Lear left at the end of April, 1847, and travelled down to Naples. From there he caught a steamer to Palermo where Proby met him, and on May 11th they set out together.

They soon found the island hot, dirty and poor, and in Calatafimi, where they stopped first, they could buy nothing but bread full of aniseed, and broad beans which they boiled and lived off for the next six days. But, though he preferred to be comfortable and well-fed, it was what he had come to see that interested Lear, and for the next month they were out each morning before the sun came up, walking and drawing until the last of the daylight had gone. They travelled right round the island, and visited the temple of

Hera at Segesta, and the six temples at Agrigento, both busy towns in the centuries when Sicily had been ruled by the Greeks; they explored the honeycomb of cave dwellings in the valley of Ipsica which had been the home of the most ancient Sicilian settlers, and they spent a night in a castle beside the wild and romantic southern seashore.

On June 8th Lear and Proby reached Syracuse, once 'the largest of Greek cities, and the most splendid of all capitals'.[14] It had stood for nearly two thousand years before being overrun by the Saracens who levelled it to the ground: now the old quarries had been made into cool green gardens heavy with flowers, and the trees were filled with nightingales. A new city had been built, and they were glad to rest there for a few days, for throughout rural Sicily the living conditions had been terrible. Worst of all had been the food; there was virtually no meat, nor any fresh fruit or vegetables, which was surprising for as they travelled they had passed acres of culti-vated fields. But because of the extreme heat the peasants kept just enough for themselves each day, and by early morning the rest had been sent into the big towns to be sold. 'Milk, do you want? The goats are driven in from the country *at sunrise*, are milked in the street, & off they go again; if then you do not run about with a milk jug, no hope of milk—for 2 hours turns it sour. Oil, vinegar, salt, pepper,—matters collected, or grown by richer people—are either consumed in small quantities by each household or exported al-together. Fish? if much is taken *at sunrise*, the happy catchers eat it, & there is none for the passer by at noon; if they catch less—so much the less chance for you. Eggs? You cannot make a hen lay when you please, & the morning produce of the hen roost is all gone by noon. Meat?—This is rarely killed & as it were *by sub-scription*, everybody taking a part & cooking it directly or it would be bad very soon . . .'[15]

From Catania, north of Syracuse, they set out to climb Mount Etna, a process which Lear didn't enjoy. In the early evening they made their way through the woods on the lower slopes, till they came to a hut where they slept for a few hours. 'At midnight we started on mules & with a light & after two hours climbing reached the snow, beyond which it is necessary to go on foot. Here the trouble begins; fancy two hours of climbing up & slipping down, over the steepest hill of frozen snow. I never was so disgusted. Sometimes I rolled back as far as 20 minutes had taken me up. It was impossible to keep one's footing, even with a spiked stick. By the aid of the guide however, we reached the top of this horrible height, & rested in another hut called Casa Inglése.

'Then we crossed a plain of snow which surround the cone, & began to climb that, an operation as difficult as the last, as it is

Mount Etna

nearly perpendicular, & made of fine ash & sulphur, into which you plunge up to your knees at each step. This however, is not the obstacle which prevents your progress—but rather the extreme rarity of the air which takes different effects on different persons. Some it stupifies, others it causes to vomit. Had it made me very ill, I should have turned back, but it only caused me to feel as if I were drowning, & made me lose my breath almost, & my voice altogether. A sort of convulsive catching was very disagreeable, & at times was so violent that for a moment or two I lost the use of my limbs & fell down. Being on the ground however, restored one's breathing, & so we got on by very slow degrees—climbing—& falling alternately.

'The fatigue is certainly immense, but one is amply repaid by the extraordinary scene above—where you look on the whole island of Sicily just like a great pink map in the sky—with the sea round it so blue, & the dark purple triangular shade of the mountains over that part furtherst from the sun which rose just before we got to the mouth of the crater.

'We did not remain long there, as you may suppose on my telling you that the sulphur we sat on burned our clothes very much, & was horribly hot—yet one was too glad to bury one's hands in it— one's body and head being wrapped up in cloaks & plaids through all which one shivered in the icy wind which blew like knives from the north. (Etna you know, is nearly as high as Mt. Blanc.) We came down ridiculously fast; you stick your heels in the ashy cone, & slide down almost without stopping to the bottom,—& with a spiked stick you shoot down the ice hill we had taken so long to surmount—in 10 minutes.'[16]

They were back in Palermo again on the eve of the festival of Santa Rosalia, and there was a week of music and fireworks and crowds, and Lear found the noise and bustle very trying. In fact both he and Proby were feeling thoroughly low: when he planned his lengthy itineraries for travel he never realised that being constantly on the move, eating badly and sleeping in primitive inns, being up before dawn and working till dusk, could leave him run down and exhausted. Whilst he was still young he could recover quickly, but later he would travel until he was unable to go on for one more day, yet it never occurred to him that he was just very tired. The walking Lear always enjoyed—it was the most certain way of keeping off attacks of epilepsy, and the world was a happier place when he was outside and on the move; it was the shuffling around, the uncertainty of whether they would find somewhere to stay or where they would be able to get a meal, that bothered him. For Proby it was even more exhausting, for he had only just got over his illness and had never travelled in this way before. 'I am sorry my companion, as his health improves, *does not* in temper,' Lear told Ann; 'he is sadly imperious & contradictory at times which is rather trying. . . . However, there is some allowance to be made, as I find he is heir to a rank which I had no knowledge of as being about to be his, or I should not have travelled with him.'[17] For Lear had discovered that Proby was heir to the Earl of Carysfoot, and his critics were quick to say that he pursued the nobility— which was true to the extent that they were more likely to buy and commission his work. But the pursuit was mutual, for he was very gifted and usually excellent company, and since people still accuse him of obsequiousness, it is worth noting that all his close friends who were peers—Carlingford, Northbrook, Tennyson, Aberdare, Westbury, Cromer—were raised to the peerage many years after Lear had come to know and like them.

When they crossed back to Naples they heard that Fortescue had gone back to England to take up a seat in Parliament, but as Lear and Proby had settled their difficulties they set off again together. As they were travelling on foot they engaged a muleteer to look after their baggage. He spoke in a strong southern dialect which they could hardly understand, but to Lear's delight he finished every incomprehensible sentence with the refrain 'Díghi Dóghi Dà'—surely the inspiration for the Yonghy-Bonghy-Bò.

Like the Abruzzi, Calabria was uncharted, and there were very few roads and practically no inns, so they had to travel from day to day relying for their accommodation on the letters of introduction that Lear had been given. But it was after they had been staying in an inn for the night that Lear overheard two young Englishmen talking. 'I say, Dick,' one of them asked, 'do you know who that fellow is we were talking to last night?' 'No,' replied the other. 'Why, he's nothing but a d——d dirty landscape-painter', a title that Lear adopted as his own: 'Edward Lear, Dirty Landscape Painter' he called himself henceforth.[18]

They decided that their best plan was to travel up the eastern side of the peninsula close to the mountains, and when they heard of anything exciting they could turn off this track and explore. Their hosts were happily hospitable, indeed often too much so,

*Pentedatilo, from the 'Journals of a Landscape painter
in Southern Calabria'*

for they would be thrown into confusion by the sudden arrival of
unknown foreigners carrying letters of introduction, and wondering
what on earth two Englishmen could possibly want in their im-
poverished corner of the world, they would set about preparing a
meal fit for travellers from a wealthy land. Whilst Lear and Proby
sat and talked with their host, answering endless questions about

the modern wonders of England, the animals were killed in the yard and then lengthily cooked, 'till you are reduced (ere it comes) to a state of torture and despair, in the protracted struggle between hunger, Morpheus, and civility'.[19] And the meals, when they did arrive, weren't always easy to eat. 'At one time a dish was exhibited full of roasted squirrels, adorned by funghi of wonderful shapes and colours; at another, there were relays of most surprising birds: among which my former ornithological studies caused me to recognise a few corvine mandibles, whose appearance was not altogether in strict accordance with the culinary arrangements of polite society.'[20] Whilst they ate, a man stood beside the table, 'and in order to dissipate the flies, which at this season are a legion, flapped a long flapper of feathers, Laputa-wise, close to our faces. No sooner did we begin to speak than whizz—flick—down came the flapper, so as to render conversation a rather difficult effort.'[21]

When they reached the south again a few weeks later they realised that the atmosphere had changed. The people were no longer so friendly, indeed they seemed nervous and strained and pressed them with questions—had they seen anything unusual, had they heard anything? They knew now that the revolution might break out at any moment, but there were still places that Lear wanted to see, and whilst Proby went for a few days across to Messina, he made a short dash on his own down to Melito on the southernmost tip of Italy. He had a letter to one of the families there, but though they made him welcome he soon realised that they were fidgety and worried. The atmosphere became really fraught when two or three gunshots were heard, but as nothing more happened they gathered nervously for dinner. As they were eating a man came in from Montebello, one of the villages further north. There was some nervous whispering, and then his host suddenly shouted: 'The Revolution has already begun.' '. . . sobs and groans and clamour followed, and the moaning hostess, after weeping frantically, fell into a violent fit, and was carried out, the party breaking up in the most admired disorder, after a display, at least so it appeared to me, of feeling in which fear and dismay greatly predominated over hope and boldness.[22]

Lear left the next day to meet Proby in Reggio, and there he saw the action for himself. It was one o'clock in the morning when he reached the city. 'How strange was that scene! All the quiet town was brilliantly lighted up, and every house illuminated; no women or children were visible, but troops of men, by twenties and thirties, all armed, and preceded by bands of music and banners inscribed, 'Viva Pio IX', or 'Viva la Constituzione', were parading the high street from end to end.

'*Cosa x'è stata*, Ciccio?' said I.

'*O non vedete*,' said the unhappy muleteer, with a suppressed groan, '*O non vedete? é una rivoluzione! Díghi, dóghi, dà!*'

'No one took the least notice of us as we passed along, and we soon arrived at Giordano's Hotel. The doors were barred, nor could I readily gain admittance; at length the waiter appeared, but he was uproariously drunk.

'Is Signor P—— arrived by the boat from Messina?' said I.

'*O che barca! O che Messina! O che bella rivoluzione! Ai! ao! Orra birra burra—ba!*' was the reply.

'Fetch me the keys of my room,' said I; 'I want to get at my roba——'

'*O che chiavi! O che camera! O che roba! ai, ai!*'

'But where are the keys?' I repeated.

'*Non ci son più chiavi*,'* screamed the excited cameriere; '*non ci sono più passaporti, non ci sono più Ré—più legge—più giudici—più niente—no x'e altro che l'amore la libertà—l'amicizia, e la constituzione—eccovi le chiavi—ai! o-o-o-o-o-orra birra bà!!.*'[23]

Throughout the night people came into Reggio, mostly young men from the mountains, gathering with banners and guns and swords and musical instruments. At the moment it was a rather strange charade, but it could get ugly and Lear was worried to find that Proby hadn't arrived. Next morning he persuaded a very reluctant boatman to row him across to Messina. Fighting had already broken out there, and he found Proby waiting anxiously in the hotel unable to get a boat to the mainland. They didn't want to stay a moment longer now than they had to, and two days later

---

* 'There are no more keys, there are no more passports, no more kings, no more laws, no more judges, no more nothing! Nothing but love and liberty, friendship and the constitution'.

they boarded a steamer en route from Malta to Naples. It was a sadly abrupt ending to a happy tour, and they were worried that the families with whom they had stayed might now be under suspicion for having entertained strangers. 'Gloom, gloom, overshadows the memory of a tour so agreeably begun,'[24] wrote Lear in his journal as they left Calabria behind.

As they were early they spent three weeks in the Kingdom of Naples, and reached Rome on October 14th, 1847. There they parted. Lear had been with Proby for five months, and he told Ann: 'I shall be exceedingly sorry to lose him, as he is a most excellent creature, & if ever he was cross as I unluckily told you, I am sure it was more than half my fault.'[25] They never met again; Proby died in 1858 when he was thirty-five, and his sister believed that he never recovered from his months of hardship travelling with Lear.

For Lear it was a busy winter. Rome was still safe, and he stayed there until the end of March working on the summer's drawings. He had twice-weekly open days in his studio, and he dined out frequently, and all the time he was planning where he would travel next: '. . . whether I go to Apulia & Calabria, or wherever I Archipela go (V.A. Archipelago, P. Archipelawent, PP. Archipelagone) or whatever I do, I strongly long to go to Egypt for the next winter as ever is, if so be as I can find a sufficiency of tin to allow of my passing 4 or 5 months there,' he wrote to Fortescue. 'I am quite crazy about Memphis & On & Isis & crocodiles and ophthalmia & nubians, and simooms & sorcerers, & sphingidae. Seriously the contemplation of Egypt must fill the mind, the artistic mind I mean, with great food for the rumination of long years. I have a strong wish also to see Syria, & Asia Minor and all sorts of grisogorious places, but, but, who can tell . . . You see therefore in how noxious a state of knownothingatallaboutwhatoneisgoingtodo-ness I am in. Yet this is clear:—the days of possible Lotus-eating are diminishing, & by the time I am 40 I would fain be in England once more.'[26]

But wherever he decided to go he knew that this would be his last winter in Rome, and he began to pack his things and send them back to England. In February he met Thomas Baring, who was later created the Earl of Northbrook and appointed Viceroy of India,

83

and who became another of Lear's closest friends. '. . . he is an extremely luminous and amiable brick, and I like him very much,' Lear told Fortescue who had arranged the meeting, '& I suppose he likes me or he wouldn't take the trouble of knocking me up as he does, considering the lot of people he might take to instead.'[27]

In February a new acquaintance, a man called Bowen who was President of the University of Corfu, invited Lear to come and stay on the island. It would be a perfect place to begin his exploration of Greece—from there he could visit the other Ionian Islands, cross to Albania and the Greek mainland, or travel down the coast to Athens.

He spent March clearing the rest of his possessions and tidying up his business in Rome. It was more than ten years since he had first come there, but he had no time to feel sad. In Rome itself the situation was becoming menacing as disillusionment grew against Pius IX who the Italians had mistakenly believed would help in the fight for unity. The revolution Lear had been caught up in in Calabria had been a flurry which died out, but by the beginning of 1848 something more forceful was building up. Early in the year there were riots in Lombardy, and in the middle of March Milan and Venice burst into rebellion. The port of Ancona was closed, and as Lear travelled down to Naples to board a boat for Corfu soldiers were gathering along the roads. He was glad to leave Italy behind him.

CHAPTER SIX

The Mediterranean

1848

For the next fifteen months Lear travelled round the Mediterranean, through Greece and Turkey, Albania and Egypt, collecting drawings as he went.

The boat taking him to Corfu wandered on its journey, and they stopped at Malta for a week. It was a happy and busy few days, for in the English community he found old friends who entertained him and showed him the small rocky island. But the scenery was terribly disappointing: 'I could not live at Malta' he wrote, 'there is hardly a bit of green in the whole island—& hot sand stone, walls, & bright white houses are all you can see from the highest places, excepting little stupid trees here & there like rubbishy bits of black worsted. The harbours are very interesting, but I don't love the water well enough to be always boating—nor can I draw ships well enough to portray such scenes characteristically. The street scenery—so white, so bright, so clean, so balconied, is really beautiful—but there the charm ends.'[1]

From Malta he crossed the stormy Ionian Sea to Patras, passing Missolonghi where Byron had died, and as they came into the shelter of the mainland the storm dropped. Then in the calm moonlight they cruised between the Ionian islands and the rocky Grecian coast, and just before dawn on April 19th, 1848, they anchored in the beautiful bay of Corfu—Prospero's Cell.

After landing, Lear went straight up to the university to find Bowen, but heard that he had left a few days earlier to visit the other Ionian islands. So Lear decided to follow him on the next boat, and for two weeks he explored Zante and Cephalonia and Ulysses' little kingdom of Ithaca, and was back in Corfu on May 10th.

Mr Lear

Corfu is a luxuriant and peaceful island. In the spring it is carpeted with millions of flowers, and in the summer it bends under the weight of dark green olives; tiny white convents perch by the pellucid blue sea, and from the shores the land climbs up into mountains and the peak of Pantokrator. At first Lear was so astonished by its loveliness that he just walked without stopping to draw. 'I wish I could give you any idea of the beauty of this island,' he told Ann, 'it is really a Paradise.'² 'The extreme gardeny verdure—the fine olives, cypresses, almonds, & oranges, make the landscape so rich—& the Albanian mountains are wonderfully fine. All the villages seem clean & white, with here & there a palm tree overtopping them. The women wear duck, black or blue, with a red handkerchief about the head; the men—the lower orders that is, mostly red capes—& duck full Turkish trousers. Here & there you see an Albanian all red & white—with a full white petticoat like a doll's—& a sheepskin over his shoulder. Then you meet some of the priests—who wear flowing black robes & beards. Mixed with them are the English soldiers & naval officers, & the upper class of Corfiotes who dress as we do; so that the mixture is very picturesque.'³

But he had been there less than three weeks when he met Sir Stratford Canning, the British Ambassador in Turkey, whom he had known in Rome years before. He and Lady Canning were on their way to Constantinople, and they invited Lear to join them as their guest. They were spending a week in Athens on the way, so he would be able to see something of Greece as well, and he would have all the privileges of the ambassador's party.

The ambassador's man-of-war sailed out of Corfu harbour on the afternoon of May 30th. Two days later they crossed the isthmus of Corinth on horseback, and on the evening of June 2nd they were in Athens.

Lear was up very early the next morning, for he wanted to see as much as he could. '. . . surely never was anything so magnificent as Athens!' he exclaimed to Ann. 'far more than I could have had any idea of. The beauty of the temples I well knew from endless drawings—but the immense sweep of plain with exquisitely formed mountains down to the sea—& the manner in which that huge mass of rock—the Acropolis—stands above the modern town with its glittering white marble ruins against the deep blue sky is quite beyond my expectations. The town is all new—but the poorer part of it, what with awnings, & bazaars & figures of all possible kinds is most picturesque.'[4]

In the afternoon the whole party went to the Acropolis, 'really the most astonishing monument of a great people I have yet seen. Poor old scrubby Rome sinks into nothing by the side of such beautiful magnificence. . . . I wish you could see the temple of the Parthenon, or the Acropolis by sunset—I really never saw anything so wonderful. Most of the columns being rusty with age the whole mass becomes like gold & ivory—& the polished white marble pavement is literally blue from the reflection of the sky. You walk about in a wilderness of broken columns—friezes etc. etc. Owls, the bird of Minerva, are extremely common, & come & sit very near me when I draw.'[5]

In Athens Lear met another friend whom he had known in Italy, a young man called Charles Church whose uncle, Sir Richard Church, had commanded the Greek forces in the War of Independence against Turkish domination. There were almost too

Athens, 1849

many opportunities at once, for now Lear had the chance of travelling round part of Greece with Charles Church, and as he couldn't speak any modern Greek at this time he would have both a guide and interpreter in his friend. The ambassadorial party would have to go on without him, but since he could follow them by boat a week or two later he decided to go with Church.

First he spent two weeks in Athens drawing as much as he could, and then they hired horses and set out north-east across the foot-hills of Pentelicon towards Marathon. The tour started badly for Lear, for on the first day his horse slipped and he sprained his shoulder. That evening they reached Marathon, '. . . which you know, is one of the famous places in the world, as that is where the Athenians defeated the Persians under Xerxes,' he wrote to Ann. 'The place like all such in Greece is quite unchanged by time, & the exact points of the battle are as exactly to be followed as those of Waterloo. A vast Tumulus still marks the site of the buried Persians. All Greece, you must know is *most thinly* inhabited,—& for a whole day you may only meet a few peasants. This is the way of travelling. We hire a man who undertakes to do *everything* for a certain sum a day; he finds us horses & has others for our baggage, & for his cooking utensils & for provisions & for beds: we were in all 7 horses. We start at sunrise after a good breakfast of coffee & eggs—& we travel till 10. Then we halt at some village, or near a fountain, & a tent is pitched, & in about 2 hours a most capital dinner—soup & 3 courses—is set forth!!—so you see there is not much hardship. Then we go on till at dusk we reach some village when any house does for our night's dwelling—for little iron bed-steads with mattresses are put up directly, & on these a large muslin bag tied to the ceiling, into which I creep by a hole which is tied up directly I am in it, so that no creature gets in & one sleeps soundly in a room full of vermin. I thought I should have laughed all night long the first time I crept into this strange bag, but soon grew used to it. In the morning—all is packed up & off we go again.

'All the great towns—except 3 or 4—are *quite* new—having been destroyed by either Turks or Greeks, or both over & over again, in the last war. They are built on no plan & look very mean & scattered. From Chalcis we made a tour of a week all over Euboea;

no such beautiful scenery can be found anywhere as the forests: you ride for days & days through whispering woods of bright green pine,—the odour of which is delightful & the branches are full of bright blue rollers. It is more like a very magnificent English park than anything else I can compare it to. The peasants—few as they are, are most obliging simple creatures. The men wear a plain tunic, but the women dress very prettily. They bind the head with a yellow handkerchief; but plait the long hair, & then tie it on to still longer plaits of silk or horse hair till it ends in bunches of silk with silver tags; in some villages they string cowries shells all down these long tails, which are confined by a girdle.

'From Euboea we crossed to Lamia—or Leitun as the Turks called it; the last town of the Turkish frontier, & very Turkey in its appearance. I wish you could see it. The strangest feature of the place is the *immense* number of storks it contains. Every house has one or more, some 8 or 10 nests, & the minarets—(now only ruins) & other ruined houses are all alive with them. The clatter they make with their bills is most curious, & makes you fancy all the town are playing at backgammon. From Lamia we came to the celebrated pass of Thermopylae where the few Spartans withstood so many Persians.'[6]

At Thebes he was suddenly taken ill, and had to be carried back to Athens, 'by 4 horses on an Indiarubber bed'.[7] He hadn't felt really well since his fall, but the illness was brought on by an insect bite followed by an overdose of sun. In fact he probably had malaria, for the fever recurred over the next few years and was treated with quinine. Lying quietly in Athens he began to recover, and had 'books, jelly, porter, & visits continual from all the English residents.'[8] He was annoyed to have missed seeing Delphi, but by the end of July he was well enough to think again of going on to Turkey.

He spent most of the voyage lying in his cabin, but as they steamed into Constantinople at sunrise on August 1st he climbed onto the deck to watch the city slide past. 'Certainly—no city is so wonderfully beautiful when you approach it—it was far beyond my idea,' he told Ann: 'I think the perpetual change as the steamer moves on, of ruined walls, immense domes—brilliantly white

Constantinople

minarets—& all mixed with such magnificent cypress, pine, & plane foliage is truly wonderful.'[9]

The Embassy was a few miles further on in Therapia, and as soon as he arrived Lear went straight to bed. Lady Canning was 'as kind as 70 mothers',[10] and fed him broth and chicken, tea and thin slices of bread and butter, and within a fortnight he was walking in the Palace gardens. But then the fever returned and he was in bed once more, and lying there looking out over a monotonous tow path, he began to think again of the future. 'What to do, my Dear Fortescue when I return to England!!??¿-¿¡! (expressive of indelible doubt, wonder, & ignorance.) London must be the place, & then comes the choice of two lines; society, & half days work, pretty pictures, petitmaître praise boundless, frequented studio &c., &c., wound up with vexation of spirits as age comes on that talents have been thrown away:—or *hard study* beginning at the root of the matter, the human figure, which to master alone would enable me to carry out the views & feelings of landscape I know to exist within me. Alas! if real art is a *student*, I know no more than a child, an infant, a foetus. How could I. I have had myself to thank for all education, & a vortex of society hath eaten my time. So you see I must choose one or other—& with my many friends it will

90

go hard at 36 to retire—please God I live for 8 or 10 years—but—
if I did—*wouldn't* the "Lears" sell in your grandchildren's time!'[11]

He could have gone on for years leading what he saw as a dilettante artist's life—although this would probably have been more
difficult in London than in Rome. Many landscape painters, including Claude Lorrain whose work he so much admired, had
employed other artists to paint in their figures, but Lear was unusually interested in the peasants and their strange and often
beautiful costumes, and he wanted to be able to draw them for
himself. As well as this he needed to satisfy his artistic conscience,
and this he could not do if he pandered to '*petit maître*' praise—
although it is arguable that the kind of topographical landscape
work that Lear liked to do was best suited at this time to just this
kind of patronage. Now he was thinking of going right back to the
beginning and working through the training that he had never had,
and at thirty-six he was perhaps fortunate to be free of responsibilities so that he could consider doing this. Not many men of his
age would have been prepared to start again, but alongside his
humility he was realistic enough to recognise the value of his work.

He had a little money saved, but still he would find it hard to
support himself throughout the lengthy training. There was just
one possibility though, for in his letters to Ann he frequently
referred to a Mrs Warner, who was apparently a friend of the Lear
family, and who lived in Bath. For years now she had hinted that
Edward was featured in her will, and she was very wealthy and
rather aged.

Gradually he began to feel really better, and as he lay in bed
recovering he wanted more than thin bread and butter. 'Hunger!
did you ever have a fever?' he asked Fortescue. 'No consideration
of morality or sentiment or fear of punishment would prevent my
devouring any small child who entered this room now. I have eaten
everything in it but a wax-candle and a bad lemon.'[12]

On August 28th he took his first proper walk, through the quiet
of a Ramadan day. The month of fasting was just ending, and the
ambassador's party had been invited to Constantinople the following
day to see the Sultan's procession to and from the Mosque of Santa
Sophia and the ceremony of 'foot kissing' in the Seraglio. It was a

brilliant, spectacular, hours-long affair with Pashas and Generals, incense and music, feathers and diamonds, an exotic and exciting introduction to eastern custom. 'I can't tell when I have passed so delightful & novel a day', Lear wrote to Ann later, '& after a long illness, one is so thankful for a change.'[13]

And now that he was feeling better he wanted to make up the time he had lost. The next morning he returned to Constantinople to explore the city on his own, and he crammed every moment of the next seven days; he saw the mosques and the ancient cypress-clad burial grounds, he sat in a boat to draw the minaretted skyline and he crossed to Scutari and back, he visited the sacred place of Ayoub where Mahomet's standard bearer lies buried and he poked through the stalls of the Stamboul bazaar for dress lengths of silk to send home to Ann. In fact, he was so absorbed and excited with all there was to see that his health improved in a great rush, and when he returned to the Embassy late at night on September 8th everybody was amazed at how well he was looking.

Lear's idea now was to visit Mount Athos with Church, then go on to spend the rest of the year in Greece. In Constantinople he had engaged a Bulgarian servant for the journey, and on September 9th they embarked together for Salonika. Church planned to join them in Mount Athos, but when Lear landed at Salonika he found the city isolated because of cholera and Mount Athos closed to all travellers. The only road out of the city still open went north-west into Macedonia, and as there was now no chance of meeting up with Church Lear decided to leave by this route and travel right across Greece to Albania then down the isolated western coast. It would be a more difficult journey than any he had yet undertaken.

They went first through Turkey, and from the beginning he found the customs weird and difficult. There were no tables or chairs and it was uncomfortable sitting always on the floor. But the Turks were understanding: 'they never stare or wonder at anything; you are not bored by any questions, and I am satisfied that if you chose to take your tea while suspended by your feet from the ceiling, not a word would be said, or a sign of amazement betrayed.'[14]

By mid-September they were in Monastir on the border of

Illyria and Macedonia. It was a beautiful place, and Lear settled down eagerly to draw. Then he discovered how difficult it was going to be to work in this primitive Islamic country where drawing was believed to be devil's work. 'I cannot but think—will matters grow worse as I advance into Albania?' he wrote in his journal, 'for all the passers-by having inspected my sketching, frown, or look ugly and many say, "Shaitán", which means, Devil; at length one quietly wrenches my book away and shutting it up returns it to me saying "Yok, Yok!" [No, No,] so as numbers are against me, I

Monastir

bow and retire. Next, I essay to draw on one of the bridges, but a gloomy sentinel comes and bullies me off directly, indicating by signs that my profane occupation is by no means to be tolerated.'[15]

From Monastir they crossed the central mountain plateau and reached Scutari in Albania on October 21st. Then they turned south along the coast. Because this part of the country was so little known Lear took on a local guide called Anástasio to show them the route and arrange some kind of accommodation for each night's stay. At Durazzo he already had a letter of introduction to the Bey, a boy of sixteen: neither could understand a word the other said, so conversation was impossible, but Lear liked the lonely, sad young man and wanted to see him smile, 'so I drew for him—& amused him immensely by drawing a steam carriage & saying—rattle-attle-attle-attle-attle—& a ship-steamer—saying wishwashsquish-squash—at which the poor boy laughed immensely.'[16]

Travelling south on the road to Dukadhes the scenery was awesome in its bleak grandeur. 'At the highest part of the pass a most singular scene opens. The spectator seems on the edge of a high wall, from the brink of which giddy elevation he looks down into a fearfully profound basin, at the roots of the mountain. Above its eastern and southern enclosures rises the giant snow-clad Tchika in all its immensity, while at his very feet, in a deep, dark green pit of wood and garden, lies the town or village of Dukadhes, its houses scattered like milk-white dice along the banks of a wide torrent, which finds its way to the gulf between the hill he stands on, and the high western ridge dividing the valleys from the sea.

'To this strange place, perhaps one of the most secluded in Europe, I began to descend, and as we slowly proceeded, halted more than once to sketch and contemplate. Shut out as it stood by iron walls of mountain, surrounded by sternest features of savage scenery, rock and chasm, precipice and torrent, a more fearful prospect, and more chilling to the very blood I never beheld—so gloomy and severe—so unredeemed by any beauty or cheerfulness.'[17]

In contrast to the landscape, the hospitality was warm and expansive, for Lear's stay was made the excuse for a celebration in the village; two gypsies were called in to play, and he was treated to an Albanian musical evening.

'At first the entertainment was rather slow. The gipsies had two guitars, but they only tinkled them with a preparatory coquettishness; till another friend dropping in with a third mandolino, a pleasing discord was by degrees created, and increased to a pitch of excitement that seemed to promise brilliant things for the evening's festivities. Anastásio, also, catching the melodious infection, led the performers by his own everlasting Greek refrain—sung at the full power of a tremendous voice, and joined in by all present in the first circle—for now, many more than the chorus had entered the room, remaining seated or standing behind, and the whole formed, in the flickering light of the wood torches, one of the most strange scenes imaginable . . . As the musical excitement increased, so did the audience begin to keep time with their bodies, which this people, even when squatted, move with the most curious flexibility.

'Presently, the fun grew fast and furious, and at length the father of the song—the hideous idol-gipsy—became animated in the grandest degree; he sang and shrieked the strangest minor airs with incredible accompaniments, tearing and twangling the guitar with great skill, and energy enough to break it into bits. Everything he sang seemed to delight his audience, which at times was moved to shouts of laughter, at other almost to tears. . .

'The last performance I can remember to have attended to, appeared to be received as a capo d'opera: each verse ended by spinning itself out into a chain of rapid little Bos, ending in chorus thus: "Bo, bo-bo-bo, BO!—bo, bobobo, BO!"—and every verse was more loudly joined in than its predecessor, till at the conclusion of the last verse, when the unearthly idol-gipsy snatched off and waved his cap in the air—his shining head was closely shaved, except one glowy raven tress three feet in length, the very rafters rang again to the frantic harmony—"BO, bo-bo-bo, bo-bo-bo, bo-bo-bo, bobobo, BO!"—the last "BO!" uttered like a pistol-shot, and followed by an unanimous yell.

'Fatigue is so good a preparation for rest, that after this savage mirth had gone on for two or three hours, I fell fast asleep, and heard no more that night.'[18]

Next morning the gaiety had gone; the sombre village was dripping with rain, and he was relieved to get away on the last stretch of the journey south. He reached Yannina at the beginning of November 1848, with 219 drawings and a diary of a strange and exciting tour. In 1851 he published *Journals of a Landscape*

Painter in Greece and Albania, a book dominated by descriptions of the landscape just as the places themselves had been dominated by the gaunt, majestic scenery.

Now it was winter and Ann was expecting him home. But he was loath to exchange the Mediterranean sun for the damp gloom of London and when John Cross, whom he had known at Knowsley, invited him to travel as his guest in Egypt and Palestine, Lear accepted eagerly.

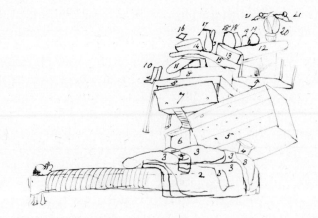

CHAPTER SEVEN

Franklin Lushington

1848-49

Cairo was astonishing. Everywhere was noise and colour, busy Arab traders shouting their strange oriental wares, hidden black-draped women, Copts and Ethiopians, donkeys, camels, mosques and minarets, exotic bright-plumed birds and brilliant oleanders.

Lear had nearly missed coming altogether for quarantine and winter storms had delayed him in Greece and he arrived in Malta to find that Cross had gone on without him. Now he reached Cairo just as Cross was preparing to leave for Mount Sinai, but he put off going so that they could spend a week discovering the city and visiting the sphinx and pyramids. Then they set out on camels for Mount Sinai, but on the way back Lear's fever returned again and though he left for Palestine with Cross, as they had planned, he soon realised that he wasn't up to the journey and turned back to Alexandria where he boarded a boat for Malta.

Lear really wanted to go back to Greece so that he could see the whole country and make drawings in every province, for he had an idea of publishing a really comprehensive book. 'The vast yet beautifully simple sweeping lines of the hills have hardly been expressed I fancy,' he told Fortescue, 'nor the *fascinating* dry foregrounds of Elgin marble peasants etc. What do you think of a huge work (if I can *do* all Greece) . . .?'[1]

He left Malta for Patras on March 3rd 1849, and told Ann: 'My companion is Mr F. Lushington—the government secretary's brother at Malta, a very amiable & talented man—to travel with whom is a great advantage to me as well as pleasure.'[2] This was the first mention of the man who was to become Lear's closest friend.

Lushington was several years younger than Lear. He had been at Rugby under Dr Arnold, then went up to Trinity College,

Mr Lear

Cambridge, where he got a First in Classics, won the Chancellor's gold medal, and was elected Fellow of his College. One of his brothers, Edmund, was Professor of Greek at Glasgow University, and another, Henry, the Chief Secretary to the Government in Malta, had been one of the select society of Apostles at Cambridge with Tennyson and Arthur Hallam.

With Henry, Franklin published three books of verse, and these contain almost all we know of his thoughts. *Points of War*, which came out in 1854, was inspired by the fighting in the Crimea, and expressed the view that though war is bad an ignoble peace is worse. It went into two editions and was followed in 1855 by *Battle Pieces*. The third volume, *Joint Compositions*, is undated and talks about reforms at home:

> They say the land is over-full—
> With wealth like this to Crown the soil—
> The bloated city sucks it in;
> And they who neither plough nor spin
> Take all the fruits of toil.
>
> .   .   .   .   .
>
> Why should the idle eat? 'tis well
> That English tempers suffer long,
> And yet it makes a plain man wroth,
> When evil laws that pamper sloth,
> Insult the poor they wrong.[3]

and on hanging:

> Oh age of boasted power,
> Of conquered land and sea—
> Ask yet a nobler birth from time—
> Be humble still—or find for crime
> A worthier remedy.[4]

Lear's friendship with Lushington later became fired with such intensity on Lear's side that he had deep unhappiness in store, but there was no hint of this now as they left together for what were probably the happiest few weeks of Lear's life.

Franklin Lushington

They landed at Patras on March 9th, and travelled south into the Morea, a land rich in the history of centuries. On the hills of Arcadia the shepherds worshipped Pan and it is traditionally the region of rustic contentment and a perfect place to be happy. In fact for most of the year it is a barren, unfriendly countryside, and the gentle happiness of the poets' Arcady is a lie. But now the hills were indulgent, for it was spring. Day after day they walked and drew—the temple of Apollo at Bassae, Sparta, Argos, Mycenae —the days were too short for all the happiness that had to be crowded into them. The countryside was green, and the occasional showers only helped to bring out the profusion of flowers. 'No one can form any idea of what the spring is in Greece; it is all very well to say that there is a mile of bright scarlet ground, then half a mile of blue or pale pink—but it is difficult for you to realise that the whole earth is like a rich Turkey carpet. As for Lushington & I, equally fond of flowers, we gather them all day like children, & when we have stuck our hats & coats & horses all over with them —it is time to throw them away, & get a new set.'[5]

Mr Lear

They crossed from Corinth to Athens then travelled up through Attica to Thebes where Lear had been taken ill in 1848. From there they went to Parnassus and Delphi and on to Patras where they parted after six happy weeks.

Left on his own Lear went north to Yannina and over the Metsovo Pass to the Vale of Tempe and Mount Olympus. He passed through beautiful countryside, but its splendour made him feel strangely sad: '. . . a keen sense of every kind of beauty, is . . . if given in the extreme—always more or less a sorrow to its owner,— tho' productive of good to others,'[6] he once said, and even as a boy this had disturbed him: 'What a mingling of sadness & admiration of landscape botheringly will persist in existing,' he wrote. 'All the unsought morbid feelings—certainly unsought—(for I knew not what even the meaning of morbid was in those days,) of past years crop up at once—such as the Hornsey fields or Highate archway, & the sad large Thorn tree at Holloway about 1819—or 1820 . . . the Mill at Arundel, or Peppering in 1824 or 5 —— the heights above Plymouth in 1836–37—the Godesburg—1837— Civitella 1839 & Nemi —— all were with me at once.'[7]

But the gentle unhurriedness of nature, peaceful blues and greens, the absence of strife—these were on the side of man. He had known this on the Campagna and in Greece, and again later in Corfu, when he wrote: 'There is everywhere a flood of gold & green & blue. This, & the breeze, blowing freshly now & then, remind one of days in many lands before *that* knowledge came which tells us we have so little, & so much conjecture. On Swiss, & Como hills in 1837—in the first years of Roman & Amalfi life /38, /9—the long Civitella sojourns—1839–40—Abruzzi 43–44— Sicily & Greece 47, 48/49.—I do not now suppose that kind of happiness can ever come back but by unexpected & unsought snatches; so I do not strive after it, nor mourn that I cannot have it.'[8]

He still wasn't able to get to Mount Athos, and had to resign himself to missing the Holy Mountain; in fact there was a lot he hadn't seen. But when he boarded the boat to take him back to England he was going home to settle down. The days of Lotus-eating were over.

Part II

SLOPES OF MYRTLE

CHAPTER EIGHT

Pre-Raphaelite

1849–53

Mrs Warner's legacy was perfectly timed, for shortly after his return to England at the beginning of June 1849 Lear heard that she had left him £500. The rest of her fortune of nearly £50,000 she had bequethed to perpetual widows. 'I thought directly I heard of this matter that I would instantly marry one of the 30 viddies,' Lear told Fortescue prudently, 'only then it occurred to me that she would not be a viddy any more if I married her.'[1] But for the first time in his life he had a little capital, and could go ahead with his plans.

He wanted to go to the Royal Academy Schools. The foundation of the Academy in 1768, and in particular its first President, Sir Joshua Reynolds, had done something very special for painting in England, and with the granting of the Royal Charter artists became gentlemen. Sir Joshua had been in Rome between 1750 and 1752 studying the work of Raphael and Michelangelo, and he believed that a revival in British art would only come through a study of great masters of the past. By copying what was good in them and rejecting what was bad, the students would learn from the experience of earlier generations, and could then go on to develop their own style. They would need a very thorough knowledge of their technique, and the course at the R.A. was spread over ten years, incidentally giving an atmosphere of refined leisure. After devoting three years to drawing and to a study of human anatomy from the antique, they moved into the Preliminary School of Painting where they learnt to handle paint, and it was only in the final stage of their training in the Upper School of Painting that they were allowed to work from the living model. For History Painters the subject matter was either biblical or classical, and as this was the age of neo-classicism in England, Reynold's approach gave painting an intellectual—and not merely artisan—status. But by the end of the eighteenth century Pope had given way to the Romantic poets, and the classical revival had been absorbed. The new thinkers were finding their truth in Nature, but at the Academy the teaching of Reynolds was still rigidly followed and was becoming increasingly academic and remote. The landscape painters had moved on, and whilst most Academicians turned out turgic academic studies in brown, Turner's paintings were singing with a brilliance of colour which burnt to a white heat.

In 1843, Ruskin published the first volume of *Modern Painters*, in which he championed the brilliance of Turner and preached a return to the study of Nature itself, and in the Summer Exhibition of 1849—the year of Lear's return to London—three strangely new paintings were hung, fresh in colour and medieval in concept, and each was inscribed mysteriously with the initials P.R.B.

Despite the criticism the R.A. Schools were unrivalled in London, and it wasn't easy to get a place there. Lear's experience might help him, but his age—for he was thirty-seven—would not. They would be selecting students in January and he had until then to prepare the drawings, from the antique of course, which he had to submit, so he enrolled again at Sass's, the school in Bloomsbury which prepared students for the Academy and where he had been fifteen years before.

The term didn't begin until September, and during the late summer he wandered from one country house to another. He went down to Maidstone to visit Lushington at his home, Park House, but the atmosphere was heavy and subdued and instead of the abandoned youth who had travelled with him in Greece he found a silent, inturned man.

It was at Park House, and probably in 1849, that Lear first met Alfred Tennyson. In 1841 the poet's family had moved to Boxley, a village two miles from Park House, and the following year his sister, Cecilia, was married to Edmund Lushington—their epithalamium forms the epilogue to *In Memoriam*. When Lear met Tennyson the poet was forty and was coming to a climax in his

life, for in 1850 he published *In Memoriam*, he was married at last
to Emily Sellwood, and he was made Poet Laureate.

Another house Lear visited was of course Knowsley, and from
there he wrote to Fortescue: 'My dear old friends Mr Hornby &
Lord Derby I found just as ever, though 72 & 75, and every day
has caused fresh shaking of hands with old friends . . . Certainly
English people do go on with friendship just where they left off,
as you go on with a book at the page you last read. So you see,
barring the queer climate I have been intensely happy, & if one
were morbidly inclined, one would think that like Dives one was
enjoying all one's good things here below.'[2]

But the good things had to end, and by mid-September he was
in London ready for the new term. His rooms were at No. 17,
Stratford Place, a cul-de-sac running north from Oxford Street
where some of the three-storey Georgian houses still stand. During
the next three months he prepared his drawings. After the kind of
painting he had been doing it must have been a wearisome task
in every way, but at the beginning of January, 1850 he sent his
work to the selectors and on the 16th he heard that he had been
accepted. He was delighted—and yet a little worried—when he
wrote to Fortescue to tell him the news:

Dear Fortescue,
    What fun!—pretty little dear—!—he got into the Academy—
he did!—Yes—so he did.
    You will be pleased to hear that the R. Academy have sate on
my drawing from the antique, and that I am a 'probationer'—&
on my trial till April when the 3 drawings I have to make will be
again sate on—and I shall be admitted for 10 years as a student—
or—rejected. *Vedermo quale sarò.*
    I tried with 51 little boys—and 19 of us were admitted. I go
with a large book and a piece of chalk to school every day like
a good little boy.

Yours affectionately,
Edward Lear[3]

Slopes of Myrtle

It must have been difficult to have been surrounded by students twenty years younger than himself, but they probably thought of him as rather special, for here was a man who had travelled widely and had published three books about his journeys, who had

Lear at the Academy Schools

illustrated numerous works of natural history and was the author of the famous *Book of Nonsense*—a man, moreover, who had been drawing master to the Queen.

Practically nothing has survived from Lear's time at the R.A. Schools, which is a pity for we don't know how he reacted to this strange interlude. We do know that he was accepted as a student after the three months' probationary period on April 26th, but it is very doubtful that he ever intended to stay the full course, for he would have been nearly fifty when he finished. It seems probable that he stayed for two and a half years, and in this time he would have done a great deal of drawing from the antique and learned something about the human form, but he would have had no tuition in oil painting.

To get extra money to help him along he published some more of his travels. In 1851 *Journals of a Landscape Painter in Greece and Albania* appeared, and was an immediate success. 'I received *heaps* and *loads* of compliments and congratulations about the book,'[4] Lear wrote to a friend, and Tennyson was so impressed that he wrote the lines, 'To E.L., on his Travels in Greece.'

> Illyrian woodlands, echoing falls
> Of water, sheets of summer glass,
> The long divine Peneïan pass,
> The vast Akrokeraunian walls,
>
> Tomohrit, Athos, all things fair,
> With such a pencil, such a pen,
> You shadow forth to distant men,
> I read and felt that I was there:
>
> And trust me while I turn'd the page,
> And track'd you still on classic ground,
> I grew in gladness till I found
> My spirits in the golden age.
>
> For me the torrent ever pour'd
> And glisten'd—here and there alone
> The broad-limb'd Gods at random thrown
> By fountain-urns;—and Naiads oar'd
>
> A glimmering shoulder under gloom
> Of cavern pillars; on the swell
> The silver lily heaved and fell;
> And many a slope was rich in bloom
>
> For him that on the mountain lea
> By dancing rivulets fed his flocks
> To him who sat upon the rocks,
> And fluted to the morning sea.

In the following year came *Journals of a Landscape Painter in Southern Calabria and the Kingdom of Naples*, the most personal and enthusiastic of his travel books. Like the book on Greece and

Albania the text here was more important than the illustrations, and he showed again how vividly he could recreate scenes with words.

It was whilst Lear was at the Academy that the dissatisfaction that some young painters felt with its principles of painting became a public issue, for a few weeks before the Summer Exhibition of 1850 the meaning of the letters P.R.B. became known, and the Pre-Raphaelite Brotherhood became a controversial part of the Victorian art scene.

The Brotherhood was the creation of three young men of unusual talent and utterly different temperament. It is extraordinary that they came together at all, and yet their very differences meant that each contributed something to the movement. John Millais— attractive and charming, yet not entirely likeable—had been encouraged to paint by enthusiastic parents who had brought him from Jersey to London so that he could study drawing. When he went to the R.A. Schools at the age of eleven he was the youngest student they had ever had, and when he left at seventeen he won the Royal Academy Gold Medal. William Holman Hunt was plain, puritanical, and rather self-consciously intense: he had to fight his father for permission to study art, and had worked for four years in a City office before going to the R.A. Schools in 1844. The third man, Dante Gabriel Rossetti, imposing and strange, was born into a house where culture seemed intuitive. His father had escaped from Italy in 1824 when King Ferdinand of Naples, whom he had openly opposed, came to power, and when Dante Gabriel was born he was Professor of Italian Literature at King's College in the Strand.

Their aims were to have genuine ideas which they sought to express well, and to study nature itself. Instead of painting onto a half-tone which absorbed the light, they used a white canvas which reflected the light and pushed it back through the paint giving a brilliance to the colour. They didn't deny the work of earlier painters, providing it was 'direct and serious and heartfelt', and they continued taking subjects from the Bible. But they discovered the little-known poetry of Keats, and found new subjects in the medievalism of Isabella and La Belle Dame sans Merci. Rossetti, the true son of a revolutionary, suggested a secret brotherhood, esoteric and dedicated to its beliefs, which they modelled on the German Nazarene painters of fifty years before, and when Collinson, Woolner, Stephens, and William Michael Rossetti were invited to join the Brotherhood numbered seven.

The first paintings exhibited with the mysterious letters P.R.B. had aroused a certain inquisitive interest, but nothing more. But now the Academicians realised that one of their brightest young painters was questioning the very foundation of the Academy, and whilst a lesser painter could be ignored—in fact the work of Hunt and Rossetti was scarcely mentioned—the new Millais could not. The critics saw in his work a rejection of the values which they had been content to endorse, so their response was entirely predictable, and they were voraciously insulting. Speaking of Millais' gentle, and to modern eyes, sentimentalized painting of 'Christ in the House of His Parents', Dickens warned the public that they must expect to see 'the lowest depths of what is mean, repulsive and revolting',[5] and—whatever one may think of the painting—his notice published in Household Words must be one of the saddest pieces of uninformed bigotry a great writer ever wrote. Perhaps it did offend against their ideas of the Holy Family, and certainly there were cries of 'blasphemy', but in the following year the same tone of criticisms met Millais' 'The Return of the Dove to the Ark', which was not, even then, a subject about which the public would have felt with passion.

This time Ruskin was persuaded to take up their cause in *The Times*, and after this the Brotherhood became more respectable. During the winter of 1851 Millais worked on his painting of 'A Huguenot', a deliberate concession to public taste, and by the middle of 1852 the fervour of the Brotherhood as a group had been spent.

The Summer Exhibition was held then in the National Gallery, and Lear who was studying in the Schools tucked away behind the Gallery was in the centre of the controversy: in fact, he had a picture in the Academy himself for the first time that year—a painting of Claude Lorrain's house on the Tiber. He had no particular sympathy for the subjects which the Pre-Raphaelites chose—his ambition was always and only to be a landscape painter—but they did seem to embody some of his own ideals: a close study of nature was essential to him and had been one reason for the extraordinary success of his ornithological paintings, and he had admired freshness of colour in Turner's work.

By the middle of 1851, when he had been at the Schools for eighteen months, Lear was feeling run down and depressed. 'I never can apply to remembering how hours of sedentary life make me boil over when I get away—a steam-force which is let off by walking, but bursts out in rage & violence if it has no natural outlet,'[6] he wrote later, for without exercise his epilepsy was always worse. London then was 'an endless roar of traffic, under an opaque sky and a steady drift of smuts, sending up, according to season, fountains of mud or whirlwinds of dust, straw and paper,'[7] an unpleasant contrast to wide Grecian valleys and Albanian hills. News of Lord Derby's death distressed him; and though his work had improved he wasn't at all happy about the way in which it was going.

He went down to Devon for the summer vacation hoping that a few months away from London would revive his health and spirits, but it was wet, he was isolated, and he felt worse than ever. 'I don't improve as I wish,' he told Fortescue sadly, 'which added to the rain, and the view prevents "happiness and tranquility". It is true I don't *expect* to improve, because I am aware of my peculiar incapacities for art, mental & physical:—but that don't mend the matter, anymore than the knowledge that he is to be always blind delights a man whose eye is poked out. The great secret of my constant hard work is, to prevent my going back, or at best standing quite still. I certainly did improve last year a little, but I aint sure if Lydford and the rain and the cows won't have made me go back this year. However I did it all for the best, as the old sow said when she sat on her little pigs.'[8]

In August Lushington came down, and they went for a walking tour through Cornwall, but when Lear was depressed he could be an extraordinarily bad companion, and it was a disaster. What he

Alfred Tennyson   *William Holman Hunt*

needed was some real instruction and encouragement in his work, for he had come back to England enthusiastic and wanting to make real use of this chance, but now he was beginning to drift. He still had another eighteen months to go in the Antique School, and he began to talk about going to a nightly academy to draw from life. His frustration was exaggerated when he tried to make considered oil paintings from the sketches he had brought back from Greece and Palestine, and he realised that he simply didn't know how to do them.

Then one day in the summer of 1852, Robert Martineau—whose picture 'Kit's Writing Lesson' painted that year hangs now in the Tate—brought Holman Hunt to Lear's studio at Stratford Place. Lear was nervous and Hunt remembered that he 'overflowed with geniality, and at the same time betrayed anxiety as we turned over the drawings'.[9] He saw that the sketches were not detailed enough as reference for large oil paintings, and his Pre-Raphaelite principles were a little shocked to think of Lear working only from sketches. The obvious thing was for Lear to find countryside which resembled what he was painting, and then he could study the scene direct from nature. The painting of the 'Quarries of Syracuse', for instance, included limestone rocks and fig trees, and both these could be found in England. He was about to go down to Fairlight, in the hills above Hastings, to work on his painting of 'The Lost Sheep', and he suggested that Lear might like to go with him and he could show him what he meant.

Lear accepted the offer excitedly, and it was arranged that he would go down first to find somewhere for them to stay. A few days later he wrote to Hunt telling him that he had found Clive Vale Farm, which was rather pokey but otherwise ideal. Hunt told him to go ahead and take it, and then came a strange letter from Lear. It was unwise, he wrote, for them to be too impulsive. Living so close might strain their friendship, and he suggested that they should have separate parts of the house and meet only at mealtimes. He was still very guarded when Hunt arrived a few days later with William Rossetti, who had come to spend the first week with them. In exchange for lessons in painting Lear was to teach Hunt Italian, and Rossetti's presence that first evening proved a blessing for he and Lear chatted to each other in Italian, and by the end of dinner Lear was no longer strained. 'Now I had intended to go to my own room,' he told them, 'but if you do not mind, I'll bring down some of my drawings and pen them out here, so that we may all be together.'[10] The suggestion of separate rooms could then become a joke, and he explained to Hunt—most unsatisfactorily—that he had been frightened that he might be a lover of bulldogs and would arrive at the farm bringing two of these detestable pets.

No more explanations were given, but perhaps it is worth noting that this was the only time, except when he was travelling, that Lear risked living closely with someone else, and that not one of his friends apparently ever realised that he was an epileptic. He had warning of the attacks, but he had to be sure of the arrangements, and to know that he could have the privacy he needed. But he must have been satisfied that his secret would be kept, for there was no more mention of separate rooms.

For the first ten days Lear went with Hunt to watch him paint, and then he decided to try on his own. It was a short apprentice-ship, and Hunt writing to F. G. Stephens was most uncompli-mentary: 'Lear is a very nice fellow but much too old to live with always—he is about 40. I am being drilled in Italian by him and in return I am letting him see me paint, which from his productions I confess myself unable to feel is a very great advantage.'[11]

Fortunately, his disdain didn't come through to Lear, nor was it apparently seriously intended, and the two men enjoyed one another's company. They lived primitively, and after their evening meal would settle down and talk, whilst Lear penned out his drawings or made notes about Hunt's technique in *Ye Booke of Hunte*. Hunt enjoyed listening to Lear's accounts of his journeyings, and they talked of one day exploring Palestine together. They discussed Tennyson's poetry and conceived the idea of illustrating his poems, a scheme that Hunt and some of the other Pre-Raphaelites went through with in the Moxon edition of 1857 in a style totally different from Lear's later illustrations. Tennyson was invited to stay but, sadly for Lear, he didn't accept. Other friends came down to see them, Martineau lived nearby in Hastings, and Millais spent a day with them, the first time that Lear had met him.

During the months that Hunt and Lear lived together, a deep and lifelong friendship grew. It had none of the emotional charge of Lear's relationship with Lushington, nor—despite the letter to Stephens—any of the condescension which later marred his relationship with Fortescue for a time. They respected each other and had much in common: 'He is very plain & uneducated, except by his own exertions,'[12] Lear said of Hunt that summer, and he might have been speaking of himself. It was a two-way relationship—Hunt could give Lear help with his painting, and Lear was able to implant in Hunt some of his own love of poetry and music: 'I am indebted to you for the amount of culture that I have got since the time I first met you,'[13] Hunt told him, many years later.

Lear never aspired to being a Pre-Raphaelite Brother, and the Brotherhood had in any case virtually broken up by 1852, but he did feel himself qualified to be called a Son, and he christened Holman Hunt 'Daddy', and Millais and Woolner were then his Uncles. 'Daddy Hunt's head would cut up sufficient for 10 men, & his heart for 200 at least. God bless him.'[14]

In the late autumn the two men split up. Hunt had to return to

Reggio, 1852. One of the first paintings Lear did under Holman Hunt at Clive Vale Farm in the late summer and autumn of 1852

London, but Lear wanted to work on the fig tree in his painting of Syracuse, and he had discovered a perfect tree in Hastings. He felt that these three months had been the most valuable of his whole stay in England, and after they parted he sent Hunt a copy of his nonsense to show his gratitude. 'I really cannot help again expressing my thanks to you for the progress I have made this autumn,' he wrote in the covering letter. 'The Reggio, and the Venosa are both done and in frames,—(except that the latter will have to benefit by some of your remarks when we meet) and I hardly believe I did them. I am now beginning to have perfect faith in the means employed, and if the Thermopylae turns out right I am a P.R.B. for ever. Indeed, in no case, shall I ever return to the old style.'[15]

The fig tree he had found was in the garden of Frederick North, the Member of Parliament for Hastings, and whilst he was working on it Lear took rooms with the gardener. He wanted to paint jackdaws perched in the tree, and had brought with him a stuffed bird which he wired onto the branches in different positions, with a delightful disregard for strict Pre-Raphaelite principles.

Pre-Raphaelite 1849-53

Frederick North had two daughters who soon became Lear's friends. The older girl, Catherine, later married John Addington Symonds, and whilst he was at Hastings Lear stated firmly and a little sadly what his own views on marriage had become. 'No, my dear Fortescue,' he wrote, '*I* don't mean to marry—never. *You* should, but there's time enough yet for you—6 or 8 years perhaps. In my case I should paint less and less well, and the thought of annual infants would drive me wild. If I attain to 65, and have an "establishmᵗ" with lots of spoons &c. to offer—I *may* chain myself:—but surely not before. And alas! and seriously—when I look around my acquaintance—and few men have more, or know more intimately, do I see a majority of happy pairs? No, I don't. Single—I may have few pleasures—but married—many risks and miseries are semi-certainly in waiting—nor till the plot is played out can it be said that evils are not at hand . . .

'In one sense, I am growing very indifferent to the running out of the sands of life. Years are making me see matters with totally different eyes than I formerly saw with:—but at the same time I am far more cheerful. I only wish I could dub and scrub myself into what I wish to be, and what I might be I fear if I took proper pains. But *chi sa?* How much will be allowed for *nature*, and early impressions, and iron early tuition? Looking back, I sometimes wonder I am even what I am. I often wonder and wonder how I have made so many certainly real friends as I have. Sometimes 6 or 8 of the kindest letters in the world come together, and the effect is rather humiliating tho' not to my peculiar idiosyncracy.'[16]

Frederick North's younger daughter, Marianne, later travelled over the world making the drawings of plants which now fill the North Gallery at Kew Gardens. She used to go and watch Lear painting, and remembered how he would 'wander into our sitting-room through the windows at dusk when his work was over, sit down to the piano, and sing Tennyson's songs for hours, composing as he went on, and picking out the accompaniments by ear, putting the greatest expression and passion into the most sentimental words. He often set me laughing; then he would say I was not worthy of them, and would continue with intense pathos of expression and gravity of face, while he substituted 'Hey Diddle

Diddle, the Cat and the Fiddle', or some other nonsensical words to the same air.'[17] Lear had no musical training and could neither read nor write music, but he was a popular after-dinner entertainer. In 1853 he published some of his settings of Tennyson's poems, including his own sad favourite, 'Tears, Idle Tears'. His were the only settings that Tennyson himself liked, 'they seem to throw a diaphanous veil over the words—nothing more,'[18] he said, and after hearing 'Home They Brought the Warrior Dead', Archbishop Tait had exclaimed, 'Sir, you ought to have half the Laureateship'.[19] But not all his listeners were so appreciative: 'Edward Lear, a charming man and author of the well-known Book of Nonsense, could hardly be called a musician', wrote one, 'but being good at "vamping" he sat down to the piano and hummed rather than sang two of Tennyson's songs to tunes of his own composing. It was a clever performance; but the really musical people there were quite surprised at the eulogistic terms in which Tennyson spoke of the compositions. I cannot help thinking, however, that it was regard for the man rather than the music which caused this unexpected outburst of praise.'[20]

He had intended to return to London in January, but when the ceiling in the London house fell in he decided to stay on until the winter was over. He wanted to submit his new paintings to the two big London exhibitions—at the British Institution and the Royal Academy—and he needed to have them finished early in the new year. Left to work on his own he quickly became disheartened, and he wrote to Emily Tennyson, 'It is a sad evil with me that I *think* I can do so much more than I ever *can* do: & that I have so little faith in my powers of improvement. Whether I shall ever see myself in a fair groove of continuous improvement is very doubtful now.'[21] He needed Hunt's constant advice to help him over the difficulties in his painting, for he never really understood what he was doing well enough to analyse what was wrong or know how to put it right. '. . . if you cannot tell me how the shadows of the blessed jackdaws will fall I don't know what I shall do,' he wrote despairingly to him. 'Also the shadows of the three blocks or necks of stone are too similar in colour,—but I don't know how to change them. Altogether I foresee the possibility of this picture being a failure and remaining unfinished, unless you can help me out of the mess. It has been so completely impossible even to see nature lately—much more to paint it, that the poor beast of painting has not had fair play. This however by no means weakens my faith as to the proper way of painting—had I been really able to follow it out.'[22]

He was back in London by the end of February in new rooms at 65 Oxford Terrace, and the sale of a painting to Richard Bethell, later Lord Westbury, helped him over the move. He had left the Academy by now, and was getting most, in fact probably all, of his tuition from Hunt. He realised that there was still a lot he didn't know and that he would soon be too old to learn, but the climate had started to worry him again and he was torn between wanting to go through and master the technique of oil painting with Hunt's help, and a hankering to be on the move again to somewhere where the sun shone.

The acceptance of his picture of the 'Mountains of Thermopylae' by the British Institution in the spring of 1853 gave him new encouragement, for it was widely praised. 'Lear has a picture at the B.I. which is capital,' Stephens told Woolner; 'he delights to acknowledge his obligations to Hunt for instruction while they were staying at Fairlight together. He goes everywhere saying that Hunt taught him all he knows and he has improved wonderfully.'[23]

Sending-in day for the R.A. was in April, and his magnum opus—the five-foot-long painting of 'The Quarries of Syracuse'—had to be ready in time for this. But his sister Sarah and her husband had decided to leave England to go and live in New Zealand, and Lear was working well on his painting when he had to put it on one side and help Sarah with her preparations. He fretted over the valuable time which was slipping away, and when he was able to get back to it he had lost the flow. Disappointed, he again asked Hunt for help, and it was ready—but not as he had wished it—in time.

Despite his misgivings, the painting was accepted, and within a few weeks had been bought by the Earl of Beauchamp who chose it as his Art Union Prize. 'Dear Daddy', Lear wrote when he heard the news, 'the Syracuse *is* sold, for £250—thanks my boy to

Lear, drawn by Holman Hunt

you. Tell Millais—and W. Rossetti from me. I am now going out—
to hop on one leg all the way to Hastings.'[24]

In March Lord Derby asked him to do a painting of Windsor
Castle, the first commission he had had since his return to England,
and at the beginning of July he left for Windsor. But working
there completely alone, his world became black. The weather was
dreadful, and this made painting difficult. 'The sky is always beastly
blueblack, and I have sent for no end of tubes of that ingredient:
—and during this week the sun has shone twice,' he told Hunt. 'It
is therefore utterly impossible to do this view in a strictly P.R.B.

principle,—for supposing a tree is black one minute—the next it is yellow, and the third green; so that were I to finish any one part the whole eight feet would be all spots—a sort of leopard landscape. I must therefore—*if ever* there is sun again, (toward evening) make out the shadows grossly and work as I can. All the distance also is blue-grey and black—dark and light by fits,—and the castle which should be in stormy light and shade has been for two days jet black—two more crumbled grey without an iota of detail, and the remaining two days wholly invisible. The difficulty of the whole thing disgusts me immensely, the more that as it is to be a portrait I can give way to no remedies of imagination.'[25]

In desperation he came away without finishing the picture, and went up to Leicestershire to make studies of rocks for a painting of the temple of Bassae. But the weather didn't improve, and in October he wrote to Emily Tennyson, 'I am turning over in every way some mode of leaving this loathsome climate & getting a living for the remainder of my life, even if as a shoeblack, so I could see the sun. Perhaps I may go & fight the Russians—perhaps go to Australia. But stay here I won't, to be demoralized by years of mud & fog & gnats and rheumatism & small beer and stupid bores and coalfires and choleramorbusses and income taxes and calvinists and steel forks and humbugs and midnight atmospheres all the year round—I have had enough of it, & forthwith I am growing moustaches in sign of going elsewhere.'[26]

He decided to go on the trip to Egypt and Palestine that he and Hunt had talked about in the evenings at Clive Vale Farm. Hunt couldn't leave at once as he was working on his painting of 'The Light of the World'; in fact, when he looked at the 'decayed returned prodigals and flourishing fatted calves',[27] he wondered if it was wise for him to leave England at all. For Lear there was no choice—his health had become so bad that he couldn't wait. 'You will be sorry to hear that my lungs & throat are so much worse that I am going off at once to see the "Palms & temples of the south",' he told Emily Tennyson. 'I wish I could see you, but I shall wait to see my friends with comfort in Heaven—for in England is none for me.'[28]

He had been home for four and a half years, and later 'rejoiced at my slavey labours at anatomy in 1849–50—for small progress as I made—I can make somewhat like figures now—& never could before.'[29] (Lear's dates are often questionable, and in reading anything of his one has to be guided by his own dictum, '. . . as the morbid and mucilaginous monkey said when he climbed to the top of the Palm-tree and found no fruit there, one can't depend on dates.'[30]) But on the whole it had been a disappointing time. He had committed himself to years of drawing from the antique, an impossible task for a man of his age with his painting experience. If he had gone to a smaller art school, one less hidebound by tradition —perhaps even the night school that he had talked about—where he could have concentrated on figure drawing, he might have learnt what he needed in one or two years. But may be it wasn't just figure drawing that he had in mind when he came home. Perhaps he felt that to qualify for acceptance as a serious painter he must have studied at the Schools where almost all the major British painters of his day had at some time been students; perhaps too he had a hankering to fulfil a boyhood ambition by going through the training that he had been cheated of then.

Sadly, for it was the end of a hopeful dream, he boarded the *S.S. Indus* on December 6th, 1855, and sailed for Alexandria.

CHAPTER NINE

The Morbids

1853–55

As Lear's boat steamed south into the Mediterranean he began to soak up the warmth of the sun. He was usually a bad sailor and it was late in the year, but the weather in the Bay of Biscay had been perfect and for the first time in his life he was really enjoying being on a boat. There were about 150 'merry & agreeable' passengers, most of them on their way out to India.

At Gibraltar there was time to make a quick dash ashore to see the Alameda and the public gardens, and then they settled back to a gentle cruise along the North African coast. To pass the time they ate breakfast at 9, luncheon at 12, dinner at 4, tea at 7, and supper at 9.30, and the rest of the time they played cards and games and got up an appetite for the next meal by walking round the deck. Each evening after supper they sat out in the warm moonlight chatting and listening to music; with the ladies in their evening gowns the deck looked like 'a great sea drawing room'[1]—colourful gaiety a few feet from the quiet rushing of the black sea as the boat cut through the water.

They stopped briefly at Malta which looked 'pretty & sunny & gay',[2] and perhaps Lear thought of his meeting there with Lushington nearly five years before.

Cairo seemed even more bustling and colourful than it had been five years before. From his hotel room he looked out over a garden of high palms and green acacia trees filled with doves and kites and crested hoopoes: this was what he had missed in London where there was nothing to satisfy his feeling for rich, colourful beauty. Thomas Seddon, one of the painters on the fringe of the Pre-Raphaelite movement, was there, and he told his brother: 'I have been very glad of Lear's arrival, both to meet him because his advice as an experienced traveller has been very useful, and also because I have been able to consult him about pictures I think of painting. He says that I have become accustomed to the language and habits of the people, and have settled down to work in much shorter time than most persons, so my conscience is at ease.'³

Lear's own conscience wasn't so easy. He really had meant to settle in England and not start wandering again, and he kept feeling that he must justify his journey to Ann. 'Of this I am sure', he wrote to her, 'that had I persisted in remaining in England, my lungs would not have recovered again. So you see I am *taking it easy*, & regarding my *exile*, as a medicinal & necessary remedy.'⁴

He dithered for a few days uncertain whether to travel up the Nile alone or stay in Cairo with Seddon, painting and learning Arabic until Hunt arrived, but then he was invited to join a party which was leaving just after Christmas and he decided to go with them. 'We start—(don't laugh!) *4* boats together, & *3* more go before, & *5* or 6 follow after!!!—so that it is a regular English company,' he told Ann. She must have been particularly anxious as he then began lengthy reassurances: 'Our Dragoman, Khaleel, is a *well known*, & *most respectable* person, & I hope you will think of me as being *quite among friends*, and also enjoying myself in seeing the wonderful temples I have so long desired to see. I wish you to know also that I promise you *not* to go into *any pits*, or *caves*; for I hate dust & mummies & dark holes.—*I will take the greatest care of myself in every way*.'⁵

They travelled up the Nile at a leisurely pace, dropping anchor each night, and by the end of the first week they had reached Minyeh. 'So far, it is a magnificent river, with endless villages— hundreds & hundreds on its banks, all fringed with palms, & reflected in the water;—the usual accompaniments of buffaloes, camels, etc. abound, but the multitude of birds it is utterly impossible to describe,—geese, pelicans, plovers, eagles, hawks, cranes, herons, hoopoes, doves, pigeons, king fishers & many others. The most beautiful feature is the number of boats, which look like giant moths,—& sometimes there is a fleet of 20 or 30 in sight at once.'⁶

The Morbids 1853-55

But it was the colour which astonished him most. It was so clear and brilliant that he found it impossible to paint, and when he went back to Egypt thirteen years later the first thing he realised was that his pictures of the Nile were drained of colour. If he could have used oils he would have been able to get more brilliance with glazes of pure paint, but oils dried almost as soon as he squeezed them onto the palette, and he had to do his best with more restricted water colour.

He was surrounded by boatloads of English people, yet he felt terribly lonely—a thing he had hardly been aware of when he was travelling by himself in the isolated mountains of Albania. He had an extraordinary way of exploring and savouring every little bit of what he saw, from the majesty of the scenery to the eccentricities of his companions, but he found nobody with whom he could share his excitement. Whenever he could he walked on his own along the river bank. 'This morning I have had a delicious walk— through never ending corn fields,' he wrote just after they had left Girga; 'at times the ground was all blue & gray with *clouds* of pigeons; & the most beautiful little plovers & kingfishers hop just before my feet. But what pleased me very much, was to find a real vulgar old English *toad*! waddling in the field!'[7]

Philae

Slopes of Myrtle

They travelled as far south as Aswan and the first cataract, and some of the party went on into Nubia as far as Wadi Halfa. But Lear wanted plenty of time to see Philae, the beautiful little oasis of ancient temples and palm trees, the home of Isis, sister-bride of Osiris. Philae is an island, and as their boat was moored upstream they couldn't return to it each night. Instead they took luggage and beds and cooking things and set themselves up in the Temple of Isis. Every day new parties were arriving or leaving, and as there were always three or four boatloads of English people they had a dinner party each evening with music on the Temple terrace.

He stayed there for ten very happy days. 'It is impossible to describe the place', he wrote, 'any further than by saying it is more like a real *fairy island* than anything else I can compare it to. It is very small, & was formerly all covered with temples, of which the ruins of 5 or 6 now only remain. The great T. of Isis, on the terrace of which I am now writing, is so extremely wonderful that no words can give the least idea of it. The Nile is divided here into several channels, by other rocky islands, & beyond you see the desert & the great granite hills of Assouan.'[8]

On February 8th he began on the return journey, and a week later the boat reached Luxor. Here he spent another ten days exploring Karnak and the ruined temples at Thebes and the tombs in the Valley of the Kings: it was all more magnificent than Philae, but not so drawable.

The rest of the journey, down stream for hundreds of miles, became very tedious. The wind kept dropping completely, and they had to heave to for days at a time. When he reached Cairo on March 16th, 1854, he had been away for ten weeks, and had grown a bushy beard. He had other beards on his travels but had always shaved them off when he reached home, but this one stayed on and he looked half way between Socrates and Sir John Falstaff.[9]

'Cairo seems like home once more.—So many friends are here,'[10] he wrote, and one of them was Holman Hunt who had finished his painting and had decided to come. Lear would have liked to have gone on with him to Jerusalem, but the Nile trip had been expensive and Palestine must wait.

The Morbids 1853-55

He reached London at the end of April feeling well, and Lord Derby's picture—which had seemed an impossible burden the previous autumn—was finished within a few weeks. But the climate soon began to tell again. 'For a fortnight I was quite knocked up by the cold east winds,' he told Hunt in July, 'but now it is rheumatism and gloom and cloud and mud and beastliness.'[11]

He wanted to try another winter in England, though, for once he made the decision to live abroad for half the year he was going to find it much more difficult to become established as a serious painter. If he got himself really fit before the cold weather he might be able to get through the winter without trouble. There was talk of his going with Lushington for a walking tour of the Pyrenees, but this had to be called off when Lushington was sent to Malta to bring back his sister who was ill. Perhaps this was as well, for he had changed completely since their carefree spring in Greece, and failing to recapture their earlier happiness would have made Lear's health worse instead of better.

Instead Lear decided to have a proper look at Switzerland which he had only passed through on his way to Italy, and Bernard Senior—who had changed his name to Bernard Husey Hunt—arranged to go with him for part of the time.

Lear left London on August 1st and waited for Husey Hunt at Thun, resting beside the lake and wallowing in the clear, clean air. In mid-August they set out together to walk over the Bernese Alps and across the Rhône Valley to Piedmulera, a few miles from Lake Maggiore. Then they turned west along the valley of Anzasca to the foot of Monte Rosa and up through Saas and the Stalden Pass to Zermatt. There Hunt left him, and Lear went north on his own to Interlaken. He had planned to cover Switzerland systematically, but the cold weather was coming on and he decided not to stay any longer. He had enjoyed the trip and the scenery had been wonderful, but somehow he wasn't enthralled by the beauty of the Alps as he had been by the wide Grecian landscape or the tumble-down splendour of parts of Italy.

He seemed to look for two things in scenery—associations with the ancient past, and tranquillity—neither of which he found in

Slopes of Myrtle

Switzerland. Horizontals and verticals in landscape give a sense of peaceful harmony and in most of Lear's work there is a recession into wide horizons. But in Swiss scenery the shapes clash diagonally, and the feeling of grand beauty combines with a fearful severity. 'I can hardly tell why I so much wished to see the Alps,' he wrote to Holman Hunt in Jerusalem—'partly because (perhaps) I was tired of having talked of without having seen them. Now that I have done so, I feel I was right in coming, as there is so much of the astonishing and majestic in Swiss scenery that no landscape painter who wishes his mind to open at the admiration and comprehension of *all kinds* of nature, should pass through life without seeing this country.'[12]

He returned to England at the beginning of October to face the worst winter he had ever known. In January London was bitterly cold and damp and dirty—a combination which went straight to his chest. His asthma was dreadful and his throat became so sore that from the middle of January until the middle of May he went out only once. 'I now imitate the conduct of marmots, dormice, truffles, tortoises & other hybernating things with the utmost strictness until summer comes,'[13] he wrote to a friend.

Tied indoors with short, dark days and only spluttering, dim gas light to work by he felt unbearably depressed, and he had to put away the large painting of Bassae on which he had started working again. Instead he painted £5 'pot-boilers' which he hoped would help to pay his bills. Friends came to visit him, and on March 18th Fortescue wrote in his diary: 'B'fast with poor Lear, whom I am v. fond of. He hardly goes out, so delicate in lungs.'[14]

For four months he lived a half-life, and he knew that he couldn't struggle through another English winter. From now on he must winter abroad and concentrate on sending work back to the big exhibitions where he might still make his name known. He would belong nowhere—to his friends in London he would be someone who lived abroad and came home for the summer months, and on the continent he would be just another of the winter visitors. Wandering—which had begun as a necessity and become an enjoyment—was now forced upon him as an exile.

Lord Derby's painting of Windsor was the only commission he had had that year, and altogether this was the most disheartening time he had known since he had begun painting. But it was only a foretaste of the chronic uncertainty which he knew for the rest of his life, and which was the result of two factors—his constant ill health which would keep him away from England for six months each year, and his inability to find even a small place in the ranks of the accepted artists of his day.

It seemed to him that year that life was going on around him, and that he was scarcely involved. In June he went to the stag party which Wilkie Collins threw for Millais before he left for Scotland to marry Effie Ruskin, and afterwards he wrote sadly to Tennyson: 'I feel woundily like a spectator,—all through my life—of what goes on amongst those I know:—very little an actor.'[15]

The gloomy winter had started him on a stream of introspection, and he seemed unable to shake himself out of it. He felt that he needed the kind of sympathetic understanding that Alfred Tennyson's gentle wife Emily could give, and he thought of spending the summer months near their new home at Farringford on the Isle of Wight. 'Do you think there is a Pharmouse or a Nin somewhere near you, where there would be a big room looking to the North?— so that I could paint in it quietly, & come & see you & Mrs Tennyson promiscuously?' he asked Alfred—'I know what you will say, or are saying—"come to us"—But that wouldn't do:—the botherations of 6 feet paintings & all the combotherations of artists' ways *do not*, & *will not* dovetail with country houses in Anglosaxnland;— I have tried the matter well—& know it to be so. Utter idleness gets possession of me body & soul in that atmosphere:—afterwards, remorse . . . If one were but a chimney pot, or a pipkin, or a mackrel, or anything respectable & consistent there would be some comfort; but the years go by without making the use of one's faculties one ought to do, & so I feel disgusted I do.'[16]

In fact it is very unlikely that the Tennysons could have coped with him that summer. In June Alfred was in Oxford receiving the honorary degree of D.C.L., and in July he was faced with an onslaught of criticism when he published *Maud*. 'If an author pipe of adultery, fornication, murder and suicide, set him down as the

Emily Tennyson

practiser of those crimes,' wrote one critic, to which Tennyson replied with splendid dignity: 'Adulterer I may be, fornicator I may be, murderer I may be, suicide I am not yet.'[17]

Instead, Lear spent the summer of 1855 moving around. He was at Eastbourne and Hurstmonceux, and at the end of July he went to stay at Park House—but that was a great mistake. Henry Lushington had been taken suddenly ill in Malta, and Lear must have decided that he could be of some help to the family. 'As Frank's friend you could not, I am sure, be in any place where you could so much wish to be,'[18] Emily Tennyson wrote to him, but the Lushingtons disagreed. The silence and gloom of Park House were even more oppressive than usual as they waited for news, and they made it quite plain that Lear was not only superfluous but a downright nuisance, and if he had arrived uninvited, their attitude was understandable. He left, deeply hurt by the way they had treated him, and when Henry died early in August, Emily wrote: 'I have a dim sad feeling we must help each other & love each other, those who at all understand each other & love each other.'[19] For the next few months she gave him the only encouragement he had.

Emily alone understood what he felt for Lushington, and she comforted him as she might have done a young boy in love for the first time. More than anyone she realised the depth of his craving for affection, and Lear came to adore her.

To help him over his loneliness she confided her own feelings of isolation when Alfred left her alone at Farringford: 'What right have I to feel so sad who have so unspeakably much to make me cheerful even when he is away,' she wrote at the end of August; 'a love tried by all the changes & chances of a more than five years marriage and if tried only to prove its unimagined worth more & more . . . Dear Mr Lear why do I say all this to you but from a feeling you are not to be always "alone" & you must now sympathise prophetically with me.'[20]

A week later Alfred had returned, and she wrote to him again:

Dear Mr Lear,
    Here is an 'alone' which I hope may comfort you by being more 'alone' than you asked for. I am expecting visitors, so farewell. Alfred's love. He sends you this. I have not sent it of myself.

Most sincerely yours,
Emily Tennyson

Courage poor heart of stone
I will not ask thee why
Thou cans't not understand
That thou art left for ever alone.
Courage, poor stupid heart of stone:
Or if I ask thee why
Care not thou to reply
She is but dead & the time is at hand
When thou shalt more than die.[21]

In October she invited both Lear and Lushington down to stay. 'I must tell you what hard work is in store for you at Farringford,' she wrote to Lear. 'Not only are you to be sofa to my shyness & Frank's silence but you are to be yourself wellest and freshest and happiest.'[22] She seemed to be planning to divert his affections somewhere more promising, and one evening she invited some friends round and included in the party a bright young woman called Miss Cotton. After dinner Emily asked Lear to play some of his settings of Alfred's poems for them, and the effect on one side was as he had hoped. 'I am afraid you will not believe me when I tell you what a hero of romance you are . . .' she wrote ingenuously after he had left. 'How Miss Cotton was found all pale after a sleepless night, how her companion came and poured into my ear a nightly river of thanks and praises and admiration.'[23]

But Lear wasn't interested, though he had spent a wonderful few days at Farringford, and when he left he wrote a long letter to Emily: 'According to the morbid nature of the animal, I even complain sometimes that such rare flashes of light as such visits are to me, make the path darker after they are over:—a bright blue & green landscape with purple hills, & winding rivers, & unexplored forests, and airy downs, & trees & birds, & all sorts of calm repose, —exchanged for a dull dark plain horizonless, pathless, & covered with cloud above, while beneath are brambles & weariness.

'I really do believe that I enjoy hardly any one thing on earth while it is present: always looking back, or frettingly peering into the dim beyond.—With all this, I may say to you & Alfred, that the 3 or 4 days of the 16th–20th Oct 55,—were the best I have passed for many a long day.—If I live to grow old, & can hope to exist in England, I should like to be somewhere near you in one's later days. I wish sometimes I could settle near Park House. Then I might have a room near Boxley, & moon cripply, cripply about those hills, & sometimes see by turns Hallam & Lionel's children, & Frank's grandchildren, & so slide peacefully out of life. Alfred, by that time would have written endlessly, & there would be 6 or 8 thick green volumes of poems.—I—possibly,—should be in the workhouse, but I know you would all come & see me.'[24]

Now it was November, and he must make his plans for the winter. Earlier in the year Lushington had been offered the post of Judge to the Supreme Court of Justice in the Ionian Islands. He would be living in Corfu, and Lear had always promised himself that he would return to that beautiful little island. After the doubts and distress of the summer he must have asked himself if he was really wise to think of a future with Lushington—but perhaps it seemed such a wonderful opportunity to combine winter sunshine and companionship that he didn't stop and think if it could ever work.

The Morbids 1853-55

Fortescue wrote him a cheerful note before he left, wishing him well. Lear had stayed with him earlier in the autumn, and Fortescue had written then in his diary: 'He spoke to me more of himself & his secret feelings than he has ever done, showed me a good deal of his great and self-tormenting sensitiveness.'[25] But he never knew the real torment that was going on in Lear's mind—the thwarted, frustrated, impossible love that he had for Lushington. On November 21st, 1855, the two men sailed from Dover.

CHAPTER TEN

Corfu

1855–57

The journey across Europe to Trieste took a week, and they enjoyed it all. In Prague the snow began to fall, and when they reached Vienna the bright moonlight shone onto a cold, white city. The Alpine railway zig-zagged its way up and up and over the Semmering Pass, and then they dropped down to the Adriatic coast. 'Nobody can be so kind & thoughtful as my dear friend all the way', Lear wrote reassuringly to Ann; '—making me take food when I did not care to leave the carriage, by buying cakes or bread & bringing them to me, & saving me all the trouble possible, although he, from being my mere travelling companion in 1848–49, has now risen to one of the very highest places of the land at the age of 33.— But he is as wonderfully good & even tempered, as he is learned & wise.'[1]

On December 3rd they reached Corfu, traditionally Homer's island of Scheria. Here Odysseus, sun-burned and weary, was washed ashore near the end of his wandering voyage. Poseidon, in his malice, threw him against the rocks, but Athene led him safely in and he fell asleep in a thicket blanketed by fallen leaves. He didn't wake until the next afternoon, when the cries of Nausicaa and her maidens disturbed his long sleep. The king's daughter gave him food and clothes, and brought him to her father's palace where he was handsomely entertained before starting again on the last part of his homeward journey.

In the centuries after the age of Greek heroes and gods, Corfu had passed from one ruler to another, for its position close to the rocky mainland of Albania guarded the important sea route between Greece and Italy. At the end of the eighteenth century all the Ionian islands were held by the French, but in 1814 they were ceded to the British after the defeat of Napoleon. During their fifty years of rule the British became heartily disliked, more by just being there than for anything they did, for in the islands they were benign imperialists and did much to improve conditions for the Corfiotes. Their own way of life revolved round the wives of the officials and was typical of so many nineteenth-century imperial courts. There were balls and dinners and petty intrigues, interminable evenings of cards and gay little picnic excursions. Most of the English had no idea of the beauty of their island, just as in Rome so few of them had explored the beauties of the Campagna.

Lushington went to stay with Bowen until his own house was ready, but there was no room there for Lear. Still, he saw a fair amount of Lushington during the next few days: they dined together, and went to look at houses, and Lear found himself some expensive but pleasant rooms overlooking the harbour. But as the new judge, Lushington was an important and sought-after man, and soon he was too busy meeting people and settling into his work to have time to visit Lear. If Lear had been happy this probably wouldn't have worried him unduly—of course he was lonely, but it was quite reasonable for Lushington to be single-mindedly absorbed in getting into his new work. As it was he became acutely and morbidly depressed.

Ever since his return to England in 1849 things had started to go wrong. He had already mastered his best work—the fresh, uncluttered water-colour drawings which are now coming into their own—and if he had taken a thorough course in life drawing he could have begun again with increased powers. But instead he had tied himself to years of working from marble statues and plaster casts, and had left the Academy dissatisfied with both himself and his work. Then he had turned to the new painters, and was deceived into thinking that the Pre-Raphaelite approach had much in common with his own, though perhaps if he had thoroughly mastered their technique he could have adapted it to his advantage.

Lear's best work was essentially *petit maître*, and he would have thrived in the atmosphere of personal patronage which he had seen as a boy, but which had died with men like Fawkes and de Tabley. Now reputations were made in large, mixed exhibitions, and his paintings couldn't hope to compete with the elaborately conceived compositions which were usually the centre of attention. And so he began painting canvases seven or nine feet long.[2] But what excited him could best be expressed with spontaneity, and it lost everything when it was put down on a large, slowly worked canvas. Indeed, in painting landscape at all he was working in the wrong age to achieve popular success, for what the public wanted now were narrative paintings like 'The Order of Release' and 'Derby Day'.

The outcome of all this was that nobody wanted his work. In Rome there had always been a sale for his paintings, and some years had been extraordinarily good, but that kind of success depended on his being known, however small the community that knew him.

Perhaps this was one reason why he now turned with such emotional craving to Lushington—if nobody wanted his work at least someone might want him. If Lushington had loved and encouraged him, theirs might have developed into a full homosexual relationship. As it was, Lear probably only partly realized his homosexuality, though in the deeper layers of his mind there was conflict as he fought to suppress it, a conflict which contributed to his constant state of restlessness and depression. He was not the philandering homosexual that some writers have made him out to be—his search wasn't for physical love, but for someone who would want him as a person in the way that his parents had not wanted him as a child.[3] Through his sensibility and charm he was sought after as a friend, and he loved to be with children because they liked him and showed it. But what he was searching for, and never found, was real spiritual involvement with another person.

And beyond even this was the terrible unhappiness of forty years, the constant epileptic attacks which still came up to twenty times a month, marked in his diary by sad little crosses and which he now had to accept would never go—and the bewildering memories of his childhood. Usually he could tuck these away into an undisturbed corner of his mind where they were gradually covered by comforting layers of dust, but when a new unhappiness found its way into that corner the dust was suddenly shaken off and the monster of memory was there.

Corfu 1855–57

Today we would say that Lear was on the verge of a nervous breakdown—what he knew was that he was so unhappy he could do nothing. For hours he walked up and down his room with tears streaming down his face. If he tried to sleep he just lay looking up at the ceiling. Nobody called, nothing happened, and day after day it rained.

In his letters to Ann he hinted at what was going on, though she had little enough to make her life happy and he was careful not to upset her. But he did ask her to write to him every week instead of fortnightly, even if only a few lines. 'I will also write every week, & your letters will be, I fear, at present the only thing I have to look for. £2.10.0 or £3 will be the utmost expense of this—even if it went on for a year, but you must let me pay this, & I know you will.'[4]

Gradually the crisis passed. The weather improved and he began to get out. People started to drop in on him and even buy his work, and on January 16th, 1856, he wrote excitedly: 'On Monday, there was a regular burst of people into my rooms, & they ran away with £28 of little drawings!! So allowing for frames, I have cleared 23—by the morning's work:—& several of the people who came wished for other views—so that it really *does* seem as if one were going to get a comfortable living after all.'[5] He could even suggest rather sheepishly to Ann that there wasn't really enough news to fill a letter every week.

In fact, he soon found himself becoming fashionable on the island. 'We have found him a most agreeable person—and a great addition to our society, and we all like him very much—especially Lady Young, who has taken to sketching with great ardour',[6] the High Commissioner wrote to Fortescue. Lady Young bought three of his drawings and the other ladies followed suit, and back came the familiar feeling of being a big fish 'in this very little fish pond of a place'[7]—the very thing he had turned his back on five years earlier, but which was after all essential to him.

He was invited to dinners and balls at the palace and he usually went, though he didn't enjoy this kind of entertainment. 'Lord! how I hate the bustle and lights and fuss of "society"—social in reality as is my nature—not gregarious. Geese, swine, gnats, etc., are gregarious.'[8]

View from above the village of Ascension, Corfu

Slopes of Myrtle

Then at the beginning of February he received a tempting offer. There was a plan to open an art department in the university in Corfu, and he was invited to become its first director. He would have a salary of £100 a year, a free house and four months' holiday: in return he would be responsible for the administration of the school, and would have to give lessons in drawing and lectures in Italian. But he would be a civil servant responsible to the Government, and this would mean no more independence—and even though that independence was risky, he valued it. Anyway, he wouldn't have time to get on with his own work, and it would mean the end of his ambitions as a painter—so he wrote and declined the offer, hoping that he had been wise.

During his terrible winter depression he had had one bright thought—there was still time for him to paint the superb picture which would catch the public imagination and establish him as a painter. At the beginning of April he sent to England for some large canvases so that he could get to work on a painting for the 1857 Summer Exhibition, and then he began to explore the island for the best view. This was an enjoyable task, for it was spring and 'lo!—all the hedges & trees have said to each other—"bless us!—here is April the 10th there is no time to lose" & out they have all come in full leaf most wonderfully!—& as for flowers, things have now reached their utmost, & I suppose there is now no more possible room for any more . . . There is hardly any green left since an immense crop of marigolds, geraniums, orchises, irises, & cannonilla have come out. The hills are positively an immense crop of geraniums all gold colour—& in the olive woods, the large white heath looks like snow, & the pale lilac asphodels in such profusion as to seem like a sort of pale veil over all the ground. The hedges are *absolutely* pink, & in fact the whole thing is almost absurd from its very oddity.'[9]

There was some beautiful scenery to choose from, with the land climbing from the lowlands of the south through gentle undulations to the mountains in the north. In the end he settled on the view from above the village of Ascension, a sweeping vista over the top of receding olive groves to the rocky peninsula and the Citadel of Corfu, with the sea and snow topped mountains of Albania beyond.

Corfu 1855–57

Whilst he waited for the canvases to arrive he worked on drawings that had been commissioned, and every day before breakfast he had a Greek lesson. At the beginning of April he found new rooms which were bigger and lighter, and as he had more space he decided to take on a servant—a man who would be valet, housemaid and cook. He chose a Suliot—Suliot guards had ridden with Byron in the last days before he died—called Giorgio Kokali, who stayed with him for twenty-seven years, went with him on all his travels, and became the tempestuous companion of his old age.

Now that Lushington had settled into his job they were seeing more of each other again, and at the end of April they went to explore the coast of Corfu in Lushington's little yacht, *Midge*. But for Lear it was a 'screwy & bumpy & squashy' agony: 'I have come to the conclusion yachting does not suit me at all,' he wrote from the safety of a little bay on the western coast of the island: 'all the week has gone without my having done one single thing of any sort, & the nuisance of knocking one's head, & being in a cramped cabin is not repaid by any society in the world. I really believe the liking for yachts is merely a fashion, just as many women will bear the utmost pain in lacing rather than not appear in the mode.'[10]

He began to make friends of his own, though there were not many people there who shared his interests. Generally they were absorbed in Court palaver, and even though they liked his drawings they didn't take him very seriously. The wives would sometimes be taken with the sudden whimsy of coming to visit him as he worked, and when he was drawing out of doors he could hardly stop them. Then the quiet olive groves would suddenly fill with horses and their gay, chattering riders, but fortunately they didn't enjoy being in one place for too long and they would leave as suddenly as they had come. But amongst all the bubbling and superficial wives and daughters he found two young women whose company he could enjoy. Their father was Italian, their mother was English and a relation of the Lancashire Hornbys. The girls' names were Helena and Madeleine Cortazzi, and Lear found himself fascinated by Helena. 'She knows every word of "In Memoriam", & indeed all Alfred's poems—& has translated many into Italian, & set many to music',[11] he told Emily Tennyson whose

139

heart must have warmed at his news. With Holman Hunt he was really enthusiastic: 'Do you know I am half in love?' he confided. 'There are two *awful* sisters here (I call the house Castle Dangerous) English, but brought up here—and so simple and good!—and so full of poetry and good taste, and grace; and all the nettings whereby men are netted—I begin to feel I must either run for it, or rush into extremes—and as neither they nor I have money, am not I a fool for thinking about it? Yet sometimes at 43 I cannot help believing that half and half life will get too wearisome to bear ere long. The older is my alarm,—but the younger is the prettier— o Papa! What a blasted old ass your son is.'[12]

Could marriage be the answer to his dreadful loneliness? He had found someone who could enjoy the things that he found important in life—painting and poetry and music, and liking people for themselves—and who was feminine without being fluffy. But marriage and a home still meant danger and almost certain unhappiness, and he didn't seriously consider it. 'Bless me—even if I could afford it, I am not sure that marriage would be a safe risk:' he wrote to Ann, 'if one could only unmarry again if it didn't suit! —only one couldn't.'[13]

He decided not to go back to England that summer, and arranged for two of his oil paintings in London to be sent in for the Academy. They were both accepted, but were hung over the door in the miniature room where they could hardly be seen. Holman Hunt's picture of 'The Scapegoat' was also in, and was the butt of much derisive comment. It is a painting of a goat standing on the shore of the Dead Sea, representing the sacrificial animal symbolically carrying the burden of man's sins. Hunt had sat for weeks in the sunken heat with an umbrella over his head and a double-barrelled gun beside him, but even Lear, who was such an admirer of his work, was doubtful about the result. 'I agree with you in not liking the subject,' he confessed to Ann, 'but where the skill & genius which Hunt possesses is so immeasurably in advance of that of the mass of painters, we must take what we can get.'[14]

In June and July he was at Ascension making drawings for his big picture, but when he got back to Corfu the canvas still hadn't arrived. Lushington was about to cross to Albania in *Midge* for a few days' holiday, and Lear decided that whilst he was waiting he would go over with him and have a third try at getting to Mount Athos.

He was at once struck with the difference in travelling through Albania and Greece since his last visit. At the start of the Crimean War the British had moved in to preserve the country's neutrality, and as most towns now had a British Consul he hardly needed the beds and cooking things he had brought. '. . . as I sit in a beautiful room in the English Consul's house here (Larissa), with sofas all round the walls, matting on the floor, & painted ceilings, & look out on a little court yard where 2 tame cranes are walking up & down—I cannot but think how much easier it is to travel in these parts now than it was in 1848.'[15]

They went straight across the mainland without stopping, but when they got to Katerina on the east coast they found that there was a local fiesta and no one would take them over to Salonika. They had to wait for two days and were running out of food: '. . . we began to speculate how Giorgio should cook the large blue jelly fish that the sea threw up. We found 2 small crabs also—& I proposed—as there were blackberries all about, to boil the jelly fish with blackberry sauce, and roast the crabs with rhum & bread crumbs—a triumph of cookery not reserved for us—for at last boats began to come, & horses appeared over the hills by scores.'[16]

This sounds reminiscent of another of Lear's feasts:

'. . . if we may take the liberty of inquiring, on what do you chiefly subsist?'

'Mainly on Oyster-patties,' said the Blue-Bottle-Fly, 'and, when these are scarce, on Raspberry Vinegar and Russian leather boiled down to a jelly.'

'How delicious!' said Guy.

To which Lionel added, 'Huzz!' and all the Blue-Bottle-Flies said, 'Buzz!'[17]

From Salonika they walked fifty miles overland and crossed the isthmus cut by King Xerxes—the X of all Lear's nonsense alphabets —when he led the invading Persian armies into Greece. A pair of

wooden gates marked the beginning of the monks' territory, and
when they had come through these Lear was at last on Mount
Athos.[18]

This strange place points forty miles into the Aegean Sea, and is
covered in dense forests of beech and oak and ilex trees which fall
away into deep, wooded ravines, and tumble down cliffs and crags
into the sea. On its southern tip is the great high peak of the holy
mountain whose white marble summit glows at sunset like a
lighted torch which can be seen from Mount Olympus and the
Plain of Troy. It was the seat of Greek gods long before Olympus,
and was called Athos after Poseidon's son. It had originally been
part of central Thrace, but one day Athos, in a fit of fury against

*Mount Athos and the Monastery
of Stavronikita, 1857*

his father, picked it up and hurled it at him into the sea. The
ancients tried to smooth out the quarrel by dedicating it to Poseidon,
but they heard rumblings of heavenly discontent and quickly
rededicated it to Zeus.

And so it became a holy mountain to the pagans, until one day
in A.D. 49 when the Virgin Mary was invited by Lazarus, then
Bishop of Kitium in Cyprus, to come and visit him. He arranged
for a boat to collect her, but on the journey back to Cyprus it
strayed from its course, and when they sighted land it was Athos
that they had found. The boat anchored in a little bay, and the Virgin
looked long and silently at the mountain. Then she said: 'This
mountain is holy ground. Let it now be my portion. Here let me
remain.' As she stepped ashore there was a terrible crash and the

143

pagan idols and statues crumbled to the ground: the whole population was baptized, and Mount Athos became a holy Christian domain. But the Virgin was jealous of her rights, and refused to allow any other female creature onto the peninsula, so that no woman, nor any cows nor chickens can go to Mount Athos.

By the Middle Ages it was the home of isolated hermits, and the first monastic foundation was set up during the tenth century. From then until the fall of Constantinople more and more monasteries were built. There was a moment of crisis in this period of fruitful expansion when it was discovered that the Vlach shepherds, who supplied the monasteries with milk and wool, were also supplying them with the services of their wives and daughters. Strict measures were taken and the situation was retrieved, but not before half the monks had left with the shepherds.

In 1430 Salonika was captured by the invading Turks, and the monks of the Holy Mountain submitted voluntarily to Turkish rule. Islamic tradition forbids the pillage of property voluntarily surrendered, so the Byzantine treasures of Athos remained intact and the Christians were allowed to keep their methods and places of worship.

Lear and Giorgio made their way up the tortuous rock path which wound through the dense woods, and the first evening they reached Kariess, the capital where the Holy Synod of twenty monks, appointed annually from each of the twenty ruling monasteries, administer the domestic affairs of the mountain. Lear went first to the 'head of the Holy Mountain', the leader of the twenty. 'He made me a tolerably civil welcome—for I had letters from consuls—bishops etc.—& gave me some supper—& a bed; first of all, they bring you a tray—some sort of sweet, & a glass of spirit; (oh! dear!—what a lot of sweets & rhum have I taken in that Holy Mountain!) then coffee . . . Next morning the Synod of 20 were assembled—& I was put at the head of the room, while my letters were read; a circular was then given to me, to present to all the convents as I chose—& in the afternoon I began my tour . . .'[19]

The monks of Athos live to pray. Soon after midnight the

144

wooden clappers of the semandron rouse them for the first service which goes on until dawn, and throughout the day they repeat prayers and intone the name of Christ. But Lear preferred the idea of attaining sanctity through other people, and he couldn't begin to share their philosophy. Soon he was feeling 'oppressed with this atmosphere of falsehood and ignorance . . . I do not say—hypocrisy; —but I say falsehood, because I am positive that living alone— banishing all women whom God has made to be our equals & companions,—passing life in everlasting repetition of formal prayers— in fact—turning God's will & works upside down—I say this is falsehood—though it may be ignorance as well'.[20]

The grandeur of the scenery was wonderful, though, and for three weeks he was walking and drawing, climbing through the thick lush woods and scrambling up rocky paths, and he discovered energies he hadn't had for years.

But only a few days after they had started, he realised that Giorgio was ill. They were staying in the dirty little monastery of Philotheo where all they could get to eat was bad bread and salty cheese and he knew that if they remained there Giorgio would only get worse. So he left his servant and rode on to Gran Lavra, the largest and most ancient of the monasteries, where he arranged a bed for him. They had a dreadful journey there on mules, but once in the monastery Giorgio gradually recovered, and whilst he lay there getting back his strength, Lear filled the time 'drawing it all round; poking about the sea shore or into the hermitages among the half witted old filthy Caloyeri; or watched the Tomcats in the galleries; or talked Greek with Melchisedek & Anthemos— smoking 5 pipes a day . . .'[21]

At the very tip of the peninsula he found the tiny monastery of St Nilo perched on the cliff: '. . . that was the queerest & saddest spot I ever beheld!' he told Ann. '2 old men lived there—neither more than half witted; they gave me a dry fish & water melon,— but only said these words all the time I was there—"are you a Christian?"—hundreds of times over and over.'[22]

When Giorgio was fit enough they moved on again up the western side of the mountain, and saw all the twenty principal monasteries and many of the smaller ones. The collection of drawings he was making was going to be unique and valuable in England, and he planned to publish them with the journal he had kept of the tour. But there was so much dirt and damp around that he was anxious now to be finished: 'O Holy Mountain! what have I not suffered to get drawings of you!'[23] he wrote, and to Fortescue he explained: 'The worst was the food & the filth, which were uneasy to bear. But however wondrous and picturesque the exterior & interior of the monasteries, & however abundantly & exquisitely glorious & stupendous the scenery of the mountain, I would not go again to the ᾿Αγιος ῾Ορος for any money, so gloomy, so shockingly unnatural, so lonely, so lying, so unatoneably odious seems to me all the atmosphere of such monkery. That half of our species which it is natural to every man to cherish & love best, ignored, prohibited and abhorred—all life spent in everlasting repetition of monotonous prayers, no sympathy with ones fellow-beans of any nation, class or age. The name of Christ on every garment and at every tongue's end, but his maxims trodden under foot. God's world and will turned upside down, maimed, & caricatured:—if this I say be Xtianity let Xtianity be rooted out as soon as possible. More pleasing in the sight of the Almighty I really believe, & more like what Jesus Christ intended man to become, is an honest Turk with 6 wives, or a Jew working hard to feed his little old clo' babbies, than these muttering, miserable, mutton-hating, man-avoiding, misogynic, morose, & merriment-marring, monotoning, many-mule-making, mocking, mournful, minced-fish & marmalade masticating Monx. Poor old pigs! Yet one or two were kind enough in their way, dirty as they were: but it is not them, it is their system I rail at.'[24]

A few months later, he thought he had discovered the remedy: 'As soon as Parliament meets,' he wrote to Fortescue, the Member for Louth, 'move that all Sidney Herbert's distressed needle-women be sent out at once to Mount Athos! By this dodge all the 5000 monks young and old will be vanquished:—distressed needle-babies will ultimately awake the echoes of ancient Acte, & the whole fabric of monkery, not to say of the Greek church will fall down crash & for ever. N.B. Let the needle-women be all landed at once, 4000 at least, on the South-east side of the peninsula &

make a rush for the nearest monastery, that subdued, all the rest will speedily follow'.[25]

He decided not to make the return journey across the mainland of Greece, and instead went by boat from Salonika. He had to wait for a few days in the Dardanelles so he was able to go quickly to see the plain of Troy. He would have liked to linger there and draw, but he wanted to get back to Corfu to begin on the large painting so that it would be finished in time for the Academy.

It had been a successful trip, and he told Fortescue: 'I have gained a great amount of health bodily & mentle, & also trust to benefit obliquely of many of my felly creatures who will hereafter peeroase my jurnles, and admyer my pigchers.'[26]

The first night back in Corfu there was a violent earth tremor, and his house was badly damaged. This gave him the excuse to move into some rooms which were vacant next door to Lushington on the Condi Terrace. 'Condi Terrace is the "West-end" of Corfu and we are all more or less swells as lives in it', he told Fortescue, and he had a 'stewjew 30 feet long: 3 windys all a looking to the North East, whereby the light is always perfect.'[27] But it might have seemed rather unwise to be so near Lushington, for only a few days earlier Lear had told Emily Tennyson, 'The impetuosity of my nature cannot always be controlled & we have had one or two sad antagonisms—though we are perhaps better friends afterwards: but our natures are so different, & he is so changed since I first knew him, while I have remained so absurdly the same . . . that I feel convinced we are best when not with each other.'[28]

It was as if he knew what was wise, but couldn't face having to act on it. A part of him was completely realistic, but then he let himself believe that one day they would be as happy together as they had been that spring in Greece—they had to be because that happiness had been real and it couldn't just disappear. He didn't realise that what Lushington had enjoyed then had been the free abandonment to life which he had never known before and which he certainly never knew again. Because he loved beautiful things so completely Lear had been part of Lushington's happiness, but in a sense he had been incidental—he had been a background to

Lushington's first real look at beauty. But for Lear it had been the other way round, and the awakening of spring had been a background to his surging new love for Lushington.

Now he settled into his new rooms and set busily to work. He laid in the drawing on his big canvas and painted several local views to get some quick money to reimburse him after the expenses of his trip, and in the evenings when the light had gone he penned out the drawings he had made on Mount Athos. He was pleased with some of the work he was doing, but was quickly disheartened with his lack of real progress. 'Dear me—I wish I could paint faster & better & had 20 pairs of hands, not to speak of an elephant's trunk to pick up any brushes when they fall down,'[29] he lamented to Ann, and to Holman Hunt he wrote: 'I wish I had gone to the Academy when you did—& had been working with you ever since! Coming so late as I did to the light of any kind of truth in painting —when my habits of life were already but too much formed, & my eyes & hands less than ever able to execute what I desired to do, I was never very likely to turn out much of a painter. Moreover, my topographical, & varied interests as to different countries—my split-application by my musical-ornithological—& other tastes— have all combined to bother & retard me—society being by no means the least of the pull-backs.'[30]

He missed the artistic companionship he had had in Rome and London, for there was nobody in Corfu with whom he could discuss his work—or indeed anything. Lushington was generally too preoccupied to talk, and they would go for long walks together without exchanging a word. But though he lacked friends he had a lot of acquaintances and was often invited out. Now that he had Giorgio to cook for him he could entertain in return, generously yet cheaply, as he told Ann: 'Soup, Ma'am, fish, Ma'am, a beefsteak pudding, Ma'am, woodcock & apple pie, Ma'am; & all very nicely done; all which sounds expensive, but isn't—because all the large dish of fish cost *5d.*, & the woodcock are *3d.* a piece just now! It does not appear to me that I ought to do otherwise than live what is called sociably & comfortably as far as I can, though an artist's life, if he has no capital—must always have its uncertainties & difficulties from month to month. So much however, of the artist's capacity & strength for going onward depends on his ordinary comforts, that if he were to live wholly alone drinking water & eating barley bread,—the money he would save by such a diet would be overbalanced by the depression which would soon prevent his getting any money at all.'[31]

But as the winter of 1856 came on again he began to feel the gloom of last year returning. Bad weather, and daylight that was

View from the One Gun Battery, Corfu,
from 'Views in the Seven Ionian Islands'

too dark to paint by, turned him in on himself and he began to brood. Gradually the sense of desperation returned. What he needed now was someone who would gentle him out of his depression by encouraging him and turning his thoughts out instead of in, keeping his mind free of the endless re-enacting of old sadnesses and hurts which he forgot when he could fill his mind with happier, more constructive thoughts. He became so throttled by unhappiness that he had to put away the large painting until he could think clearly again. 'O dear! I find Corfu very like a prison I do',[32] he told Ann, but the impenetrable prison was in his own mind.

Just after Christmas he spent a few days in Albania with Lushington, and though it poured with rain most of the time the change did him good. He enjoyed the 'solitary quiet of nature' just across the water from the fuss and flurry of garrison life, for he sometimes felt that the people and the ridiculous life they seemed to enjoy destroyed the beauty of Corfu. '. . . what a place this might be if there were any good people to give it a twist!' he told Ann. 'As it is—a more disorganised fiddlefaddle Poodly-pumpkin place never was . . . at the Palace they are active—dancing & rushing about pauselessly & continually. I suspect Lady Young would not be happy in Heaven if she did not get up an immense ball & land & water picnics, among the angels. It is sadly frivolous work—this life for "amusement" & that only.'[33]

Of course, when spring began to reawaken the island he felt better at once—'we are all sunshine & anemones & clear skies & asphodels & little green frogs just as usual'[34] he wrote with relief. The world was better, people were all right and the Corfu painting was the finest he had yet done. He had come on so well with his daily Greek lessons that he could read the New Testament in old and modern Greek, fulfilling a long-standing ambition and renewing his desire to see the holy places in Palestine which he had missed. In fact he wrote to Clowes, a friend from Knowsley days, suggesting that they might travel there together, but Clowes couldn't get away, so instead Lear decided to go to England for the summer. His painting wouldn't be ready now in time for the Academy, but he had been invited to put work into the International Exhibition in Manchester. He wanted to arrange for the publication of his Athos drawings and the engravings of some of his Corfu drawings which he could sell when he got back to the island, and he was hungry for the companionship of friends.

On May 1st he wrote to Fortescue: 'I am coming to England fast as I can, having taken a redboom at Hamsens 16 Upper Seymour Street, Squortman Pare, and also a rorkwoom or Stew-jew at 15 Stratford Place. My big picture is in a mess, & without Holman Hunt's help I can't get on with it, though it is done as to what must necessarily be done here, and requires but 2 months of cropping and thought. Pray heaven I may sell it . . . Why are you coming say you? because I can't stay here any longer—without seeing friends & having the communion of heart & spirit—with one who should have been this to me, I have none. And I can't bear it. And I want to see my sister. And also another sister who is going to N. Zealand before she goes. And some Canadian cousins. And *you*. And my dear Daddy Holman Hunt, & other people. So I'm off.'³⁵

Then just before he left Corfu, he wrote jubilantly to Ann:

Dear Ann,
    At half past one o'clock THE CORFU PICTURE WAS SOLD—TO
        W. EVANS ESQ. M.P.
        FOR 500 GUINEAS!
        HURRAH!

Your affect., Grandfather
Edward Lear³⁶

CHAPTER ELEVEN

The Holy Land

1857-58

Lear was in England by the end of May, 1857, and at once began on a busy round of visits: 'Mr Lear is in town but I have not yet been able to see him,' Woolner wrote to Emily Tennyson; 'he is so very busy and says he ought to go to 756 places on every evening.'[1]

One of the places was, of course, the Tennysons' home at Farringford, where he spent three happy days. Another was Nuneham in Oxfordshire, the home of Mr Harcourt and his wife, Lady Waldegrave. In the spring of 1850, Fortescue had been walking down Piccadilly when an open carriage passed him. Riding inside were an elderly gentleman, and a beautiful young woman. She was Lady Waldegrave, daughter of the famous tenor Charles Braham, and widow of both John Waldegrave and his younger brother George, the 7th Earl. She had inherited both their fortunes and now, at twenty-nine, was married to the dull and elderly Mr Harcourt.[2] Fortescue arranged to be introduced to her, and was soon invited to become a member of the theatrical company that she ran for her amusement at Nuneham. Before long he was desperately in love with her. Within the limits of propriety she encouraged her young suitor with coquettish tête-à-têtes, and he filled his diary with descriptions of what she said, how she looked, and exactly what she wore. He was a frequent guest at one of Lady Waldegrave's homes—Carlton Gardens, Strawberry Hill, Dudbrook, or Nuneham—and sometimes Lear was invited to join the party. He found them kind, but rather patronising. 'Lear came today,' Fortescue wrote in his diary on August 8th. 'I am glad Lady W likes him so much. He has sold his Corfu to Evans M.P. for 500 guineas—poor old boy. When I told Mr H it gave him greatly increased respect for L.'[3]

Frances, Lady Waldegrave   *Chichester Fortescue*

But the visit was fruitful, for Lady Waldegrave commissioned two paintings in Palestine if he went there in the spring. The trip began to look possible now, for the sale of the Corfu painting had cleared his debts and left him with £100. The visit to Nuneham also gave him an opportunity to talk at last with Fortescue, who wrote in his diary: 'I have sat with old Lear both nights, he in low spirits, longing for "sympathy", which means a woman, specially a wife.'[4] Before they went back to London he invited Lear to go with him to Ireland and stay for six weeks at his home in Ardee.

Lear spent a busy fortnight in London, and they left for Dublin at the end of August. The party at Ardee was very quiet—just Lear, Fortescue, his aunt Mrs Ruxton who was a widow of 85, and an aged governess. He was given a room where he could paint during the day whilst Fortescue got on with his business on the estate, though he found it hard to concentrate on painting and be sociable at the same time and he didn't get much done.

But he hadn't gone there to work, and the times he looked forward to were the evenings when he could go with Fortescue for long walks through the beautiful green Irish countryside. Then he would unburden the weight of loneliness which he had been bearing for so long. He talked endlessly about Lushington—though

Fortescue didn't seem to grasp the meaning of what Lear told him, and saw more significance in his mention of Helena Cortazzi.

Whilst Lear was at Ardee his dear friend Robert Hornby died. Lear mourned him sadly, and as thousands of other Victorians had done he fingered through *In Memoriam*. One night he and Fortescue sat up until the small hours to read the poem right through—this was the 'consistent kindness & reciprocity' he had been yearning for.

He stayed in Ireland until the beginning of October, then crossed back to Liverpool and spent a few days at Knowsley. From there he travelled across to Manchester to see his painting of 'The Quarries of Syracuse' in the International Exhibition, and then went on to London.

By now it was well into October and he had done none of the things he had planned to do. He hadn't published the Athos drawings or had engravings made of his Corfu drawings: instead he had spent the time with Fortescue—and that, after all, had been his reason for coming.

He dreaded the return to Corfu, for during the summer the Cortazzi family had left and he would be even lonelier than before. He stayed on in England until the middle of November when he knew he must get away south. 'Come back soon well & happy',[5] wrote Emily Tennyson, and Lear must have echoed her wish.

Back in Corfu he was soon choked by the feeling of stagnation and he wrote in desperation to Fortescue: 'My dear Chichester, I do not know how I shall bear it, being an ass: —& if you don't write, & if others don't write, I really can't tell what I shall do.

'Just figure to yourself the conditions of a place where you never have any breadth or extent of intellectual society, & yet cannot have any peace or quiet. Suppose yourself living in Piccadilly, we will say, taking a place with a long surface, from Coventry St. to Knightsbridge say. And suppose that line your constant & only egress & ingress to & from the country, and that by little & little you come to know all & every of the persons in all the houses, & meet them always and everywhere, & were thought a brute & queer if you didn't know everybody more or less! Wouldn't you wish every one of them, except a few, at the bottom of the sea? Then you live in a house, one of the best here it is true, where you hear everything from top to bottom:—a piano on each side, above and below, maddens you:—and you can neither study nor think, nor even swear properly by reason of the proximity of the neighbours. I assure you a more rotten, dead, stupid place than this existeth not . . . L is just as ever: perfectly calm—& although doubtless intending to be kind is as ever more & more indifferent & passive to all but his own routine of life. I vow I never felt more shockingly alone than the two or three evenings I have staid in.

'Yet all this must be conquered if fighting can do it. Yet at times, I have thought of,—I hardly know what. The constant walking and noise overhead prevents my application to any sort of work, & it is only from 6 to 8 in the morning that I can attend really to anything . . . And then, if I can't sleep, my whole system seems to turn into pins, cayenne-pepper, & vinegar & I suffer hideously. You see I have no means of carrying off my irritation: others have horses, or boats, in short:—I have only walking, and that is beginning to be impossible alone. I could not go to church to-day. I felt I should make faces at everybody, so I read some Greek of St John, wishing for you to read it with—some Robinson's *Palestine*, some *Jane Eyre*, some Burton's *Mecca*, some *Friends in Council*, some Shakespeare, some *Vingt ans Après*, some Leake's *Topography*, some Rabelais, some Tennyson, some Gardiner Wilkinson, some Grote, some Ruskin—& all in half an hour. O! doesn't "he take it out of me" in a raging worry? Just this moment I think I *must* have a piano: that may do me good. But then I remember Miss Hendon over my head has one, & plays jocular jigs continually. Then what the devil can I do? Buy a baboon & a parrot & let them rush about the room?

'I still hold to going to Palestine if possible. If I could but get myself comfortable and untwisted by the noise & general discomfort of these houses, I think I could bring myself right yet, but I cannot tell. Sometimes I think I must begin another big picture, as I want something to gnash & grind my teeth on. If Helena Cortazzi had been here, it would have been useless to think of avoiding asking her to marry me, even had I never so little trust in the wisdom of such a step . . .'[6]

But if she had been there he wouldn't have done so. The few amorous sentiments Lear expressed towards unattached women faded when he was actually with them and they were no longer safely unattainable.

The next few months were, as he had expected, of profound unhappiness. He went on seeing Lushington but each meeting left him more wretched, and on February 28th he wrote in his diary: 'Dined at L's—but wearied myself with talk, & when after dinner, in that cold room, he took a good cigar himself from a box at the other end, but offered me none,—& when coffee came $\frac{3}{4}$ of an hour after, I grew black & silent, & went away at $9\frac{1}{2}$.'[7]

Preparing for his visit to Palestine was the one thing that cheered him that dreadful winter. As usual he read everything he could find about the countries he was visiting, then he had to buy medicines and a tent, leather saddle-bags and cooking things, and it was all very expensive. He did think of a way to get more money, as he told Ann: '. . . nothing is talked of by the Corfu world but the Marchioness of Headford's diamonds, which cover her up so much, that few people have seen their wearer. As for me, I sat next to her at dinner yesterday, but she hadn't got no diamonds; only about 200 big turquoises & emeralds & bangles & spangles & chains & griggly-miggly dazzling messes, a few of which I should have liked to have had for the fun of turning them into pounds & shillings for my Holy Land trip.'[8]

He needed to go armed because travellers were being attacked and robbed by Arab tribesmen. Lushington offered him his revolver and taught him how to use it. 'I have been practising shooting at a mark (I can hardly write for laughing), & have learned all the occult nature of pistols,' he told Fortescue. 'Don't grin. My progress is slow—but always (I trust) somewhat. At 103 I may marry possibly. Goodbye dear 40scue.'[9]

They reached Alexandria at sunrise on March 17th, but there wasn't a boat to Jaffa until the 26th so they decided to fill in a few days by going down to Cairo. Lear knew the city well, but to

Giorgio, brought up in peaceful Corfu, it must have seemed astonishing. The steamer when it came was absolutely crammed with pilgrims going to Jerusalem for Easter. Luckily it was a short voyage and in less than a day they were at Jaffa, a scrubby little place with no proper harbour. They dropped anchor offshore, and were at once surrounded by boatloads of shouting, waving Arabs: it was a milling, pressing, clambering scrabble of people and baggage, and Lear heaved a sigh of relief when at last they were out on the road to Ramleh.

They stayed there for the night, but found that all the prices were up for Easter and it was both uncomfortable and expensive. 'During the night I did not sleep at all,' he told Ann, 'but passed the time in catching innumerable animals, which,—with the sagacity & desire of knowledge a zoological landscape painter should combine,—I placed upon a sheet of paper—wishing to know what manner of insects they were, & rejoicing to find on the first break of day, that 17 were fleas, 3 mosquitoes, 8 ants, only 2 bugs, & nothing at all of a less creditable nature. You may suppose I was not sorry to leave Ramleh at 6 in the morning of the 27th; yet it is a *most beautiful* place; reminding me strongly of many spots both in Sicily & in the Campagna of Rome. The same glorious corn plain is journeyed through for 3 more hours after leaving Ramleh, untiring in its morning brightness. Group by group we began to pass the body of the pilgrims—who travel slowly with their luggage; & by degrees we began to enter the edge of the hills, the road becoming stonier & steeper as we went on. The corn grows scantier, but is soon exchanged for olives—& now we wound up a narrower pass—like many another in Greece—beshrubbed & beflowered on all sides.'[10]

After riding for several hours they began to ascend 'the last steep tiresome pull of all—before conquering which we could not see the Holy City. . . . It was 2.30 before I saw all the places I at once recognised as portions of the scene I so long have desired to paint,— & when we were opposite the west side of the city—I at once found it far more beautiful than I had expected.'[11]

Because of the crowds it was impossible to pick and choose accommodation, so he took the first room he was offered. The city

Jerusalem, May 3rd, 1858

was so thronged with pilgrims he decided not to try and draw there at the moment: he would stay for two or three days, then visit some of the places that he wanted to see outside Jerusalem and come back again when the crowds had gone.

The next day, Palm Sunday, he crossed the rocky valley of Jehosophat to the Mount of Olives and climbed 'to the spot Christ must have been on when he "saw the city"—on coming from Bethany'.[12] From the top he could look across to the Dead Sea—'clear pale milky far blue, with farther off all rosy mountain—fretted & carved in lovely shadow forms,—this long long simple line melting into air towards the desert.'[13] When the light had gone he went back to his room tingling with the excitement of what was all around him: '. . . as I came up the stairs, how glorious was the full moon of blessed Israel—& how beautiful the dim pale film of Moab!—the round domes of the city & a thousand other glorious quietudes recalling other days.'[14]

He left Jerusalem on April 2nd and travelled south to Bethlehem, which he liked, and Hebron which he didn't. There he found a guide called Abdel who would take him on to Petra. He was offered an escort of altogether fifteen men, which he was going to need, for travellers then were frequently attacked by Arab tribes-

men, They asked £30 for the trip, a big extra on his budget, but he decided that it would be worth while.

The journey on camels took them through some of the lowest, hottest land on earth. Lear loathed the animal's heaving, swaying motion and the fifteen Arabs turned out to be argumentative and quarrelled constantly amongst themselves: when he could he got away from them and walked, as he had done from his incompatible companions on the Nile. Each night they pitched their tents on the sand, and after dinner he would sit outside in the quiet stillness watching the large round moon and the stars in the vast desert silence. Dawn had a different kind of beauty: 'What a strange calm world was the tawny hollow glen landscape, dusky-tufted and be-camelled with ghostly wanderers, before the sunlight came gloriously bursting over the dark sapphire heights of Moab!'[15] he wrote in his journal.

They travelled for five days and on the morning of the sixth they came to Petra, the ancient centre of caravan trade between Arabia and the countries west and north. 'About 9 we reached the highest part of the mountain ascent, and passing the ridge immediately below the rocks of Gebel Haroun (Aaron's mountain), now upon our left, entered the first or upper part of Wady Mousa on its western side. But it was nearly another hour before, still descending by winding tracks, we reached the first cavern tombs and the first coloured rocks. The slow advance chills with a feeling of strange solitude the intruder into the loneliness of this bygone world, where on every side are tokens of older greatness, and where between *then* and *now* is no link. As the path wandered among huge crags and over broad slabs of rock, ever becoming more striped and glowing in colour, I was more and more excited with curiosity and expectation. And after passing the solitary column which stands sentinel-like over the heaps of ruin around, and reaching the open space whence the whole area of the old city and the vast eastern cliff are fully seen, I own to having been more delighted and astonished than I had ever been by any spectacle. . . . The singular mixture of architectural labour with the wildest extravagences of nature—the excessive and almost terrible feeling of loneliness in the very midst of scenes so plainly telling of a past glory and a race of days long gone—the vivid contrast of the countless fragments of ruin, basement, foundation, wall, and scattered stone, with the bright green of the vegetation, and the rainbow hues of rock and cliff—the dark openings of the hollow tombs on every side—the white river bed and its clear stream, edged with superb scarlet-tufted blossoms of oleander alternating with groups of white-flowered broom—these combine to form a magical condensation of beauty and wonder which the ablest pen or pencil has no chance of conveying to the eye or mind.*

'What art could give the star-bright flitting of that wild dove and rock-partridge through the oleander-bloom, or the sound of the clear river rushing among the ruins of the fallen city. I felt, "I have found a new world—but my art is helpless to recall it to others, or to represent it to those who have never seen it." Yet, as the enthusiastic foreigner said to the angry huntsman who asked if he meant to catch the fox—"I will try".[16]

And try he did: until it was too dark to see any more he drew

* ' "Oh master", said Giorgio (who is prone to culinary similes), "we have come into a world where everything is made of chocolate, ham, curry-powder, & salmon" '.

one scene after another, and only when the light had gone did he go back to where the Arabs had pitched the tents. And then he saw, on one of the rock terraces above the camp, a line of ten black squatting figures silently watching them. A small goatherd boy who had seen their party had told the Bedouin that they were there, and now they had come to demand money as tax for travelling across their land. Lear had already paid a levy to the Sheikh of Haweitât, but these Arabs were from Dibdiba and wanted their own payment. They told Abdel, the leader of Lear's men, that if they weren't paid they would return with fifty men, and Lear realised that his journey to Petra which was already so expensive, might become both exorbitant and useless. He refused to pay any more and told them that the Sheikh of Haweitat would divide the money he had been given amongst them all. They left muttering belligerently and one man stayed behind perched above the camp, watching them until it was too dark for them to move on again that night: then he too disappeared.

Lear went uneasily to bed, and at midnight was wakened by shouting. The scene outside his tent was strange and almost comical: fifty or so Arabs were dismounting noisily from their camels, and after cheerily greeting Lear's men, they lit fires and settled down to wait for the morning. All through the night more kept arriving, and it was impossible to sleep. Instead Lear repacked everything so that he could move quickly if he had to, and at dawn he cautiously opened his tent flap and saw more than a hundred Arabs squatting outside.

Now a group of Haweitât rode into the camp. Their Sheikh was coming and he had the money with him. It looked as though there wouldn't be trouble after all, and as his one thought was to get drawings of Petra, Lear slipped quietly away. It was still very early, and he drew until ten o'clock, when he went back to the camp to see what was happening. Now there were nearly two hundred Arabs, and the Sheikh, dressed in scarlet robes and riding a white Arab stallion, had arrived. But they were quarrelling violently over the division of the money, and Lear could see that it would be impossible to stay on. He gave orders for the tents to come down, and then disappeared again to draw, and in the chamber of Khasmé he

Petra

melodramatically wrote his name on the wall so that a search party would know that he had reached Petra.

When he got back his men were ready to leave, but the money had still not been divided. The Sheikh was in a cave with some of the other leaders, and furious arguments were going on. Now the Arabs grabbed Lear's camels and gathered menacingly in on him. On and on went the argument in the cave, and he was pushed and thrust from one Arab to the next, and had time to think what splendid studies their expressions would make. Then a cry went up and he was seized by the arms and his pockets emptied—except surprisingly for his watch and Lushington's pistol. The same happened to Giorgio, and Abdel was pulled to the ground and his turban wrenched off. Lear managed to get away and into the cave, and he pulled the Sheikh outside so that he could see what was

162

happening. 'You must pay twenty dollars at once to these men of
Dibdiba or I can do nothing for you;' he told Lear; 'after that I will
help you on if I can.'[17]

Lear no longer cared about the expense and he told Abdel to
fetch the money. When it had been paid the Sheikh helped them
to their camels and led the way out of the camp. But it wasn't all
over. First one group and then another and another, dissatisfied
with their share, came after them and demanded more. He paid
them all he had, and when at last they realised that he had nothing
more they turned back and left him.

Their route back took them along the western shores of the Dead
Sea to Masada then north to Jerusalem. The crowds had gone, and
he could move easily round the city: '. . . there is enough in
Jerusalem to set a man thinking for life, & I am deeply glad I have

been there,' he wrote to Lady Waldegrave. 'O my nose! O my eyes! O my feet! How you all suffered in that vile place! for let me tell you, physically Jerusalem is the foulest and odiousest place on earth. A bitter doleful soul-ague comes over you in its streets. And your memories of its interior are but horrid dreams of squalor & filth, clamour and uneasiness, hatred & malice & all uncharitableness. But the outside is full of melancholy glory, exquisite beauty & a world of past history of all ages:—every point forcing you to think of a vastly dim receding past, of a time of Roman war & splendour, (for Aelia Capitolium was a fine city) or a smash of Moslem & Crusader years, with long long dull winter of deep decay through centuries of misrule. The Arab & his sheep are alone the wanderers on the pleasant vallies and breezy hills round Zion:— the file of slow camels all that brings to mind the commerce of Tyre & other bygone merchandize.'[18]

But the tragedy of Christian dissent there saddened him—the bickering and the scandalous quarrels, the hypocrisy and the shows of power and wealth which denied everything that Christ had ever taught. It was only five years since the disputes over the holy places of Jerusalem had precipitated the Crimean War.

They went north towards the Sea of Galilee and Nazareth, but when they stopped in Jericho it was hot and insect-ridden, and he couldn't sleep. He began to feel exhausted and unwell, and when the next day a party of Arabs stopped them to demand money it seemed like a nightmare. He couldn't go on, and turned back to Jerusalem without seeing Nazareth or Galilee.

After he had rested there for a few days, he decided to go on to the Lebanon, which should be more peaceful. To avoid travelling overland through Palestine they went by boat from Jaffa to Beirut which they reached on May 11th, 1858. But the country was a disappointment and the scenery like any he had seen in Greece or Albania, though the Cedars—ancient and enormous—were a marvellous sight, and Damascus too was beautiful, like '16 worlds full of gardens rolled out flat, with a river and a glittering city in the middle'.[19] The hottest time of year had begun, and he was moving from the oppressive heat of the plain to the extreme cold of the mountains—suddenly he had had enough.

CHAPTER TWELVE

Rome

1858–60

It had been an extraordinary and exciting three months, and back in Corfu a deep post-travel depression settled on him. 'O! that this blank of life would break into some varied light or shade!!'[1] he wrote in his diary. He was run down and developed a sty: 'My mind is confused between cause and effect,' he wrote to Fortescue, '& I don't know if my being a pig has produced the sty, or whether the sty makes me a pig. But I know I am a pig.'[2]

Whilst he had been away the intrigues and island bothers which had helped to make Lushington so exaggeratedly morose had come rushing to a head, and now he had resigned his post and was going back to England. Lear wondered if he should stay on there alone, or find somewhere else for the winter. Clowes had asked him to go with him to Rome, but it was a long time since he had left there and it could be a mistake to go back now.

Early in August he travelled to England with Lushington, and they parted at Dover. He was alone again. Of course there were friends by the score for him to visit, and one of the first was Holman Hunt. He stayed at Hunt's rooms at Campden Hill, and even wondered if he could live with him permanently. 'One thing is a fact,' he wrote, 'living with Daddy Hunt is more a certain chance of happiness than any other life I know of.'[3] But it wouldn't really work. He visited Helena Cortazzi, and indulged in a 'world of thought'[4] about her—but there was no solution there either.

He felt more and more desolate, and entries in his diary ached with unhappiness. 'Wake, to impatience, blindness & misery. Incapable of deciding whether life can be cured or cursed—I totter giddily, refusing to take any road, yet agonized by staying irresolute.'[5] His painting went badly, and he felt desperate at the thought

165

of the unending struggle which faced him on and on into the future.

In the autumn he decided to accept Clowes' invitation, though he wasn't happy about going back to Rome. 'You have no idea, my dear boy, what a grief this going to and fro is,' he told Fortescue. 'I had rather, methinks, come and [settle] and die straight away, only the half life half death of physical hell and worrying is a trial one flees from as yet.'[6]

At the beginning of November he packed his things. Before he left he went to the Zoo, and he drew—vultures.

When Lear had left Rome in March 1848, the threat of nationalist revolution had been drawing in on the city. The new pope, Pius IX, had at first been welcomed by Italian patriots who believed that he would join in their fight for his country's unity, but he was absorbed in reforming papal administration and the government of his territories and he didn't want to be involved in a war. Anyway, his position was an impossible one—as an Italian he supported the idea of unity, but if he went into a war against Austria he would compromise his position as leader of the universal church. All he could hope to do was to steer an uncommitted middle course, but in a time of crusading revolution lack of support means opposition, and the papacy was seen as the reactionary bulwark which would hold back the revolutionary tide. To try and placate the people he appointed popular ministers, but this wasn't a time for watery half-measures and in November 1848 he had to flee from Rome when Garibaldi's nationalist troops over-ran the city.

Louis Napoleon, anxious to woo Catholic support in France, decided to send soldiers to win back Rome for the pope, and in the summer of 1849 the French defeated Garibaldi's men, the Republic collapsed, and Pius IX was brought back with a French garrison to protect him and guarantee his territorial rights. For nine years now the city had been quiet, but the balance was unreal and would inevitably topple.

Lear and Clowes reached Rome on December 1st, 1858 almost exactly twenty-one years after Lear had first arrived there, flushed and excited. Then the world had been bursting with expectations and hope which needed only time to be fulfilled. Now he knew what he had almost forgotten then—that life was unhappy and that it would never change: '. . . so dismal has been the return here,' he told Fortescue, 'that only the friendlyness of ancient acquaintances, & the even temper and kindness of Clowes could have kept me above water.'[7]

But two weeks after their arrival Clowes fell from his horse and broke his collar bone, and for the next few weeks he was in bed. Lear felt so lonely that when letters began to arrive from England he couldn't help 'the tears a busting out of my eyes incontinent'.[8] Even visiting friends was a sad task, for they had grown older and tireder, and though they were pleased enough to see him, he had been away for a long time and after the first pleasantries they weren't really very interested in his return.

When he began to search for rooms he saw that changes had been made in the city since he'd left. The Tiber still overflowed its banks in winter, and carts were still pulled through the city streets by buffaloes—but the streets were cleaner and there were new houses and shops. There were new prices too, and he had to pay £80 a year for the apartment he found in the Via Condotti, opposite the Spanish Steps. He moved in on December 21st, and when Giorgio arrived three days later his life began to run smoothly again.

He had a three-year lease on the rooms and now he carpeted all the floors and bought a new wall-covering for the study, he ordered fenders for all the fireplaces, blinds for all the windows and green beize curtains for all the doors, he hired a piano and then went shopping for 'a portable bed-stead, six chairs, a pair of bellows & a pepper-box.'[9] It seems strange that he should have gone to so much trouble and expense when he didn't yet know if he would like living in Rome again, but he was longing to find a permanent winter home and Rome had one overriding advantage, for '. . . everyone comes here with an express purpose to buy something in the way of painting'.[10]

When he had set up a room where he could show his drawings he began holding twice-weekly open-days. At about mid-day on Wednesday and Saturday the bell would start to ring, and Giorgio would open the door to twenty or thirty or sometimes even more than forty people. They would be shown into the gallery where a fire had been lit and seats arranged in front of a folio stand, and when everyone was settled Giorgio would go to Lear, and announce gravely 'the Arabs are come'.[11] For the next hour and a half Lear would show his drawings of Palestine and Egypt. He sold a few paintings, but not many, and generally he found that the process just wasted a lot of his time. 'I grow so tired of new people, & silly people, & tiresome people, & fanatical people, & robustious people, & vulgar people, & ugly people, and intriguing people, & fussy people, and omblomphious people—and people altogether,' he told Emily Tennyson. 'Fancy a society of 2000 people all bursting (for the first time mostly—) into a conviction of the necessity of seeing & talking about Art night & morning,—or if not that, of who is here & not here, & how such a party or ball can be attained to. Not that there is any lack of nice or clever people—only as they all aim at one scrambly jumble knowledge of Sculpture—antiquities etc.—& as I had already heard exactly the same questions and replies from 2000 people every year for 10 years when I lived here, —the repitition of it after one has been to the great & wonderful East, & to Egypt—is not a little sickening.'[12]

But there were some whose company he could enjoy. The Stratford Cannings, with whom he had stayed in Constantinople, were there, and so was the American actress Charlotte Cushman, who gave excellent dinner parties.[13] He met Robert Browning, and went to visit Elizabeth Barrett Browning, but found her so smothered with bores and snobs that he asked Emily Tennyson, 'what good does one get of anyone's society when it is merely like a beautiful small rose tree planted in the midst of 43 sunflowers, 182 marigolds, 96 dahlias and 756 china-asters?'[14]

The guest of honour in the English community that winter was the young Prince of Wales. He had been four when Lear had given his mother drawing lessons; now he was seventeen and on his first trip abroad. Queen Victoria wasn't at all sure about her son: he seemed rather slow, and though she scarcely liked to admit it, at times she almost found herself disliking him. But the English in Rome had none of her doubts: he had won their hearts on the very

Edward Lear and the Prince of Wales in about 1860

day he arrived by going out for a walk in the rain and refusing both a mackintosh and an umbrella.

On March 29th Lear received a note from the Prince's tutor, Colonel Bruce, saying that his Royal Highness would like to come and see his drawings. It was three in the afternoon—would it be convenient if they arrived at four? At once Lear and Giorgio set to work with brooms and dusters, then Giorgio was sent to put on his Sunday suit so that he could open the door to the Prince, whilst Lear stood on the landing to greet him when he arrived. 'Nobody could have nicer & better manners than the young Prince, nor be more generally intelligent & pleasing,' he wrote that night. 'I was afraid of telling or shewing him too much, but I soon found he was interested in what he saw, both by his attention, & by his intelligent few remarx. Yet I shewed him the Greek pictures, & all the Palestine oils,—& the whole of the sketches, & when I said,— "please tell me to stop, Sir, if you are tired by so many"—he said— "*o dear no!*" in the naturalist way.'[15]

It was a good thing for Giorgio to have this extra excitement, for he was becoming very unhappy in Rome. He had never lived in a city before and didn't know anybody there apart from Lear. He didn't like the Italians, he thought Roman laundries quite ridiculously expensive and the workmen shamefully lazy, and he was very distressed that Roman bread rolls could only be broken in four pieces instead of three like bread rolls in Corfu—in fact Lear was dreading that he would ask if he could go back to the island.

During that winter, Cavour and Louis Napoleon were making secret plans to drive the Austrians finally from Italian soil, and by the late spring rumours of war had begun to spread. The English started to pour out of the city to Civita Vecchia where they waited in crowds for enough boats to take them all off. Lear scorned their rush, and was alarmed to see the disappearance of the people who should be buying and commissioning his work—exactly the same had happened to him there in 1848, and he realised that if it went on for any time he was going to be left with two years' unexpired lease and no income. War was declared at the end of April 1859, and a month later he left safely for London.

He began the summer with a round of visits to friends, and for six weeks he rattled round the countryside from one country house to another, from Lewes to Wells, and from Winwick to the Isle of Wight, showing his drawings and collecting commissions. He spent a happy few days at Farringford, striding over the downs beside Alfred with his tousled black beard and flowing cloak, booming out his new 'Idylls of the King' in a deep measured voice, or playing with the two boys who were now seven and five and 'very darling chaps indeed'.[16]

Emily seemed tired and ill, and he thought Alfred should have realised that she was wearing herself out working for him. 'I should think computing moderately,' he wrote to Fortescue, 'that 15 angels, several hundreds of ordinary women, many philosophers, a heap of truly wise and kind mothers, 3 or 4 minor prophets, and a lot of doctors and school-mistresses, might all be boiled down, and yet their combined essence fall short of what Emily Tennyson really is.'[17] There was an atmosphere there of sadness mingled with 'a kind of sensitive excitement',[18] yet he felt happier at Farringford than anywhere and when he left a heavy post-happiness depression settled down on him. 'I am doing little, but dimly walking on along the dusty twilight lanes of incomprehensible life,' he wrote to

Fortescue, 'I wish you were married. I wish I were an egg and was going to be hatched.'[19] And perhaps if he could begin life again he would have a mother like Emily Tennyson.

In July he began to look for rooms in London where he could settle to work. He was already in debt and now he had spent £20 travelling round England, and though it brought him work it was money he could ill afford. Fortescue offered to help him through the summer, but Lear told him: 'My dear boy:—I don't want any money & fresh borrowing would only distress me more. I am thought wrong by some for want of independence in ever borrowing at all, but, I am sure that is not a right view of things, for my whole life from 14 years has been independentissimo, & on the other hand, the man who will not put himself under obligation of any kind to even the friends who entirely sympathise with his progress—nourishes in my opinion, a selfish & icicle sort of pride.'[20]

He felt cross and disheartened by London life, and decided that he must go somewhere with fewer distractions so that he could get down to work. This always meant either Sussex or the north, the two places where he had been happiest, and in July he found rooms in St Leonards on Sea. From there he wrote to Fortescue, '. . . although the queer solitude in which I live & the displeasing mill-round of toil is not particularly joyful, yet apart from the thorough necessity of the daily life, (in order that I may be out of debt if possible before November,) I quite believe it is a better extreme for me than the lounging existence to which I can look back with no comfort. . . .

'This is what I do here:—rise at $5\frac{1}{2}$, & after 6 or so am at work till 8, breakfast then work till 5—occasionally obliged to leave off on account of sight, or from utter weariness, when I do a line or two of Sophocles, or compose some new song music, & at 5 dinner— to $5\frac{3}{4}$ at most. Then to $7\frac{1}{2}$ paint again, and by the time the brushes are washed it is nearly dark, & I potter out to the post with some notes I may have written, or puddle along the shingly beach till $9\frac{1}{2}$—Then, half an hour Sophocles, & bed. This is unvaried, barring the Sundays, when I go to Hastings to dine with somebody or other—No "followers" or visits allowed in the week, nohow.'[21]

Really he was rather enjoying it. There was a beautifully mellow late summer and autumn, and the gentle warmth sank into his soul. 'Of all the very loveliest days of this wonderfully loftiest summer-endless—perhaps this might be the softest & calmest & brightest',[22] he wrote one day in the middle of October. It was a year now since he and Lushington had parted; emotionally he was disengaged, and for the time being his mind was freed from its obsession of unhappiness.

Throughout the summer the newspapers had been filled with reports from Italy. In July the nationalists were betrayed when Louis Napoleon made peace with Austria behind Cavour's back, but the news did mean that Lear would be able to go back to Rome for the winter.

When he had finished his work at St Leonards he returned to London to deliver the paintings and clear himself of debt. November was settling in, London was odious and he wanted to get away south as soon as he had tied up his business and said good-bye to his friends. He wrote to Fortescue telling him his plans:

O! Mimber for the County Louth
Residing at Ardee!
Whom I, before I wander South
Partik'lar wish to see:—

I send you this.—That you may know
I've left the Sussex shore,
And coming here two days ago
Do cough for evermore.

Or grasping hard for breath do sit
Upon a brutal chair,
For to lie down in Asthma fit
Is what I cannot bear.

Or sometimes sneeze: and always blow
My well-developed nose.
And altogether never know
No comfort nor repose.

Rome 1858-60

All through next week I shall be here,
To work as best I may,
On my last picture, which is near-
er finished every day.

    .   .   .   .   .

So then I hope to hear your ways
Are bent on English moves
For that I trust once more to gaze
Upon the friend I loves.

(Alas! Blue Posts I shall not dare
To visit ere I go—
Being compulsed to take such care
Of all the winds as blow.)

But if you are not coming now
Just write a line to say so—
And I shall still consider how
Ajoskyboskybayso.

No more my pen: no more my ink:
No more my rhyme is clear.
So I shall leave off here I think—

Yours ever,

EDWARD LEAR[23]

Someone—probably Lushington—had suggested that his painting of the Temple of Bassae should be presented to the Fitzwilliam Museum, and he had to spend some time in London writing to ask his friends if they would subscribe towards the purchase. '. . . the "Bassae Septuagent" or as some call it "the subscription to the 70 Elders"—or "The Bassaerelief" is riz to 50'[24] he told Holman Hunt on December 9th, and a few days later he went up to Cambridge to see where the picture would hang.

His final task before leaving was to arrange for the publication of his settings of the 'Idylls of the King'. On December 22nd, 1859, Lushington saw him off to Rome.

*The Temple of Bassae. Bought by subscribers and presented
to the Fitzwilliam Museum, Cambridge in 1859*

Lear travelled across France in the fast new express to Marseilles.[25] It was a relief to get that part of the journey over quickly, for he always found it a great strain sitting in a train or coach for hours on end. At Marseilles he boarded a boat for Civita Vecchia. The weather had suddenly worsened, and he had a dreadful yet magnificent passage across the Ligurian Sea: 'The waves are really a wonderful sight!—a deep blue-black, with silver crests—valley making, gulfing—vast, forcible, opal-vitriol hued above, solemn inky below,—gull-abounding—ever moving—terrible. But I lay & held on—as the vessel swooped & circled.—No rest: no food: & so day went on, till, toward sunset, the dismal-wave-chase seemed to lull,—& then came the golden sunset, calm, & with one long purple, orange lighted cloud above, & many a golden flecked streak at the waters edge—the sun going down one full orb of sublimity—: above the delicate new moon, & one star.'[26]

In Rome there was an uneasy peace, and he returned to a half deserted city. Usually there would be nearly 2,000 English residents, but that year he thought there were probably no more than

250. The artists who relied on casual sales to visitors were going to have a hard winter, and Lear was glad that he had come back with commissions to work on. But even though he was busy he found Rome oppressive.

'O dear Emily T! & various people!
How I live a living death here!'[27] he wrote in his diary.

The weather was 'abomminnable: filthy: beeeeeeeeeestly: so I shan't talk about it. I am always in a rage—always.'[28]

Giorgio was gloomy and cross as well—and early in March he suddenly told Lear that he had a wife and three children in Corfu. Lear had employed him now for four years but had had no idea of this—even though part of this time had been spent in Corfu where Giorgio's family lived. He realised now that his servant wouldn't want to come back to Rome for another winter. It had been a mistake coming at all, and he told Fortescue: 'I hate and loathe this place so utterly—from its pettiness, its cliquiness—its art before nature,—its faith pro works,—its wet and dirty atmosphere,—its compulsory boredom,—its imprisoning life,—and thousand more reasons,—that I know I do right to quit it at all risks.'[29] Next winter he would have to look for somewhere new. 'I am convinced of this more and more,' he had written, 'if you have a wife, or are in love with a woman, (both phases of the same state of self division, the only real and proper state of life in this world) if I say such be your condition, 'ὦ ἄνθρωπε' ['O man!'] then you may stay in any place & in any circumstances: you are raised out of the necessity of contemplating the cussed nuisances of poverty or bores by sympathy:—but if you are absolutely alone in the world, & likely to be so, then move about continually & never stand still. I therefore think I shall be compulsed . . . to go to Japan & New York, or Paraguay, or anywhere before long.'[30] Part of him longed to stop wandering—though another part wondered if he ever could. 'How I wish I had some settled abode, at least until the last narrow box,' he told Fortescue. 'But if I settled myself I should go to Tobago the next day.'[31]

If he didn't come back to Rome he would lose a whole year's rent, but luckily he had managed to save £350 from the previous summer's stint of work. It would mean that he couldn't think of going back to Palestine yet—as he had vaguely hoped that he might. Instead he would start on another large painting, for he had had nothing in the Academy since 1856. He was pleased with the progress he had made during the winter; for the first time he had been using white paper instead of his usual half-tone.

On April 13th, 1860, he began to pack 'furibundiously' and tie up everything ready to leave. Then he spent a fortnight travelling with Giorgio round the Bay of Spezia. Despite the bad weather he thought the bay superbly beautiful, and the walk did him good and helped to ease off the few inches of extra weight he had put on during the winter. At the end of May he saw Giorgio on his way to Corfu, and then he turned back for England.

CHAPTER THIRTEEN

Landscape Painter

1860–63

Creative artists are strangely placed. There is a lingering mystique of their apartness—the idea that they are men of vision and that with the great leaders, and now the great scientists, they will be the people most remembered by other generations. Because of this, and the dignity of their talent, they may find their way into the highest layers of society. Yet they are also tradesmen who must sell their goods, and in Lear's time—indeed sometimes even now—tradesmen were considered quite simply beyond the pale.

And so they find themselves in an ambivalent situation in which they may be both admired and despised, and where as a result they will often be regarded with magnanimous condescension. When an artist is in demand he can afford to ignore this and this in its turn will inspire confidence in his value, for a man who allows himself to be patronised, who is inordinately grateful to anyone buying his work, can leave the purchaser with an uneasy feeling that he has taken an inferior work off a second-rate artist's hands.

Viewed objectively now, Lear's water-colour drawings are enjoying a reputation they never had in his lifetime, and one reason for this—one amongst several—is that Lear let himself be patronised. The trouble, of course, was that he simply couldn't afford to upset anyone who was thinking of buying his work, but the result was that though many of the people who had his paintings derived a great deal of pleasure from them, few came away feeling that they had bought anything of value.

There were other reasons for this, of course. His water-colour drawings varied in quality a good deal—particularly later in life when his sight was going and he had rheumatism in his right arm—and he would cheerfully exhibit the very bad beside the good.

But he underestimated the value of even the best of them and tended to see them either as slight, inexpensive 'pot-boilers' or as sketches for the oil paintings which he regarded as his real achievement. He never fully understood what he was doing when he painted in oils, and in his anxiety he often overworked the pictures until all the sparkle had gone and the fluid, rhythmical movement which made his water colours so delightful had been ground to a standstill.

But Lear was certain that it was with his oil painting that he would become known, and in a sense he was right, for his water-colour drawings stood no chance in the great exhibition halls and galleries. His mistake was in even trying to compete with the fashionable painters of his day who surpassed him in both sentimentality and mastery of their medium. If he had concentrated on water-colours he might have enjoyed in his own lifetime the respect that he now commands, and he would probably have made a steady if undramatic living. But he never realised this, and when he came back to England in 1860 he was planning to paint the large and conspicuous oil painting which would finally establish him as the respected and sought-after painter he felt he should be.

He didn't settle to work at once. In the middle of June he was invited with Lushington to stay at Farringford. It was the first time they had been together for more than an odd hour or two since they had left Corfu, but Lear felt easier with him now: '. . . fanatical-frantic caring overmuch for those who care little for us, is a miserable folly. And after all ordinary natural pride revolts at selfish coldness,'[1] he wrote in his diary.

It was a strange and rather unhappy visit. Emily was as perfect as ever but as Lear was sinking back into the rare contentment of family life, Julia Cameron, the photographer, swept into the house followed by eight men carrying a grand piano so that Lear could play and sing for them: '. . . odious incense palavar & fuss succeeded to quiet home moments', he wrote sadly. 'After all, it is perhaps better now, never to feel happy & quiet; so one gradually cares less for life.'[2] And then he added the phrase which he quoted over and over again as he found earlier happiness slipping away: 'We come no more to the golden shore, where we danced in days of old.'

*Ann Lear, Edward's eldest
sister who brought him up*

The next day was Sunday, and the three men—Tennyson, Lushington and Lear—set out to walk across the Downs. Tennyson had begun to loathe the strangers who wanted to devour him, and the walk was miserable: 'AT was most disagreeably querulous and irritating and would return, chiefly because he saw people approaching,' wrote Lear. 'But FL would not go back, and led zigzagwise toward the sea—AT snubby and cross always. After a time he would not go on—but led me back by muddy paths (over our shoes,) a short cut home—hardly, even at last avoiding his horror,—the villagers coming from church . . . I believe that this is my last visit to Farringford:—nor can I wish it otherwise all things considered.'[3]

Back in London he was alarmed at how old and tired Ann was looking. It was a warm summer and the close June weather seemed to be crushing down on her. She had moved now to Stonefield Street in Islington where she shared a house with two of her oldest friends, but in her gentle old age she was lonely.

In August Lear was invited to stay at Nuneham, where Lady Waldegrave had asked him to do two paintings of the grounds. There was to be a house full of people, and he could combine work with the chance of talking with Fortescue. He wasn't always at ease with Lady Waldegrave, though she was beautiful and kind and

179

commissioned a great deal of work from him. She had been delighted with the paintings he had done for her in Palestine, and sent him a letter of doubtful praise: 'I fell in love at first sight with your beautiful pictures,' she had written. 'They far and far surpass my expectations and I am miserable at not knowing where I can find a good place for them.'[4]

> 'Bother all painting! I wish I'd 200 per annum!
> Wouldn't I sell all my colours and brushes and
>   damnable messes!
> Over the world I should rove, North, South,
>   East and *West*, I would
> Marry a black girl at last, and slowly prepare to
>   walk into Paradise!'[5]

he wrote to Fortescue on July 9th. But—unlike Tennyson who had an annual grant from the Exchequer—he didn't have £200 a year and he must get back to work.

He arrived at Nuneham at the beginning of August, and found the house gurgling with people. But then he heard that the whole party was moving on to Strawberry Hill and that it had been arranged for him to stay on with the housekeepers, the governess and Lady Waldegrave's seven-year-old niece, Constance: he was expected to eat with the governess, and apparently this was considered his rightful position. He hadn't been treated like this since his earliest days at Knowsley and as he wandered in the rain under the dripping trees and across the sodden park he was reminded of lonely days there. He became so despondent that he couldn't get on with the paintings; instead he made a few drawings to work from and left as soon as he could.

Back in London he began to concentrate on his plans for the large painting. In fact, he had decided to work on two pictures— one nine feet long of the Cedars of Lebanon, and another seven feet long of Masada and the Dead Sea. 'One *must* plan & risk & think something,' he wrote to Emily Tennyson, 'or if not, turn into a stagnant snail.'[6]

He needed some cedar trees that were within easy reach of London, and he found them at Oatlands Park Hotel at Walton-on-

Thames. 'It stands upon elevated Terrace land, within its own
grounds of forty-four acres. The rooms are spacious, and replete in
every comfort, and the Mansion being placed on a dry, gravelly
subsoil, is particularly well adapted for a winter residence.'[7] So
ran an advertisement in *The Saturday Review*, and since it looked
as if Lear would be working there through the winter, it sounded
ideal. The oldest cedar, still there today, was reputed to have been

Lear feeding 'unfortunate birds' at Oatlands Park Hotel, Weybridge

one of the first imported into England from the Lebanon, and was
planted to commemorate the birth of Prince Henry, the son of
Charles I, in the royal palace which had stood on the site.

At the end of September 1860 his things were sent to the hotel,
and he went down and settled in. He didn't usually like hotel life,
but he was well and busy and he found himself rather enjoying it.
It was 'a large & sumptiously commodious place, in a part of the old
Oatlands Park—with nice broad terrace walks, & a wonderfully
lovely view over the river Temms & the surroundiant landskip.'[8]
He was given a large light bedroom, 'delightful to behold, & wanting for nought.'[9] Each morning he was up at six o'clock. '. . . what
deep strange delight in the morning air & sun,—& bird singing,
& tree rustling freshness!!!!'[10] he wrote in his diary. His first
job was to feed the 'unfortunate birds' then he would get in an
hour or so on small commissioned works before breakfast at eight.
He would 'breakfast audibly in the public coughy-room',[11] and

immediately afterwards begin working outside. He painted until six in the evening on the Cedars or the Masada, or on two big commissioned works of Damascus and Beirut. Dinner was at a quarter to seven and afterwards he would be sociable downstairs until nine o'clock. Then he would spend one hour translating Plato and one hour penning out his Mount Athos drawings, and at eleven o'clock he went to bed.

It was the kind of full, regular life which most satisfied him, and he was getting through the winter remarkably well: '. . . the soil is so dry at present I have neither Asthma nor roomatizsim when I am there—— On the contrary I have been making some new nonsenses in my old age,'[12] he told Lady Waldegrave. It was fourteen years since *A Book of Nonsense* had been published, and he had been writing new limericks all the time. Now he wanted to bring out a revised and larger edition with a lot of new rhymes, and this time he thought he would offer it outright to a publisher instead of publishing it himself.

Right through December and into January he painted out of doors, feeling remarkably fit. Christmas had been unusually cold, and when the thaw came it was disastrous. 'Lo! as I began to write this afternoon', he told Emily Tennyson, 'horrible borrible squashfibolious meligoposhquilous sounds were heard, & ever increasingly, like 5000 whales in hysterics.

'Then—huming screams & shouts.—Then stamping; roaring;—rushing;—bouncing;—booming;—by-go-bustling;—

. . . O! . . .

the great cistern, along of the sudden thaw—had bust all the pipes —which spouted forth arm-broad torrents of water like fire from cannons.'[13]

His room was all right, but when workmen arrived to repair the mess and began hammering all around, he decided that it was time to get back to London.

During the winter he had taken out a new lease on some rooms at 15 Stratford Place, two down from the house where he'd lived whilst he was at the R.A. 'Exhibitions in a mass of thousands of paintings—the greater part of which are painted so as to look well as regards the surrounding pictures,—seem to me more and more a false practice,'[14] he told Lady Waldegrave wisely, and now he set up one of his own rooms as a gallery. Then he sent out invitations and settled back to wait for visitors. They came, 'sometimes 20 at a time—of all kinds of phases of life: sometimes for 3 hours no one comes:—so then I partly sleep, & partly draw pages of a new Nonsense book. If I sleep, I wake up savagely at some new comer's entrance, & they go away abashed. If I write nonsense, I am pervaded with smiles, & please the visitors.'[15]

Ann called frequently, just to sit quietly with him. Sometimes he would walk back to Islington with her, and she would tell him about their brothers and sisters and the years in Pentonville before he was born. She revelled in his company and they spent some of the most contented days together that they had ever known. In January she had her seventieth birthday and she looked little and frail. On March 2nd she came as usual to his studio and sat with him through the morning whilst he painted, then they lunched together and at 3.30 they parted.

Two days later she began to have terrible bouts of sickness, and a swelling appeared on the back of her neck. She became really ill, and each day Edward went up to Islington, sometimes taking flowers to brighten her room, and would sit quietly with her holding her hand. She seemed calm and contented, '& speaks of dying as a change about to bring such great delight that she only checks herself for thinking of it too much. She has always been indeed as near Heaven as it was possible to be.'[16]

On March 9th the constant sickness began to tell and her strength seemed to fall away. Edward sat with her, and she was happy just to have him there. 'Dear dear Ann! Always joyous at seeing me,' he wrote in his diary. '. . . Sometimes she spoke suddenly—"What a blessing you are here!—not among the Arabs!" . . . "bless you my dear Edward: what a comfort you have been to [me] all your life!" '[17]

The next day she grew weaker. 'The dearest Ann *never* murmurs: thanks us for all we do:—always thinks of us!—"Go to bed Ellen dear! you are tired!"—"Nurse have you had your supper?"— "Edward my precious—take care that you do not hurt your head against the bed iron".'[18]

Slopes of Myrtle

In the early hours of March 11th she sank into a coma, and he couldn't bear to watch what was happening to her. He went back to Stratford Place to wash and make an attempt at eating breakfast, then went back to her; he walked up to Highbury to see the Nevills, and then went back to her again. As the morning wore on she grew weaker, and he knew that' he couldn't be with her when she died. Instead he went out into Stonefield Street and walked up and down the pavement opposite the house, and just after noon he looked up and saw the blinds in her room being drawn across. '. . . she died as a little infant falls asleep! Painless— motionless! As her life has been one of good & blessing—so is her death.'[19]

He wrote at once to Fortescue: 'My dear Ann is gone—she died a little after noon today—in such quiet!

'I am going down to Lewes to try to get Husey Hunt (who is her executor) to come on Saturday to my darling sister's funeral— for I shall be so terribly alone.'[20]

He stayed two nights at Lewes, glad to be with someone who had known Ann, and then he went up to sort her meagre belongings. So many of them related to him—his drawings from the age of four, letters, all the hundred and one trinkets and mementos he had sent her from every place he had been to—necklaces and scarves and brooches and carved paper-knives—they had all been faithfully kept. How she must have longed for his company in the years that he was away, though she had never tried to persuade him to come home to live. 'Ever all she was to me was good:—& what I should have been unless she had been my mother I dare not think'.[21] he wrote.

The funeral at Highgate cemetery was quiet, and afterwards he went for a few days down to Oatlands Park Hotel.

Lear didn't feel like being alone. Emily Tennyson had written to him, 'come to us when you feel equal to it',[22] and she was the person who would most understand his loneliness. He reached Farringford on March 19th—but it was the wrong moment. Alfred's brother, Horatio, was expected with all his family, and the house was in a bustle of preparation. Lear found himself a room at the

Landscape Painter 1860–63

Royal Albion Hotel at Freshwater, and on the first day he was able to have a talk with Emily. After that he was in the way. Then there was a misunderstanding about an invitation for dinner, and he was so distressed by the whole atmosphere that on the 24th he slipped away without going up to the house to say goodbye. For the next two weeks he wandered from one friend's house to another, and on April 11th he came back to London.

Gradually he began to work again, and by the middle of May the 'Cedars' were finished. This was the first large painting he had done without any help from Hunt, and it was going to be his crowning success. Since the sale of his first large oil painting— 'The Quarries of Syracuse' which had sold in the Academy in 1853 for £250—both the size and the price of his paintings had been going up. In 1857 he had been paid 500 guineas for the 'Corfu', and the following year he asked the same price for Lady Waldegrave's painting of Damascus. Now he was thinking of asking a larger sum for the 'Cedars', but he hadn't finally decided, when one evening in May he was invited to dinner with Millais and his wife, Effie.

A drawing of the Cedars of Lebanon

He didn't enjoy the evening, for he had begun to dislike the successful young painter who had betrayed Pre-Raphaelite principles, and whom he considered, with determined blindness, to be far inferior to Hunt. 'He, at 30, is like a crafty French dancing-master,' he wrote in his diary, '& has neither depth nor softness in his character.'[23] Millais' painting, 'Apple Blossoms', had just been sold for 450 guineas, and Lear decided that if that was worth 450 then the 'Cedars' were worth 700. 'If the Cedars don't sell for £735 now I shall put a higher price on them if exhibited and shall be wholly indifferent to their not selling,'[24] he told Fortescue. But there was one important difference—Millais was the most popular painter of his day and people were eager to spend their money on his work, but Lear was known to only a very few, and as the pound then would have bought more than five times what it will buy today the price was exceedingly high.

With the big picture out of the way he felt he needed a change, and as Lady Waldegrave had asked him to paint two views of Florence he decided to spend the next few months on the Continent.

The Folkestone train rocked and swayed and jumbled along, and two small children travelling with their nurse were frightened and unhappy. So Lear lifted them onto his knee, '& told them my long name & all kinds of nonsense till they forgot the shaking bother. I NEVER saw 2 SWEETER & more intelligent children than those 2: I LONGED to keep them both,'[25] wrote the lonely man.

Giorgio joined him in Florence, and he worked there for two weeks. 'Plumpudding—treacle, weddingcake, sugar, barleysugar, sugar candy, raisins & peppermint drops would not make a more luscious mixture in the culinary world, than Florence & its Val d'Arno does as Landscape,'[26] he told Holman Hunt contentedly.

It seemed odd to be away from England and not be writing long and frequent letters to Ann, and he told Fortescue, 'the want of the constant journal I have sent my dear sister for so many years, makes every hour seem very strange and sad and blank'.[27] From America, where the Civil War had broken out earlier in the year, came the news that four of his nephews had joined the Northern army and another the Southern, and then he heard that his sister,

Florence, 1861

Mary, had died on her way back from New Zealand. Lear had often sent her money, for whenever he could he would send money to anyone who needed it, especially anyone in his own family.

He was back in England at the beginning of August and went straight down to St Leonards to work on the Florence pictures. When he had been young he had enjoyed his work, but now it was becoming an odious and objectionable task. 'No life is more *shocking* to me than the sitting motionless like a petrified gorilla as to my body & limbs hour after hour—my hand meanwhile, peck peck pecking at billions of little dots & lines, while my mind is fretting & fuming through every moment of the weary days work,'[28] he told Fortescue. In fact it came back to money, for painting, painting, painting to pay the bills took away every ounce of creative enjoyment—if he had had just a small private income he knew he could have painted so much better.

But one thing did cheer him—it seemed that he had been right about the 'Cedars'. The painting was on exhibition in Liverpool and a critic there had written: ' "Mr Lear has in this great picture not only achieved a professional success, but he has also conferred an obligation of the highest order on the whole Christian world." (!!!!!!—After that take care how you speak or write to me.)' he warned Fortescue. 'I shall not be surprised if the Cedars are purchased at Liverpool.'[29] But they weren't—they were too highly priced.

By the beginning of October the paintings of Florence were finished, and he was back in London. Now he had one more task before the winter began, and that was to find a publisher for the revised edition of *A Book of Nonsense*. He took it to Smith & Elder, and then to Routledge & Warne—but neither of them wanted it. This was rather a shock, for however he might turn out as a painter he had thought that his success as a nonsense writer was assured. As no one would take it he asked Dalziel to make wood-engravings of the drawings—this was cheaper than the lithography he had used in earlier editions—and to print and bind the book, and now that he was paying for the entire book production, Routledge said that they would take 1,000 finished copies for distribution.

Winter was coming on again, and as there was nothing now until the Great International Exhibition in London in the spring he thought it was time to get away south. He had decided to try another winter in Corfu: the past was over, for at the beginning of October Lushington became engaged. Instead he would look to the future: the nonsense book would be out in time for Christmas, and with the 'Cedars' he was approaching the climax of his painting career.

He wished he had never come. He was weary and lonely and

missed Lushington's sombre company, for though it hadn't made him happy it had given a purpose to his life. The weather certainly was marvellous—'All without,—the sea, mountains, olive woods—are as lovely as colour and calm atmosphere and cloudless sky can make them:—but within I confess to being blank & weary and sad to a choking amount—: and perhaps a lesson may be learnt from this state of things—that the outside is not so much that we should think of—but then how the Devil is it to be otherwise with a dirty landscape painter.'[30]

But he began to settle in, and after the dullness and heaviness of his Roman exile he actually enjoyed the bustle of the garrison town. There was a new High Commissioner, Sir Henry Storks, and he had as one of his aides a zealous young Royal Artillery subaltern. This was Evelyn Baring, a cousin of Lear's close friend, Lord Northbrook, and later created Earl of Cromer for his work in making modern Egypt. He was young, intelligent and enthusiastic, and despite the thirty years difference in their age he and Lear formed a spontaneous and happy friendship which lasted until Lear's death. A few of Lear's letters to him have survived, like this one:

'Thrippy Pilliwinx,—Inkly tinksy pobblebookle abblesquabs? Flosky? beebul trimble flosky! Okul scratchabibblebongibo, viddle squibble tog-a-tog, ferrymoyassity amsky flamsky ramsky damsky crocklefether squiggs.

Flinkywisty pomm
Slushypipp.'[31]

But having military friends had its disadvantages, as he told Fortescue: '. . . just now I looked out of the window at the time when the 2nd were marching by—I having a full palate & brushes in my hand: whereat Col. Bruce saw me & saluted; & not liking to make a formillier nod in the presence of the hole harmy, I put up my hand to salute,—& thereby transferred all my colours into my hair & whiskers—which I must now wash in Turpentine or shave off.'[32]

The nonsense book was out in time for Christmas, and within a few days five hundred copies had been sold. But a critic writing in *The Saturday Review* described the verses as 'anonymous, & a reprint of old nursery rhymes',[33] which made Lear cross and sad. 'I wish I could have all the credit due to me, small as that may be,'[34] he wrote. 'I wish someone would review it properly & funnily.'

It was a quiet winter. He had a few small commissions to work on, and as usual he opened his gallery twice a week to visitors, but he soon realised again the one advantage of Rome—for he sold absolutely nothing. He had gone back to his Greek lessons again, and told Fortescue, '. . . if I had my way & wor an axiom maker & Lawgiver, I would cause it to be understood that Greek is (or a knowledge of it) the first of virtues: cleanliness the 2nd., and Godliness—as held by parsons generally—the 3rd.'[35]

When the spring came round he crossed the island to do some drawing at Palaeokastrizza, a village on the western coast, perfect and utterly peaceful, 'excepting only a dim hum of myriad ripples 500 feet below me. On my left is the convent of Paleokastrizza, and happily, as the monkery had functions at 2 a.m. they are all fast asleep now . . . to my left is one of the many peacock-tail-hued bays here, reflecting the vast red cliffs and far above them—higher and higher, the immense rock of St Angelo rising into the air, on whose summit the old castle still is seen a ruin, just 1,400 feet above the water.

'It half seems to me that such life as this must be wholly another from the drumbeating bothery frivolity of the town of Corfu, and I seem to grow a year younger every hour. Not that it will last. Accursed picnic parties with miserable scores of asses male and female are coming tomorrow, and peace flies—as I shall too. . . . One thing, under all circumstances I have quite decided on— ἀποφάσισα ἀκριθως*—when I go to heaven—if indeed I go—and am surrounded by thousands of polite angels,—I shall say courteously 'please leave me alone!—you are doubtless all delightful, but I do not wish to become acquainted with you:—let me have a park and a beautiful view of sea and hill, mountain and river, valley and plain, with no end of tropical foliage:—a few well-behaved small cherubs to cook and keep the place clean—and—after I am quite

* 'I unconditionally surrender.'

established—say for a million or two of years—an angel of a wife.'[36]

In April he began to be anxious about his paintings in the Exhibition. Their success now depended very much on how well they were hung and lit, for exhibition walls then were always crammed with pictures and a badly hung painting could hardly be seen. Anxiously he wrote to Fortescue: '. . . please let me know, unvarnishedly, how my Cedars and Corfu look:—for the sale of the Cedars depends much on its place and *my* plans on *its* sale for £735.'[37] The reply came back—the pictures are hung high.

In the middle of May 1862 he left for England, ground down with disappointment. His great painting, lionised in Liverpool the year before, was not only hung high—it was slated by Tom Taylor reviewing the exhibition for *The Times*. When Lear saw this he was desperate. He had believed that this painting would establish his reputation. He also had to live and he had spent most of one winter working on it, expecting to see an ample return for his time and the expense of staying at Oatlands Park Hotel. Now he was practically out of money for he had hardly sold a thing since he left Rome in the spring of 1860: the large paintings of Beirut and Damascus on which he had worked in 1860 and 1861 had been paid for in advance to get him to the Holy Land. Ann's property had been sold and this brought him in an annual income of £50, and he had money saved for the day when his sight was too bad for him to paint any more, but he didn't want to break into this as he knew that he would never be able to replace it.

He began to talk of declaring himself bankrupt. He thought of cutting all his picture prices by half. In the next breath he considered buying one of the houses in Stratford Place from his savings and setting himself up there with two servants and a permanent exhibition of his work. His quandary was dreadful. However much he might dream of it, he couldn't seriously think of buying a house in England as he couldn't stand the climate: but to get enough money to live—and though his tastes weren't extravagant, they were at least generous—he needed to be where people bought pictures, and that meant either London, or else Rome which he hated.

One thing he did know: he couldn't again spend months working on one large, important, but uncommissioned work. Instead he must paint the small water-colour drawings which he knew he could sell. There is a popular fallacy that artists are stimulated by poverty, and that enough money saps their creativity: as Lear saw and experienced it, lack of money meant that he must bury his real creativity and produce instead pot-boilers just so that he could pay his bills.[38] 'I agree with you Daddy,' he wrote to Holman Hunt, 'Art is the Devil. I believe that originally in the Hebrew version of Job, the Devil was made to set Job about a painting, & that that excellent & unfortunate individual took it in hand until he was worn out, & bust into curses no end. But the later transcribers of the Bible could not see the sense of this; so they cut it out. More fools they.'[39]

At the end of September the exhibition came down. 'What to do with the Cedars I do not know,' he wrote to Fortescue, 'probably make a great coat of them. To a philosopher, the fate of a picture so well thought of and containing such high qualities is funny enough.'[40]

Even the nonsense was becoming a millstone, for Dalziel was pressing him for money, and though the whole edition had sold Routledge had so far paid him nothing. Then they decided, after all, to buy the copyright, but Lear refused now to let them have it for the £100 he had originally asked. Instead, he sold the entire rights of a book which went into nineteen editions in his own lifetime, for £125. 700 guineas for the 'Cedars', £125 for the copyright of *A Book of Nonsense*—he didn't realise where his unique value lay. But he was pleased. 'I went to the city today, to put the £125 I got for the "Book of Nonsense" into the funds,' he told Lady Waldegrave. 'It is doubtless a very unusual thing for an artist to put by money, for the whole way from Temple Bar to the Bank was *crowded* with carriages and people,—so immense a sensation did this occurance make. And all the way back it was the same, which was very gratifying.'[41]

Lady Waldegrave was now a widow, for Mr Harcourt had died

the previous winter, and as it was considered improper for a widow to become engaged until at least a year after her husband's death and Fortescue was having an anxious time. He knew that he had rivals, including the Duke of Newcastle under whom he worked in the Colonial Office, and as the summer wore on he began cautiously to push his suit. Lady Waldegrave encouraged him, and in September she accepted his proposal. It was to be kept a guarded secret which Lear, who had been a confidante all along, was entrusted to keep. And so another dear friend was marrying. 'Every marriage of people I care about rather seems to leave one on the bleak shore alone,'[42] he wrote, and the shore was becoming a very lonely place.

> ' "but never more, O! never we—
> Shall meet to eggs and toast and T!"

Never mind. I don't grumble at the less I see of friends—so they gain by it.'[43]

But there was a germ of an idea coming into his own mind. Early in November he went to see Richard Bethell, who was now Lord Westbury, the Lord Chancellor. He had a twenty-four-year-old daughter called Augusta whom Lear had known from a child, and now he began to notice her: '. . . dear little Gussie, who is absolutely good & sweet & delightful,' he wrote in his diary, 'BOTHER'.[44]

In the middle of November he left for Corfu, and as soon as he had settled in he began a completely new system of work. First he sorted through the sketches he had made on his travels, and chose sixty from which to work. Then he prepared and mounted thirty pieces of paper of one size, and thirty more rather larger. Next he drew in thirty outlines and a few days later thirty more. Then, moving from one picture to the next he painted in all the blues, and all the greens and all the browns. The process wasn't entirely unenjoyable: '. . . worked all day—to 4: getting the whole of the larger 30 tyrants—another step forward. This sense of progress—however dark the terminus—is inspiring.'[45] His plan was to make a large number of pleasing paintings which would sell, 'small

Carrara, July, 1861

10 and 12 guinea drawings calculated to attract the attention of
small capitalists.'[46] 'They are an odd sort of drawings—in as much
as they recall vividly other places & times—yet have no "upward
aspirations" as vorx of hart.'[47]

As usual when he worked hard, Lear was much happier.
'January is nearly gone', he wrote in his diary, '& I must say I have
never passed one so serenely for many many years.'[48] 'I lead as
quiet a life as I can being strongly convinced that a regular application to some kind of self improvement by way of work is more
necessary to ensure comfort than any great variety of social life.'[49]

Whenever he could, he committed himself to things completely:
when he travelled he pushed himself on and on until he was exhausted, when he was painting he might work from 6 in the morning until the evening light had gone, when he wrote letters they
would be several carefully composed pages and he might write
more than twenty at a time until he 'became like unto a spawned
salmon, & was exhausted, & could work no more'.[50] 'The beaver,
the Ant, the Bee, and suchlike brutes are my model communities,'[51]
he once wrote, and for him work was a 'universal panacea for the
ills of life'[52]—it left no time for brooding or recrimination. Physio-

logically, too, he couldn't cope with an empty, idle life, and he never felt better than when he was working hard and able to get out walking: then he could keep both 'the morbids' and his epilepsy at bay.

It took him sixty days to complete the sixty Tyrants as he called them, and by the end of February they were all framed and hung in his studio. Throughout March they were on exhibition, and within a few days £120 worth had been bought. Some of the visitors were most provoking, especially one 'who saw all 60 drawings in 19 minutes, calling over the names of each and saying "£700! why you must give a ball!" Fool! As yet I have sold £120 worth—but have not received one farthing—for great people generally suppose that artists gnaw their colours and brushes for food.'[53]

He found new friends that winter. Sir Percy Shelley, son of the poet, was there 'in a yott' and he set down the music Lear had composed to Shelley's words, 'O world, O life, O time!' Other friends were a family called De Vere who had a small daughter, Mary. Lear was always happy when he was with her, making up nonsenses and drawing pictures, and delighting in her childlike appreciation. 'Would *one* have been as happy as *one* fancies if *one* had married & had had children?'[54] he pondered sadly.

Really it had been a marvellous season. 'The same perfect weather. Hardly a cloud in all the sky: every crag & winkle of Salvador—every gull & goose—every sail & boat, reflected clear & calm in the bright sea from 7.30 to 6 p.m. It is not possible to imagine greater beauty of nature.'[55] 'So happy a "winter" as this— one thing with another—passed I never,'[56] he summed up on March 6th.

He seemed at last to have found a way of combining a happy winter home with making enough money to live, and of all the places he had tried none suited him as perfectly as Corfu: '. . . the more I see of this place, so the more I feel that no other spot on earth can be fuller of beauty & of variety of beauty. For you may pass your days by gigantic cliffs with breaking foam-waves below them . . .—or on hills which overlook long seas of foliage backed by snow-covered mountain ridges . . . or beneath vast olives, over-branching dells full of fern & myrtle & soft green fields of bright grass: or in gardens dark with oranges & lemon groves, those fruits sparkling golden & yellow against the purple sea & amethyst hills: —or by a calm sandy shore below aloe-grown heights—rippling— sparkling curves of sea sounding gently around all day long.'[57]

He was thinking now that he would settle permanently abroad and not come back to England each summer, for the expensive double journey brought him nothing. '. . . the few friends I care much for, I see only for a few hours, and really don't communicate with as much as when abroad:—the sitting for six weeks or two months in a room on the chance of purchasers coming is far from pleasant:—and the country house life is rattling and expensive . . . and moreover cannot be carried on by those who have ever to work for life.'[58]

At the end of March 1863 he took the exhibition down, and as he had enough money he decided to make a tour of the Ionian Islands before they ceased to be under British rule—for in 1862 the Cabinet had decided that they must be returned to Greece. He was away for two months, walking and drawing on each island so that if the next summer in England brought him no new commissions he would have material for another book.

Mount Skopo, Zante. From 'Views in the Seven Ionian Islands'

He returned to Corfu for a few days early in June, and then left for England. The journey took him nearly a month, for he was taken ill in Italy. He had landed at Ancona which was a free port, but he couldn't leave by the road out of the town until he had had all his baggage examined. It was noon and the sun pulsed down on him as he struggled to undo the straps and bindings on his cases. He managed to get to Turin, but there he collapsed with sunstroke. For a few days he was really ill, and he was still feeling horribly weak when he reached England at the end of June.

The large paintings had been on exhibition throughout the winter at Stratford Place, but there was no sign of their being sold, and as he had no other work he settled down to the Ionian Islands book. Instead of using lithography, a task he dreaded, he decided to experiment with photography. This meant doing the drawings in black and white so that they would photograph, and he tried using charcoal, lampblack, pencil, chalk—but they were all hopeless. Instead he made a delightful water-colour drawing of Paxo which couldn't be reproduced by any method, then sat back and wondered what to do. 'All other years I have had some large work to do and have had to go through with it and look forward to its completion by gradual progress and labour:—but this year I have nothing of the kind:—and the only work I wish to pursue seems to elude my search by the difficulty of its execution. . . . Squiggs. Bettles, Bother. Bullfrogs. Buttercups. Let us change the subject.'[59]

But really he had no choice. Nobody wanted his work, and at least he should make some money from the book. Besides, if he did it well, it 'would keep up my prestige as a draftsman of Mediterranean scenery—and would, moreover, hold up or pave a way to my more general smaller-sized Topography of Greece, to be one day printed with my Journals'.[60] This work covering the whole of Greece had been in his mind since his very first visit there in 1848.

He knew that he must simply start on the book and stay in England until it was finished, and as his photography experiments had been failures he would have to use lithography again. 'The 60 drawings I began in December last were a longer toil,—but then I could often get out & walk, & see the mountains. Now & here, that is not possible,—& I am in a prison.'[61] 'I go grinding on most sadly and painfully, for it is not altogether the physical allowances of banishment from fresh air and nature combined with many hours daily work of a constrained kind, that bothers and depresses me,— but beyond these the impossibility of getting any compensation-dispiritual from the views I am doing, since their being all executed reversed causes them to seem unreal, and without any interest.

'You may ask—then why undertake a task so odious? The reply to which would be, what else could I do?—The remains of my water-colour gains could not carry me through the winter, and therefore, as ever the case with artists who have no settled income, —something else was necessary. And as it would be folly to commence more oil works—those I have done being still unsold,—or to begin more water colours when there are none to see them,— the Ionian book was my only apparent open-door of progress.'[62]

He made up his mind to see nobody until he had finished. He did go up to Highgate to see Ann's grave, and as he walked back through Holloway he passed Bowman's Lodge. The gardens and paddocks had already gone to make room for new roads and buildings, and now the house was advertised for sale as building materials. He decided to take one last look over it. 'Some of the steps were gone:—a woman showed me in to the hall. The parlour at once annihilated 50 years. Empty—but—there were the two bookcases, and the old "secretary" my father used to write at. I saw every possible evening for years. Would I could see the pictures as they were!!—then I went upstairs—the Drawing room is really a fine good room—but spoiled now by the back buildings. *My* room—ehi!—ehi!—Henry's, Mary's, mother's, and the spare room. Down stairs again—the Nursery, a large low room—just as it was—only with no view. Dear Ann's—& the painting room—the happiest of all my life perhaps—the "dark room"—and the "play ground". The little parlour was shut—& the study & greenhouse now extinct. Gave the woman 2 shillings—a cheap & wonderful lesson.'[63] Unless several other rooms were also extinct, it seems to have been a very small house for such a large family; in fact it sounds as though most of them didn't live there. The Bowman's Lodge days are certainly a mystery.

The last of the lithographs was finished on October 20th, then he wrote six hundred letters asking people to subscribe. This too was an endless task, and he confessed to Fortescue, 'if I were an angel I would immediately moult all my quills for fear of their being used in calligraphy'.[64] He was still in England in December, and on the 17th he went to Strawberry Hill for dinner. 'The people I sate next to bored me to death . . . the large drawing room was *horribly* cold: & all things horribly dull. Society at Strawberry Hill —unless a great fete,—is a misery.'[65] Compared with this a quiet visit to Holman Hunt was perfect, '. . . a really delightful evening— very rare nowadays . . . Daddy always seems semifabulous to me; either qua goodness—or for depth of thought: conscientiousness:— talent etc. etc.'[66]

On December 1st, 1863, *Views of the Seven Ionian Islands* was published. It was similar to the second volume of *Illustrated Excursions in Italy*, and had twenty plates each with a short descriptive text. It had been a test of his endurance, and it wasn't all over yet, for he had to chase up fifty subscribers who hadn't bothered to pay, and 'who naturally think 3 guineas can be nothing, forgetting that 150 guineas are much'.[67] But from the book he was able to put £300 into the 3 per cents for his old age. Ten days after Christmas he left once more for Corfu.

CHAPTER FOURTEEN

Wanderer

1864–66

During the summer of 1863 the seventeen-year-old Prince William of Denmark had accepted the Greek throne, and when Lear reached Corfu early in January 1864 he found the British preparing to leave. Hopeful that he could stay on he had written to Fortescue: 'I want you to write to Lord Palmerston to ask him to ask the Queen to ask the King of Greece to give me a "place". As I never asked anything of you before, I think I may rely on your doing this for me. I wish the place to be created a-purpos for me, and the title to be δ ’Αρχανοηδιφλυαρίαποιος, * with permission to wear a fool's cap (or mitre)—3 pounds of butter yearly and a little pig,—and a small donkey to ride on. Please don't forget all this, as I have set my heart on it.'[1]

But he had to leave with the rest of them. The members of the garrison would receive new postings, and some of the civilians were moving on to Athens to live and Lear wondered if he should go there to look for a home for himself. It wouldn't be perfect, for it was a long way from England and the political atmosphere was still unsettled, but he was hoping to be known as a painter of Greek landscape and from Athens he could travel easily over the country. Besides, the English there should be art-conscious as they had been in Rome—which would mean that he should be able to sell his work.

He would have been content to settle in Corfu, for since his return at the end of 1861 he hadn't been happier anywhere. Sadly he packed his things. 'Goodbye, my last furniture is going. I shall sit upon an eggcup and eat my breakfast with a pen . . .'[2]

He left the island on April 4th, and watched 'the loveliest place

* The Lord High Bosh and nonsense maker.

in the world'³ diminishing into the horizon. After dinner, he and Evelyn Baring sat out on deck under the stars, and before he went to bed he composed a sad little ditty, perhaps the purest piece of nonsense he ever wrote:

> She sits upon her Bulbul
> Through the long long hours of night—
> And o'er the dark horizon gleams
> The Yashmack's fitful light.
> The lone Yaourt sails slowly down
> The deep & craggy dell—
> And from his lofty nest, loud screams
> The white plumed Asphodel.⁴

Athens wasn't as he remembered it. It seemed pervaded with 'a queer analytic dryness of soul & mind & atmosphere',⁵ and he knew he couldn't make a home there. But winter was still a long way off so there was no hurry to find somewhere else, and as it was too early to go back to England he decided to visit Crete. Within a week Giorgio had joined him, and they left together for Khania.

'Out in the dark blue sea there lies a land called Crete, a rich and lovely land, washed by the waves on every side, densely peopled and boasting ninety cities . . . One of the ninety towns is a great city called Cnossus, and there, for nine years, King Minos ruled and enjoyed the friendship of almighty Zeus.'⁶ So wrote Homer in the *Odyssey*, but King Minos was no more than legend to people travelling in Crete in Lear's time. 'Its antiquities are *so* old as to be all but invisible,'⁷ he wrote sadly, and with more truth than he realised, for it wasn't until the end of the century that Arthur Evans began to excavate and reconstruct the palace at Knossos.

Today we know that the Minoan civilisation was the forerunner of the Mycenean and Athenian cultures and that they were a colourful, uninhibited people apparently free from the fears of wrathful gods and the worries of convention. If Lear had known this too he would have respected them for the very characteristics he most admired: but he didn't, and he was disappointed with the island. Indeed, even the description 'rich and lovely' seemed legendary, for when they arrived it was windy and wet and altogether horrible, and ten days later it was no better. 'Alas! for Crete, it seems a sell,' he wrote, '& when I think of Sicily & its every step & every moment of interest, while here is so little, except that of floral nature & the delight of the sweet morning air & thorough calm.'[8] The only good thing was that the peasants didn't bother them as they had done in Albania and Palestine—though one did call out to Giorgio, 'Why don't you draw?' to which the Suliot replied inconsequently, 'Don't you see, I am too short.'[9]

One place Lear could see and draw was Mount Ida, the birthplace of Zeus, and as they crossed from the northern coast the island seemed to brighten. 'Lovely leafy thickets & glens! Birds! birds! other sorts of birds is wonderful & most delightful, as is the mountains: sitting below oaks——, —a cornfield sloping down to the stream & to thick groves of walnut & cherry:—above these, opposite to where I lie, rises a steep hill, slanting off into a summit of rox, but the sides are covered with plane, walnut, olive & oak, —cornfields,—& here & there rocks, & a few cypresses. Far off, the cawing of rooks—which brings back days—"days that are no more"—so long gone as those of 1832—when I first heard the voices of rooks in Sussex.—O life!—o earth! o time!—on whose last steps . . .'[10]

Lear with the moufflons in Crete

He made drawings of Mount Ida and watched the antics of the mountain moufflons, and at the end of May he left for England.

One of the first people he went to see was Gussie Bethell. 'There is but one Gussie so one need not comment,'[11] he wrote in his diary, and thoughts of her wandered unhurried through his mind. More pressing was the decision about a house. Now that his things were on their way back from Corfu he had to decide between taking bigger rooms at Stratford Place or putting everything, including the large oil paintings, into store whilst he concentrated on finding a permanent winter home. In fact, he had a chance that summer of selling the big paintings, for John Chaworth Musters—one of the family connected with Byron—was building himself a new house and he wondered if he should put the 'Cedars' into the dining-room and the 'Beirut' into the drawing-room. He was wealthy but he was young with small children, and Lear found himself suggesting 'economy & thoughtfulness as to coming children's fortunes'.[12]

But though the paintings were unsold Lear was still certain of their value, and he decided to take the larger rooms on a three year lease, exhibit the 'Cedars' and the 'Masada' in them during the winter whilst he was abroad and use them as a gallery each summer to show his winter's work.

He wanted now to get enough money to finish his travels in Palestine, so he decided to work towards a large exhibition of small water-colour drawings the following summer. He would spend the winter somewhere where he could make a new collection of drawings, and he thought of trying the Pyrenees or Gibraltar, or southern France and the Corniche. But he felt himself getting tired, and told Holman Hunt: 'Few seem to realise the constant necessity of work in an Artist life.'[13] He didn't enjoy the mechanics of painting: he knew that it was hard, slogging work, and the popular idea that artists were genteel, effete daubers infuriated him.

He chose the Riviera for the winter, and at the beginning of November he left for the south of France. He found the prices there very high, and the rooms he settled on in Nice were horribly expensive. It was always a problem for him finding the right sort of accommodation, for if he was in the wrong place the right kind of people didn't come to look at his paintings.

He got down to work at once. The previous winter he had produced sixty water-colour drawings—this time he was going to do 240, and he set out paper in batches of eighty at a time. It was a dreadful way to work: '. . . the constant change of subject, & the inability—according to this system,—to work out any improvement or feeling, worries & drives me wild,'[14] he wrote in his diary. For a month he drummed through this soulless task, then he and Giorgio set out to walk along the coast to Genoa.

It was bitterly cold, and on the whole he was disappointed with what he saw—'Obscure torrents, & unpleasant villages: roaring sea: —but no peacock hue bays nor any other pleasure.'[15] They walked between sixteen and twenty miles a day, and were back in Nice again on New Year's Eve. Despite the wintery weather and the disappointing scenery he had 144 drawings.

Before getting back to the Tyrants for the summer exhibition he made a collection of 'slight small £5 pot-boilers'[16] of local views to sell in Nice, and soon the local 'swells' began to crowd into his room. 'At 12 came Ld. & Ly. Fitzwilliam, in the simplest kindest way, wanting 6 more drawings, & to give me a cheque for £100,' he wrote in his diary on February 11th, 'dear old Mrs Wentworth of Woolley would have rejoiced.'[17] It was strange that he should have mentioned Mrs Wentworth at this point. She had helped him at the very beginning of his career, and now he was beginning again but on something quite different, for in February 1865 he wrote the first of his nonsense stories, 'The History of Seven Families who went round the World,' and he presented it to Lady Fitzwilliam's little son.

He found some old friends wintering in Nice. Helena Cortazzi was there, but that particular flame, which had never burnt very high, had quite gone out. More exciting was Gussie Bethell, who travelled through with her sister on their way to Rome, 'to my delight, who with them walked and drove about thro' all the livelong day'.[18] But on the whole the winter was a lonely one, and he had few interruptions in the task he had set himself. 'I sometimes wish I were able to study more & so produce more nature-like work,' he wrote to Holman Hunt, 'but the whole groove & tenor of my life is against that, & it is perhaps better to aim at extensive Topographical representation, of a better order than has hitherto been called such, than at producing fewer paintings of a more perfect class.'[19]

In April he returned to London, and spent the first few weeks completing the Tyrants. 'Unpacking and arranging has been a long and hardish work, and now there is the fitting, framing, finishing of the Drawings I have brought over, which are wonderful in number even for your humble servant.'[20] 'If I am not repaid for the great outlay of rooms, fittings up—frames—wintering abroad with double rent—etc. etc.—I think I shall collapse in the Autumn, & go & live at Para on the Amazon. There . . . are abundance of fat caterpillars highly edible & refreshing—& thus life for its few remaining years, would be cheaply sustained.'[21]

But when the exhibition opened the drawings sold quickly. At one point Lady Ashburton toyed with the idea of buying the 'Cedars', but then she decided that after all they were too expensive. He was given a commission for a painting of Jerusalem, and the Prince of Wales came again and this time he bought ten drawings. But London gallery life depressed him, and he told Emily Tennyson, '. . . even if I get enough tin to cover all expenses, the method of doing so is so harrassing & odious—seeing the vapid nature of swells, & the great amount of writing; & the close confinement to the house . . . The walking—sketching—exploring—novelty perceiving & beauty appreciating part of the Landscape painter's life is undoubtedly to be envied:—but then the contrast of the money-tryingtoget, smokydark London life—fuss—trouble & bustle is wholly odious, & every year more so.'[22]

In July he went to stay with the Westburys. Gussie was home from Italy, and he seriously began to wonder if he should ask her to marry him. 'Poor Gussie!—but how to decide? if her life is sad,—united to mine would it be less so? or rather—would it not be more so? . . . The risk of marriage—the marriage itself so gt. a risk of making 2 people more unhappy than before?'[23] He left the next day, still wondering. 'Poor dear little Gussie. I know not what to do.'[24]

Slopes of Myrtle

Holman Hunt, the last of his close friends still unmarried, became engaged in August, and in September Lear was again at the Bethells. 'Gussie—poor dear—played the "Cloches du Monasterie" & for a moment one's heart returned. But no. It would not do. Better suffer alone, than cause sufferings in others.'[25] And so it seemed that his brief thoughts of marriage were over, and

Santa Maria della Salute, Venice

when Lady Waldegrave commissioned him to do a painting in Venice, which he had never visited, he decided to leave and begin the winter in Italy.

Venice was foggy, but as it cleared he was excited by the magnificent architecture and the splendid sunsets. Lady Waldegrave had left the choice of subject to him, and he gondoled slowly up and down the canals trying to decide what to draw, but 'thickphoggs' kept coming down making it impossible to see. In the end he chose a canal scene, but he didn't much enjoy drawing it for there was none of 'the poetry of plain or mountains—or woods—or rocks, Man-work—not God work'.[26]

Whilst he was there he picked up *The Times* at breakfast one morning and saw that Fortescue had been appointed Irish Secretary, a post which gave him a seat on the Cabinet: '. . . being of an undiplomatic and demonstrative nature in matters that give me pleasure, I threw the paper up into the air and jumped aloft myself —ending by taking a small fried whiting out of the plate before me and waving it round my foolish head triumphantly till the tail came off and the body and head flew bounce over to the other side of the table d'hote room. Then only did I perceive that I was not alone, but that a party was at breakfast in a recess. Happily for me they were not English, and when I made an apology saying I had suddenly seen some good news of a friend of mine—these amiable Italians said—*"Bravissimo Signore! ci rallegriamo anche noi' se avessimo anche noi piccoli pesce li butteremmo di quâ e lâ per la camera in simpatia con voi!**—so we ended by all screaming with laughter." '[27]

When he had finished the drawings he decided to go on to Malta. Sir Henry Storks, who had been High Commissioner of the Ionian Islands, was now Commander in Chief in Malta, and Evelyn Baring had gone with him as one of his aides, so there were friends already there, and if he liked it he might make it a permanent winter home.

But Malta was dreadful. Sir Henry Storks had been invited to preside over a commission of enquiry in Jamaica and had left for the West Indies. Baring had gone with him, and Lear arrived to find that his friends had just left.

The only suitable house he could find was across the bay from Valetta and three miles by road from the town, and, as he remembered, there was practically no scenery on the island. He drew whatever he could find, 'more because I happened to be there, and some work had to be done, than for any good it is likely to do me',[28]

---

* Hurrah, Signore, we also are delighted. If we had only got some little fish, too, we would throw them all about the room in sympathy with you.

and the only good part of the winter was a trip with Giorgio to the island of Gozo, where the 'Coast scenery may truly be called pomskizillious and gromphibberous, being as no words can describe its magnificence.'[29]

In the whole three months he was there he sold only £25 worth of work, but this was probably because he was thoroughly cross and grumpy with the visitors who came to see his studio. 'The Anglo-Maltese intelligence does not seem ever to have heard that Artists

Malta, April 3rd, 1866

require particular light, aspect, quiet, etc.: and because I cannot have some three or four hundred visitors lounging in my rooms— I am dubbed a mystery and a savage:—tho' the very same people can understand that they could not go to a Lawyer's or Physician's rooms to take up his hours gratis. Were I to ask a Military Cove, if this climate on account of its dryness required him always to pour water down his gun before firing it, or a Naval one if he weighed anchor before he sailed or a week afterwards, I should be laughed at as a fool; yet many not much less silly questions are asked me. No creature has as yet asked for even a £5 drawing, nor have I sold even one of my few remaining Corfu books. My rooms though spacious are painted, one blue—one orange—one green—so that my sight is getting really injured as to colour, just as if a musical composer should have to work in the midst of hundreds of out of tune instruments.'[30]

Wanderer 1864–66

He left Malta with relief in April. The boat taking him to Trieste via Dalmatia and Montenegro, where he spent a few days exploring, stopped on the way in Corfu. The island made an overwhelming impact on him. 'The beauty of this place would strike a savage: how much more *me*, & me fresh from Malta!!' he wrote in his diary, 'a regular intoxication of beauty! Walked up towards the hill church, & down, down, where terraces of close green sward with large patches of bright yell: gr: fern, & sheets of blooming rosy & white asters spread away. Myrtle also. Over head ever the loved olive: far below "bowery hollows" of green—ever & ever retreating: spotless blue above: glimpses of darker blue sea, & pearly radiant mountain through the transparent foliage. No wonder the Olive is undrawn—unknown: so inaccessible-poetical-difficult are its belongings. So bright & glorious is all I now see & feel, it seems to overpay any outlay of pain—time—money! Can I give *no* idea of this Paradise island to others? Would Gussie like to live here?'[31]

CHAPTER FIFTEEN

A Proposal of Marriage

1866–67

His first thought when he reached England was of Gussie. The loneliness of the winter had helped to crystallise his feelings, and he had made up his mind that he would propose to her. The day after his arrival he called on the Westburys, but she was out. A few days later he dined there '. . . passed a pleasant evening. Pleasant did I say?—This—the last dream—to burst in a bubble or flourish into reality—is indeed a strange matter.'[1] Three days later he was there again:

> 'Like a sudden spark
> Struck vainly in the night—
> & Back returns the dark
> With no more hope of light.

Alas the building seems to fade away & the dream to flit.'[2]

But the next day he wrote, 'the "marriage phantasy" will not let me be.—yet seems an intangible myth. To think of it no more, is to resolve on all the rest of life being passed thus—alone—& year by year getting more weary—to encourage it, is to pursue a thread leading to doubt & perhaps more positive misery . . .'[3]

He simply couldn't make up his mind. He longed for companionship, and she was so unlike most women he knew: she was kind and gentle, 'poor little Gussie' he called her, and she was far happier sitting and talking than rushing into society. But for Lear it wasn't easy. She might refuse him which would be distressing, or accept him which could be worse, for he would have to tell her about his epilepsy—and then she might change her mind.

'Lady Jingly! Lady Jingly!
Sitting where the pumpkins blow,
Will you come and be my wife?'—
Said the Yonghy-Bonghy-Bò.
'I am tired of living singly,—
On this coast so wild and shingly,—
I'm a-weary of my life:
If you'll come and be my wife,
Quite serene would be my life!'—
Said the Yonghy-Bonghy-Bò,
Said the Yonghy-Bonghy-Bò.[4]

Lady Jingly Jones and the Yonghy-Bonghy-Bò

He went to see Lady Waldegrave to ask what he should do, and she warned him that as Gussie had no money it would be too much of an extra burden for him. He became anxious and depressed, and developed nervous symptoms of neuralgia and an itching skin. If he couldn't propose to Gussie then he didn't want to come back to England again. There was still a year to go on his Stratford Place lease, but he had had an offer from Maclean's Gallery to exhibit his work there. He could accept this, close Stratford Place, and wander away.

211

He didn't let himself sit and think. As usual he had more dinner invitations than he could possibly accept. 'I believe if I were the last man—someone would be created to ask me to dinner,'[5] he wrote. During the day he worked through 250 new Tyrants for Macleans to exhibit during the winter, then he went on to finish some limericks which he offered to Routledge again. At first they didn't want them, but then they changed their minds though in fact they were never used. Really Lear had satisfied the public with his old favourites, and the book of limericks, which he published as *More Nonsense* in 1871, was never as popular as *A Book of Nonsense* had been. Routledge were constantly reprinting this earlier book though, and one afternoon in October when Lear went by train to see Husey Hunt in Lewes, he shared a compartment with a globular gentleman, and two ladies with some children who were reading *A Book of Nonsense*. The gentleman explained that 'thousands of families were grateful to the author (which in silence I agreed to) who was not generally known—but was really Lord Derby: and now came a showing forth, which cleared up at once to my mind why that statement has already appeared in several papers. Edward, Earl of Derby (said the Gentleman) did not choose to publish the book openly, but dedicated it as you see to his relations, and now if you will transpose the letters LEAR you will read simply EDWARD EARL.—Says I, joining spontaneous in the conversation— "That is quite a mistake: I have reason to know that Edward Lear the painter and author wrote and illustrated the whole book." "And I," says the Gentleman, says he—"have good reason to know Sir, that you are wholly mistaken. *There is no such a person* as Edward Lear", "But," says I, "there *is*—and I am the man—and I wrote the book!" Whereon all the party burst out laughing and evidently thought me mad or telling fibs. So I took off my hat and showed it all round, with Edward Lear and the address in large letters—also one of my cards, and a marked handkerchief: on which amazement devoured those benighted individuals and I left them to gnash their teeth in trouble and tumult.'[6]

He had already accepted Maclean's offer for the gallery that winter and had finished the 250 Tyrants for them to show, but now Husey Hunt persuaded him that he should come back and try one more summer in England in case he could still sell the large paintings. Probably Lear was pleased to be talked into this, and he told Gussie: 'Some of my friends think I had better hang on another year, to give the large picture a chance of sale.'[7]

'I have never been so utterly weary of 6 months as of these last,' he wrote to Fortescue, 'never seeing anything but the dreadful brick houses—and latterly suffering from cold, smoke—darkness —ach! horror!—verily England may be a blessed place for the wealthy, but an accursed dwelling place for those who have known liberty and have seen God's daylight daily in other countries. By degrees, however, (if I don't leave it by the sudden collapse of mortality) I hope to quit it altogether, even if I turn Musselman and settle in Timbuctoo.'[8]

He left England at the beginning of December 1866, just too soon to be cheered by a notice reviewing the seventeenth edition of *A Book of Nonsense* which came out in time for Christmas: 'Never was a book published that so exactly hit the child's mind as this one,' it read, 'the fine artist that produced it, is without doubt prouder of the joy these sketches and nonsense rhymes have given to a million children, than of the powerful pictures with which he has delighted the artistic world.'[9]

Cairo

Now, as he had planned, he was off on his long-delayed trip to see the rest of Egypt and Palestine.

It had been nearly thirteen years since Lear had left Egypt. 'It seems like a dream that I am about to see the blinding brightness of the south once more!'[10] he wrote as the boat neared Alexandria.

As soon as he reached Cairo he began to enquire about the cost of boats to take him up the Nile. This time he wanted to go through the Nubian desert to the second cataract, but it was a long way and the cheapest price he was quoted was nearly £400. He didn't have so much money at the moment, but he knew that if he didn't go now each year would just add to the price. There were two hundred and fifty of his water colours on exhibition at Macleans, so he should be earning money in London whilst he was away: he would risk borrowing some now, and hope to repay it when he got back to England. So he sat down and wrote to eight of his friends asking each of them for a loan of £100. 'Verily I am an odd bird,'[11] he thought.

Giorgio joined him in Cairo, and they spent a few days looking round the city. 'O! dear! what wonderful street scenes—& scenes of all sorts!' he wrote in his diary. 'And to me what wonders of broad beautiful green & lilac vegetation & far hills & mosques— see thro' & beyond gt. palms & acacias! O sugar canes! o camels! O Egypt!'[12]

This time they didn't drop anchor at night as they had much further to go, and Lear had already seen the lower Nile. He had arranged to stop at Luxor to pick up a cousin from Canada called Archie Jones, who was touring Europe and the Mediterranean. Lear hadn't yet met him, but he was glad to have some companionship on such a long, tedious journey.

Again he was amazed by the Nile scenery. Each morning he rose early and watched the dawn come up. As the sun broke over the horizon the shadows of the palms stretched across the sand in exaggerated leanness, and the moving leaves touched by the morning sun glittered against the darkness of the shadows like slivers of beaten silver. The colours of the day were superb, and when he saw the places that he had drawn so often in the last thirteen years

Nile scene

he realised that his work was too red, or not richly gray enough, or just simply dull. The whole scene was vast in its atmosphere of disappeared greatness. 'The intense deadness of old Egypt is felt as a weight of knowledge in all that world of utter silence . . . looking down on the great green valley with its modern life beyond,' he wrote. 'The Myriad bees are the only living world here, & when one peeps into those dark death-silent giant halls of columns—a terror pervades the heart & head.'[13]

But there were hundreds of birds, and they were very alive. Sometimes they stood in lines along the narrow sand-pits, '4 black storks—one legged: apart.—8 pelicans—careless foolish. 17 small ducks, cohesive. 23 herons—watching variously posed : & 2 or 3 flocks of lovely ivory ibis.'[14] Sometimes they were busily absorbed; 'Here & there are bits of desert sand with a few palms, & some of the poisonous euphorbia, a few geese & ducks now & then in the still water—with ever a long necked Heron peering to keep watch, & informing the more busy ducks, who perhaps pay him in fishes for his assistance in saving their lives.'[15]

215

Slopes of Myrtle

We live on the Nile. The Nile we love.
By night we sleep on the cliffs above;
By day we fish, and at eve we stand
On long bare islands of yellow sand.
And when the sun sinks slowly down
And the great rock walls grow dark and brown,
Where the purple river rolls fast and dim
And the Ivory Ibis starlike skim,
Wing to wing we dance around,—
Stamping our feet with a flumpy sound,—
Opening our mouths as Pelicans ought,
And this is the song we nightly snort;—
　　Ploffskin, Pluffskin, Pelican jee,—
　　We think no Birds so happy as we!
　　Plumpskin, Ploshkin, Pelican jill,—
　　We think so then, and we thought so still.[16]

Cousin Archie came aboard at Luxor, and they went on to
Esneh and Edfu and then to Philae, 'more beautiful than ever'.[17]
Archie finished Philae in three hours, which Lear found sorrow-
fully unbelievable. In fact he was finding his company a bit of a
strain. He rushed in and out of temples declaring that they had 'an
affle bad smell',[18] and in the evening he sat on deck and whistled,
beating out the rhythm with his finger-tips. 'I often feel—any
amount of loneliness is necessary at times,'[19] Lear wrote sadly in
his diary.

They went on south to Wadi Halfa, a place of desolate loneliness
with long lines of hills and great expanses of sand. In fact the
Nubian desert was a complete contrast to the green-fringed Nile of
Egypt. Here there was 'sad, stern, uncompromising landscape, dark
ashy purple lines of hills, piles of granite rocks, fringes of palm, and
ever and anon astonishing ruins of oldest temples'.[20] And life
seemed 'a casual gift, not a necessity of the district'.[21]

From Wadi Halfa they turned north again, and on February 8th
they came upon the magnificence of Abou Simbel. 'I was absolutely
too astonished & affected to draw—so I lost my sketch & must go
back for it. Happy I am to feel that I nearly cried with a burst of

amazement & delight—even after all I had seen & heard & read of these statues';[22] '. . . all other visible things in this world seem to me to be as chips, or potato parings, or any nonsense in comparison.'[23]

Cousin Archie left them near Luxor, and on March 8th, 1867, Lear and Giorgio were in Cairo. They made a short trip to Sakkara and Memphis, and with this Lear's Egyptian work was done.

Now he turned his thoughts again to Palestine. His plan was to cross the desert to Gaza and go inland to Jerusalem, then travel north to Galilee. In Cairo he took on a dragoman called Abdul, and on March 22nd they set off on camels across the desert. 'Some things in this world *are not* pleasant,' he wrote philosophically in his diary, three days later: 'to wit beetles in your hair,—the odoriferous nature of respected domestic fleas: and the grumpy roarygroanery of camels.'[24] These weren't the only things, for he soon discovered that Abdul had brought only one tent, no curry powder, and not nearly enough warm blankets.

He was glad to reach the sudden greenness of Gaza, and at Askalon they turned east to Jerusalem. It was now mid-April and Lear had been travelling since the beginning of December. 'I don't feel up to much of it—mentally & physically,'[25] he wrote in his diary. But he thought Jerusalem more exquisitely beautiful than ever, though two days later he felt exhausted and low again. But he'd missed Nazareth and Galilee before, and he must get there this time. On April 15th they left Jerusalem for the north and as they came to Bethany they saw that the road ahead was crammed

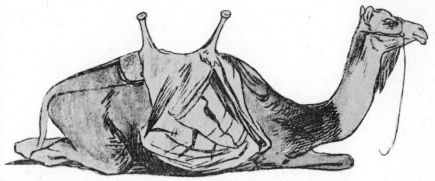

with long lines of pilgrims coming up to Jerusalem for Easter. Suddenly he knew that he couldn't go on any further—Nazareth and Galilee would have to wait. By nightfall he was back in Jerusalem and by noon on the 20th they were in Alexandria again.

It was too early in the year to go to England so they went by boat to Brindisi, and for a month wandered quietly along the coast. They saw the Forest of Ravenna where Byron had lived, then travelled to Rimini before turning back to the Lombardy Lakes. At the beginning of June Giorgio left for Corfu and Lear returned to England.

The large painting hadn't sold, and he told Fortescue: '. . . sometimes I consider as to the wit of taking my Cedars out of its frame and putting round it a border of rose coloured velvet, embellished with a fringe of yellow worsted with black spots, to protypify the possible proximate propinquity of predatorial panthers—and then selling the whole for floorcloth by auction.'[26]

He was able to repay most of his debts within a few weeks, and with each £100 he sent a small picture by way of thanks. It was a sad summer, as they all were now, for each year he had less and less contact with his old friends, and he must often have been depressing company. At Strawberry Hill Fortescue asked him to sing, but he refused, '& was disgusted at their tiresome upper 10000 ways'.[27] He found no more happiness in his visit to the Tennysons; the Laureate's poetry seemed to be a repetition of the old, and he loathed the brutal and snubbing way in which he treated Lionel and Hallam. He went to Lord Northbrook's home at Stratton, but he wrote in his diary: 'Vainly, vainly I strive to keep merry & lively: it is *not* always possible.'[28]

'. . . the recollection of past days—& the worry about the few to come—all conspire to depress me horribly. Happily I can bear up against this better than of old—yet it is hard work. Yet when I look back on life—even from my 5th year, I know step by step how all has occurred—& knowing (what I alone know,) it seems to me wonderful that I have gone on thus far as well as I have!'[29]

The only spark in his gloomy blackness was Gussie. He had seen very little of her that summer, but in October he received a letter from her which gave him a sudden new hope. Within a week his mind was made up. He would go to the Westburys and he would propose to her—at least he would go to the Westburys—and then he could decide.

He packed two trunkloads of clothes for he didn't know how long he might stay. 'It is absurd to think that at 54 years old I am within a point of doing what will fix the rest of my life—be it short or long—in one groove—good or bad,' he wrote in his diary before he left. 'I do not say I am decided to take this leap in the dark, but I say that I am nearer to doing so than I ever was before.'[30]

It was Saturday evening when he arrived at the Lord Chancellor's house. He had decided to talk to Gussie's sister, Emma, before he spoke to Gussie herself, as he couldn't face an outright refusal. On Sunday morning he managed to get her on her own. We don't know what was said, but by the end of the interview all Lear's hopes were crushed. The marriage couldn't work, they could never be happy together, he mustn't think about it. It was all over. 'Accept a lonely destiny—ordained perhaps—or the clear result of causes—& make the best of it,'[31] he wrote resignedly in his diary.

Would Lear ever have married? It is really very unlikely—though if Emma had encouraged him it is difficult to see how he could have backed out, and it does seem very likely that Gussie herself would have accepted him. Money would have been no problem after all, for Gussie was to receive £20,000 on her marriage. Certainly he would have liked to have married, to have had children of his own instead of the world's children, but there would have been too much possibility of new suffering, of his children going through the terrors that he himself had gone through. In fact, the whole human situation was so sad that perhaps it was cruel to have children anyway. 'I have come to the conclusion,' he wrote once to Emily Tennyson, 'that nobody ought to marry at all, & that no more people ought ever to be born, & so we should be gradually extinguished, & the world be left to triumphant chimpanzees, gorillas, cockroaches & crocodiles . . .'[32]

And then there was the terrible possibility that another woman might leave him one day as his mother had once done. As far back as 1851 he had told Fortescue: '. . . there is nothing of which I have so distinct a recollection as the fearful gnawing sensation which chills & destroys one, on leaving scenes & persons, for which & whom there are no substitutes till their memory is a bit worn down. I say, there is nothing I so distinctly remember, because those feelings are with me already taking the form of past matters, never again to recur, like cutting ones teeth, measles &c. Not that one has actually *outlived* the possibility of their repetition, but rather, I *prevent* them by keeping them at arm's length:—I *won't* like anyone else, if I can help it, I mean, any new person, or scenes, or place, all the rest of my short foolish life.'[33] He hadn't lived up to his resolution, and because of this he had to suffer all the unhappiness of his love for Lushington.

He didn't leave at once, in fact he stayed until the following Thursday, and the day before he left he sat down and wrote a story for Gussie's brother's children. 'Once upon a time, a long while ago, there were four little people whose names were Violet, Slingsby, Guy and Lionel; and they all thought they should like to see the world . . .'[34]

On November 26th, 1867, he left England for the south of France.

> Down the slippery slopes of Myrtle,
> Where the early pumpkins blow,
>   To the calm and silent sea
> Fled the Yonghy-Bonghy-Bò.
> There, beyond the Bay of Gurtle,
> Lay a large and lively Turtle;—
>   'You're the Cove,' he said, 'for me
>   'On your back beyond the sea,
>   'Turtle, you shall carry me!'
> Said the Yonghy-Bonghy-Bò,
> Said the Yonghy-Bonghy-Bò.[35]

CHAPTER SIXTEEN

The Greatest Nonsense

1867

He went to Cannes this time, and found a suite of rooms over-looking the bay with 'sun-aspect for health—light to work, and position etc. for swells to come to'.[1] The air there was unpleasantly cold, like 'cayenne pepper frozen',[2] and for a month nobody bought anything.

But he found a kindred spirit with whom he could talk. John Addington Symonds, later the author of a seven-volume history of the Italian Renaissance, was there with his wife Catherine, daughter of Lear's old friend Frederick North of Hastings, and they sat together discussing Byron and Shelley and the modern writers, Swinburne and Walt Whitman. Although in many ways quite unalike, Lear and Symonds had much in common. Both had been separated from their mothers at the age of four and had been brought up in predominantly female households; both were often ill as children and carried psychosomatic illnesses into adult life; each was inclined to self-dramatisation and craved affection; both sank into periods of abysmal depression and they were both homo-sexual, though as Lear never seems to have discussed this aspect of himself with anyone, and Symonds at this time was desperately trying to suppress his longings, it is unlikely that they ever touched on the subject when they were together. They certainly grumbled together though, and this Lear found most satisfying.

EDWARDUS: What makes you look so black, so glum, so cross?
Is it neuralgia, headache, or remorse?
JOHANNES: What makes you look as cross, or even more so?
Less like a man than is a broken Torso?

.　　.　　.　　.　　.

John Addington Symonds

EDWARDUS: Why did I leave my native land, to find
Sharp hailstones, snow and most disgusting wind?
JOHANNES: What boots it that we orange trees or lemons see,
If we must suffer from *such* vile inclemency
EDWARDUS: Why did I take the lodgings I have got,
Where all I don't want is:—all I want not?[3]

The Symonds' small daughter, Janet, was ill in bed, and just before Christmas Lear went up to see her, taking with him a picture poem to make her feel happier. It was 'The Owl and the Pussy-cat'—the first of his nonsense songs.

It is difficult to establish the dates when Lear wrote his later nonsense. Occasionally he mentioned in his diary that he had just written a new song or an alphabet, but generally we have to go by the earliest surviving manuscript copy that he made to give away to his friends, and this could have been made days or even years after he had written the song. He 'sang nonsense for the children'[4] as far back as September 1860, seven years before the earliest of his nonsense songs appeared in manuscript form to be given away, and in October 1866 he told Fortescue, 'I have been preparing a little book for some time past, (but which unfortunately cannot be brought out for some months) the originality of which will at least strike those who may not approve of all its contents'.[5] The earliest mention of anything more than limericks was in February 1865 when he wrote 'The Story of the Seven Families from Lake Pipple-popple'. In August 1866 came 'Mr Lear, the Polly and the Pussybite',[6] in December 1867 'The Owl

222

and the Pussy-cat'. By 1869 copies of other nonsense songs were in existence, and at the end of 1870 *Nonsense Songs, Stories, Botany and Alphabets* was published.

When Lear was first writing there was no such thing as an established literary genre of nonsense.[7] To him the word meant something happy and inconsequential like the limericks, but he and Carroll both altered that meaning. Even now it is difficult to define succinctly, and any definition needs qualifying clauses: perhaps it could be said that incongruity of characters, situations, or words, plus a predictable, stable element such as numbers, choruses, alliteration or, paradoxically, an insistence on the correct use of words, equals nonsense. Without this unifying element it tends towards dream: with it, it is more logical, and nonsense is a game played by a rational, methodical mind. Carroll was a professional mathematician, and though Lear wasn't trained in logic his mind was 'concrete and fastidious'.[8]

We do not know if Carroll was influenced by Lear, or Lear by Carroll, for neither seems to have spoken of the other though they could scarcely have missed one another's work. *Alice in Wonderland* was published in June 1865, and the only nonsense we know for certain that Lear had written before then were the limericks and the 'History of the Seven Families'. Without this story it would have seemed likely that it was from *Alice in Wonderland* that Lear realised how much larger was the field of nonsense over which he could roam, for in *Alice* he would have discovered a new world of strangeness—the caterpillar smoking his hookah, the Mad Hatter's Tea Party, the game of croquet played with flamingoes and hedgehogs and the sad sad Mock Turtle with his Lobster Quadrille. But five months earlier—after *Alice* had been written but before it was published—Lear himself had created the Land of Gramblamble, the Lake Pipple-popple, Soffsky-Poffsky trees, the Plumpudding Flea, the Clangle-Wangle, the blue Bosswoss, the gardens full of Goose-berry bushes and Tiggory-trees. And so it really does seem that these two men were at this stage creating their nonsense at the same time but quite independently.[9] It would be fascinating to know if Lear acquired any of his feeling for nonsense as a child from someone in his own family as Carroll probably did. 'Then what a bawling & a tearing of hair there will be!' wrote Canon Dodgson to his small son, 'Pigs & babies, camels & butterflies, rolling in the gutter together—old women rushing up chimneys & cows after them—ducks hiding themselves in coffee cups, & fat geese trying to squeeze themselves into pencil cases . . .'[10]

Nonsense is a universe of words. Lear was unusually aware of the sounds words make and he would analyse them phonetically. He was regarded by his friends as a dreadful punster and he enjoyed making up riddles. 'What is the difference between the Czar and the "Times" paper? One is the type of Despotism: the other is the despotism of Type.'[11] With his strong musical sense he would mull over the words and phrases he heard, so that Díghi Dóghi Dà reappears twenty years later as the Yonghy-Bonghy-Bò, and Mr & Mrs Discobbolos are named after the Grecian sculpture a cast of which still stands in the Royal Academy Schools. He would use words incongruously as in 'The Cummerbund', and he liked rounded words like promiscuous and pusillanimous which he used out of their place as meaningless, musical adjectives. And of course he invented words, like runcible, because he liked the sound they made: he had a runcible goose and a runcible wall, a runcible spoon and a runcible hat, a runcible raven and even a runcible state of mind.

One of the characteristics of pure nonsense is detachment—neither the writer nor the reader is to be involved with the characters. To establish this Lear showed quite clearly by his drawings that the hero, even when human, is not for a moment to be treated seriously,[12] and he created imaginary characters like the Quangle Wangle and the Pobble. Once this detachment has been established it is quite acceptable and not at all distressing to find a man being baked in an oven or coiled up like a length of elastic. In the same way nonsense characters can have alarming physical defects, and Lear returns often to the feature of himself that most bothered him—the size of his nose. There are people with noses which reach to the ground, noses which finish in tassels, noses like trumpets and noses which simply disappear out of sight, and the Dong gathered the bark of the Twangum tree and 'he wove him a wondrous nose'. But though in the limericks, which are pure nonsense, violence and distortion leave us unmoved, in the nonsense songs they begin to bother the reader for here the detachment is no longer complete.

Lear's nonsense falls into three overlapping groups. The first, begun at Knowsley or even earlier and going all through the rest of his life, comes under the original classification of the happy and inconsequential. Here are the limericks, the botany, the cookery, the alphabets and the nonsense he put into letters to amuse his friends. Humour, though not an essential ingredient of nonsense, is often found in this group, but in the other two it gradually diminishes.

In the second group are stories, in both prose and verse, nearly always of wandering and travel, and either with happy endings— 'The Owl and the Pussy-cat', 'The Duck and the Kangaroo'—or sad endings which don't worry us for they are pure nonsense—'The Story of the Seven Families from the Lake Pipple-popple'.

Between this and the third group the unhappiness becomes disturbing, for the detachment is beginning to break down. 'The Daddy Long-legs and the Fly'

> Sat down in silence by the sea,
> And gazed upon the sky.
> They said, 'This is a dreadful thing!
> The world has all gone wrong,
> Since one has legs too short by half,
> The other much too long![13]

By the time we have reached the third group the detachment has gone. Here are verses which express Lear's deep personal feelings, written no longer for children but for himself, songs like 'The Pelican Chorus':

> And far away in the twilight sky,
> We heard them singing a lessening cry,—
> Farther and farther till out of sight,
> And we stood alone in the silent night!
> Often since, in the nights of June,
> We sit on the sand and watch the moon;—

She has gone to the great Gromboolian plain,
And we probably never shall meet again!
Oft, in the long still night of June,
We sit on the rocks and watch the moon;—
She dwells by the streams of the Chankly Bore,
And we probably never shall see her more.[14]

'The Dong with the Luminous Nose', also in this group, begins
in the usual nonsense way with a creature quite outside our experience and a drawing which suggests that here is a character we need
not worry ourselves about. But from the very first verse something
has gone wrong and the mood quickly changes:

When awful darkness and silence reign
Over the great Gromboolian plain,
Through the long, long wintry nights;—
When the angry breakers roar
As they beat on the rocky shore;—

When the Storm-clouds brood on the towering heights
Of the Hills of the Chankly Bore:—
Then, through the vast and gloomy dark,
There moves what seems a fiery spark,
A lonely spark with silvery rays
Piercing the coal-black night,—
A Meteor strange and bright:—

Hither and thither the vision strays,
A single lurid light.
Slowly it wanders,—pauses,—creeps,—
Anon it sparkles,—flashes and leaps;
And ever as onward it gleaming goes
A light on the Bong-tree stems it throws.
And those who watch at that midnight hour
From Hall or Terrace, or lofty Tower,
Cry, as the wild light passes along,—
  'The Dong!—the Dong!
  'The wandering Dong through the forest goes!
  'The Dong! the Dong!
  'The Dong with a luminous Nose!'[15]

Again they are songs of wandering, but now the emphasis is on looking back to a time of happiness that has gone for ever, or wandering grief-stricken like Demeter in search of Persephone, seeking someone who in Lear's songs will never return. In fact, his development as a nonsense writer is increasingly away from pure nonsense into sad and moving poetry.

Lear was proud of his nonsense and it is not true, as is sometimes said, that whilst he took his painting seriously he regarded his nonsense as frivolous and unimportant. His assertion that he was the author of *A Book of Nonsense* that day in the railway carriage was much more than a claim to fame—these verses were very particularly his and no one else's. The day he sold *A Book of Nonsense* to Routledge & Warne Lear went to dine with some friends: 'Bye & bye, on showing the receipt for the Bk of Nonsense, they seemed to think it was nil,—wh. distressed & disgusted me, & made me cross,'[16] he wrote in his diary. He may not have tried to make a living from his nonsense, but he took it every bit as seriously as he did his painting.

He did have to make a living from his painting, however, and nobody in Cannes was buying any of his work. By Christmas he had used practically all his ready money. 'It is really absurd at 55 to be so utterly without prospects for the future,'[17] he wrote. But on

Boxing Day he heard that Lady Ashburton had decided to buy the 'Cedars'. She wrote offering him £200, which wasn't even a third of the price he had asked, but he was glad that at last the painting was sold, and he told Fortescue: 'They will be well placed and thoroughly appreciated.'[18] This was important for Lear, partly because it might bring him work, but also because he cared about where his pictures were hung. He spoke of them as his 'children', and they were something of himself.

With the sale of the 'Cedars' his luck seemed to turn. Within a few days he had begun to sell some water-colour drawings, and the new year was beginning well.

CHAPTER SEVENTEEN

Last Travel Book

1867–69

'By degrees I want to topographise all the journeyings of my life, so that I shall have been of some use after all to my fellow critters besides leaving them drawings and pictures which they may sell when I'm dead,'[1] Lear told Fortescue and he spent the rest of the winter writing up his journals of Crete and his two trips down the Nile. By the end of March these were finished, and though he now had eight unpublished journals he decided to spend the spring in Corsica getting material for another book.

He left on April 8th, 1868, and travelled with John Symonds and his family who were going to Ajaccio. They arrived in the rain, and all the people seemed to be wearing black. In fact the only sign of colour was the French sailors' scarlet trousers, and their brisk walk and busy chatter was a complete contrast to the dour drabness of the Corsicans: '. . . this is truly the land of the *Helix tristis*, the melancholy snail,'[2] he pondered sadly.

Instead of going on horseback or on foot, as he had always done, Lear hired a two-horse carriage to take them swiftly round the places he wanted to see. This was a way of travel he usually deplored, but his excitement in exploring new scenery had been replaced by a calculated decision to see and draw as much as he could as quickly as possible—not a good beginning for a book.

Before he left Ajaccio the weather cleared, and as they travelled south things improved even more. Birds and flowers and mountains began appearing one after another, and though the people were still dour they were 'thoroughly kindly and obliging'.[3] This may have been partly because the coachman, a bad-tempered man called Peter, was telling the villagers that Lear was the Finance Minister of England. 'But why?' asked Lear. 'Oh, partly because you wear

The Forest of Bavella, from the 'Journals of a Landscape Painter in Corsica'

spectacles, and have an air of extreme wisdom, and partly because one must say something or other,'[4] he replied.

On April 28th they reached the pine forests of Bavella, which grew 'as it were in the pit of an immense theatre confined between towering rock-wall, and filling up with its thousands of pines all the great hollow'.[5] Whilst they were there there was a sudden thunderstorm, and they sheltered from the downpour in a forester's cottage: '. . . when the storm ceases for a time, and the sun gleams out through cloud, the whole scene is lighted up in a thousand splendid ways, and becomes more than ever astonishing, a change-ful golden haze illumines the tops of the mighty peaks, a vast gloom below, resulting from the masses of black solemn pines standing out in deepest shadow from pale granite cliffs dazzling in the sunlight, torrents of water streaming down between walls and gates of granite . . . profound silence, broken only by the cuckoo's notes echoing from the crags, and from the fulness of melody chanted by thousands of blackbirds.'[6]

But Peter's temper didn't improve. A few days after they lett Bavella he took the carriage on up a narrow mountain road ahead of Lear and Giorgio, and when they caught up with him again he was beating the horses wildly over the head. At each stroke the animals backed in terror, and suddenly there were screams and a splintering crash as they fell shattering over the edge, cascading down the rocks until they came to rest in a clump of chestnut trees. Pieces of coach and cases were scattered about, one horse was cut and the other lay dead, and on the road Peter knelt appealing to the Madonna and saints whom only moments before he had been blaspheming.

Lear spent a month in Corsica, and on June 7th was in Cannes once more with 350 drawings and a journal of his travels: a few days later he left for London.

Only one of his paintings had sold during the winter and as there were no new commissions awaiting him it seemed sensible to spend the summer working on a new book as he had done in 1863. His choice was between Crete and Corsica, perhaps the least interesting of all his unpublished tours: it seems strange that he didn't decide to publish his tour of Mount Athos which so few people had visited, or Egypt which had really interested him, or that he didn't begin on the book about Greece which he could have done so well and which never did materialise. Instead he settled on Corsica.

Symonds had given him an introduction to the publisher Smith & Elder who had turned down his nonsense in 1861, and at the end of July he went to see Mr Smith to talk over the idea of the book with him. He was interested, but would only consider it if the expenses were kept very low. Lear had published all his other travel books himself and had never economised on their production, and he wasn't at all happy at the thought of doing so now. But never again could he write hundreds of letters asking people to subscribe to his work—so he asked Smith how he would like the book done. He was told that instead of the two volumes he had in mind he could have one small volume, and he must use wood engravings and not the more expensive lithography. Ever since his book of *Parrots*, Lear had used lithography for he knew that his work lost almost all its sweeping grace and subtlety when it was engraved. It was bound to be inferior to anything he had done before, and it is a shame that he should have agreed to accept these conditions, especially as Smith & Elder hadn't even accepted the book. But he went ahead as they suggested, and sent some of his drawings to be engraved.

At the end of July he decided that it was stupid for him to keep on even the small rooms at Stratford Place: the lease on the large rooms had run out the previous year. Macleans had now taken over the sale of his drawings and he didn't need a London home any more. 'Verily this coming to England is Hell,'[7] he wrote, and each visit made him realise his loneliness a little more. He was beginning to find that he preferred receiving letters from his friends to actually being with them—there was a kind of harsh reality in being with people from whom he had grown away which could be disguised in letters. Yet, in spite of this he thought of buying a plot of land near to the Tennysons' new home at Aldworth, and he even went down to look at a site—but he knew that he could never live in England. 'I am very dimbemisted-cloudy-besquashed as to plans,' he told Fortescue. 'Nevertheless, they go on slowly forming like the walls of Troy or some place as riz to slow music.'[8]

Meanwhile, he had seen samples of the engravings, and they were terribly disappointing. They were also very expensive, for the small vignettes alone were going to cost nearly £7 each. But as the alternative was for him to draw his own lithographs he decided to go ahead, and by December they were done and ready to take to Smith & Elder. On the spot they decided that they weren't inter-

ested. They were too expensive—Lear could have told them that—
and the book wouldn't pay. If the blocks were any less good it
couldn't be called an illustrated book, and it wouldn't pay as a
literary work. Poor Lear! he had done as they had suggested, in-
curred a bill of £130—and now they didn't want them.

But he couldn't afford to waste all this time and money, and he
became dreadfully worried. 'I have one of my cruellest fits of
depression,' he wrote in his diary on December 10th, '& can only
say—God's will be done. Yet, looking back to, & carefully analysing
all the curious physical phenomena of myself from 4 years old, &
the consequent effects on the mind, I ought to see I am little to
blame & therefore must hold on & abide.'[9]

Now there was only one thing he could do—he must publish the
book himself. A few days before Christmas he went to see a
printer called Bush who agreed to do it 'if cheaply got up'.[10] This
would mean beginning again and cutting smaller, cheaper blocks,
and at this point Lear should have cut his losses and left it. A
'cheaply got up' book would do him no good at all, and he would
have to add the cost of new blocks to the £130 he had already spent.
Besides, he would have to go through the dreadful process of finding
subscribers. But he decided to persevere.

By now it was late into December, and as his rooms in Cannes
were paid for and waiting he would finish writing the book in France
and see about getting some cheaper wood-engraving done over
there.

In Cannes he felt happier at once. The sun was shining and the
sea was blue. 'Every sunset beautiful, & certainly the view from
these rooms *is* something in life. I am not sure though that it is
good to have such a violent weight in the one scale, because, when
the weight is taken out,—how low goes the other side!'[11]

His epilepsy was better, at least he was having fewer attacks,
though when they came they were more violent than they had
ever been and when they were over he would fall into a deep
sleep. Giorgio was there to look after him, and Lear began to ask
him in each Sunday evening for half a glass of wine and a cigar—
after all, he was the only companion Lear had.

He worked on the book until the end of February, then he began

Cannes, 1869

on a group of sixty Tyrants: it was the first painting he had done for nearly two years. Meanwhile he sent for some wood-blocks so that he could start on the vignettes himself, and a friend—Prosper Merimée, the distinguished French writer—recommended some wood-engravers in Paris for the big engravings.

He was in Paris at the end of June 1869, spreading the work around and hoping that some at least would be passable. 'Of course the cuts will be coarse & queer, & the book will not have the shadow of a pretention to merit qua art, but it will give a good notion of the scenery of an island little known,'[12] he told Holman Hunt. In fact, the quality did vary considerably, but even the best brought out nothing of the delicacy of Lear's drawings.

In London he accepted Bush's estimate for the work, but before giving him the manuscript he went to stay with Lushington to ask his help in tidying up the text and the notes.

Since Lushington's marriage, this friendship had changed in character—it had come, perhaps, more as Lushington had always wanted it. The intensity of Lear's love had declined after their parting at Dover in 1858 when he had had to realise that Lushington didn't return his feelings, and later, when he could think more dispassionately, he was grateful to Lushington for not allowing the

friendship to develop as he might have dreamt: '. . . when I, who know all, remember how much more a friend he has been to me than even he himself knows:—I have reason to be grateful,'[13] he wrote. For some years they had seen one another occasionally, but it wasn't until after Lushington's marriage that they began to develop a more satisfying relationship. It began gradually with Lear, as now, going to stay for a few days to talk about business or to ask Lushington's advice in negotiations with publishers. He was able to help Lushington in return, for in the autumn of 1869 when Lushington applied to be made magistrate for the Thames Police Court Lear wrote to Lord Aberdare who in turn recommended him for the appointment. Lear was god-father to Lushington's daughter, Clare, and after her death to another child, Gertrude; and still later Lushington took upon himself the responsibility of helping Lear with all the problems which beset his old age. In the sad Corfu days Lear had thought him 'a diamond as to value, yet hidden in a tortoise's shell',[14] and as they grew older the shell was drawn slowly back.

Back from the Lushingtons, Lear began writing the letters to possible subscribers and he did over a hundred a day: '. . . rest there is none,' he told Fortescue. 'When shall we fold our wings, and list

235

to what the inner spirit says—there is no joy but calm? Never in this world I fear—for I shall never get a large north-light studio to paint in. Perhaps in the next eggzi stens you and I and My Lady may be able to sit for placid hours under a lotus tree a eating of ice creams and pelican pie, with our feet in a hazure coloured stream and with the birds and beasts of Paradise a sporting around us.

'I can't help laughing at my "position" at fifty-seven! And considering how the Corfu, Florence, Petra, etc., etc., etc., are seen by thousands, and not one commission coming from that fact, how plainly is it visible that the wise public only give commissions for pictures through the Press that tell the sheep to leap where others leap!'[15]

He was able to fold his wings a little when he visited an old Knowsley friend, a Mrs Greville Howard, at Ashstead. Before dinner he went to his room: 'The evening's all gray—no sun: & when I put my head out of the window, the sweet air, the rooks' voices, & the quiet, bring back memories of "days that are no more": —but as those were wont to bring with them regret, & as I have for a good time past felt that regrets are absurd,—I do not encourage sights sounds & sentiments which in reviving regrets of the past, do more harm than good to the present. What is past is past— gone—gone:—I, being alone ever, & having never now any with whom to talk on these subjects—(not E.T. nor A.B.*—the two last with whom one *could* talk)—cease as much as I can from thought during the last few years of remaining life . . . And on the whole as calm brings with it inevitable recollections & their pain,— it is perhaps better that calm should be as rarely found as it nowadays is . . .'[16]

Calm certainly seemed to have vanished on his visit to the Tennysons. Alfred had chosen two drawings of Corsica, but whilst Lear was in his room putting away his work the poet changed his mind— he wanted water-colours. Lear didn't mind—but then Tennyson began to wonder if he should have any at all, after all the money might be better used on the outside of the house. Anyway, it was Emily who wanted them, and not he—Lear lost his temper— Tennyson said he was irritable (undoubtedly true)—Lear told

* Augusta Bethell—'Gussie'.

him 'he was given to worry and everyone knew it'—they both exploded in rage and Lear went upstairs to pack. When he came down Emily had written out a cheque for £10 for one picture, and she persuaded him to stay. Before he went to bed Lear apologised for speaking so angrily—Tennyson said 'how characteristic'—it wasn't that that worried him, but that *'everyone'* said he was a worrier.[17]

In fact, the relationship between Tennyson and Lear had been deteriorating over the years. They had never been close friends, but they had got on well and admired one another's work. Perhaps things began to go wrong when Lear turned to Emily for consolation over his frustrated love for Lushington. Certainly Tennyson found Lear trying. He had written a poem called 'Northern Farmer, Old Style', and when he followed this up with 'Northern Farmer, New Style', Lear remarked that if he wrote any more he might publish them all in a Farmacopoeia—'wh. disgusted him'.[18]

> Vex not thou the poet's mind
> With thy shallow wit;
> Vex not thou the poet's mind,
> For thou canst not fathom it[19]

Tennyson had written to a fellow undergraduate who had made some witticism about a poem he had written at Cambridge—and he might well have addressed the lines to Lear.

Despite this Lear never ceased to admire his poetry, though he thought his later work less good than his earlier writings. 'The way to enjoy Tennyson is to look to him for what he is—a superb landscape-painter, a consummate musician,'[20] wrote F. L. Lucas, and on these grounds alone Lear could appreciate his work.

But he did become disillusioned by Tennyson as a man, and he found his harshness and egocentricity hard to bear—'I would he were as his poems,'[21] he remarked sadly on one occasion, and on another when he had just left Farringford, he wrote, 'I suppose it is the anomaly of high souled & philosophical writings combined with slovenliness, selfishness & morbid folly that prevents my being happy there.'[22] Yet, he was probably happier when he was with the Tennysons than in any other home; Emily remained his perfect ideal of womanhood and he worshipped her.

During November he was buried in correcting the proofs of his book, and on December 8th he paid a last visit to Bush to give him the remaining third of his money. *Journal of a Landscape Painter in Corsica*, Lear's last travel book and far and away his least successful, was nearly finished at last and would be out in time for Christmas, 1869, modestly priced at 30*s*.

The next day he left London, and on the 10th he crossed to France.

Part III

SAN REMO

CHAPTER EIGHTEEN

Villa Emily

1869–72

In Cannes he settled down to do two oil paintings of Corsica, the first he had done for years. Then he sat back and looked carefully at his situation. 'I can't decide "in my mind"—if it be wiser to await death in one spot,' he had written two years earlier, 'making that spot as pleasant as may be, & varying its monotony by such pleasant gleams of older life as can be obtained—or—to hurry on through constantly new & burningly bright scenes, & then dying al'improviso as may happen.'[1] But what he wanted now was a home where he could just paint.

He had £3,000 saved, and this was bringing in £90 a year, but he was spending £30 on storage and insurance in London and another £70 on lodgings in Cannes—£90 in, £100 out—it would be cheaper to buy himself a house. Then where should he build? 'The extreme beauty of the Bay of Cannes is a great temptation to fix here—but if a house be built opposite your windows, no good would come of such fixing'[2]—these were prophetic words. Besides, Cannes was hopeless as a place to sell pictures and he wasn't sure that he could stand the people there, for when they did come to his studio to look at his work they were most provoking. 'What books did you copy all these drawings from?' asked one woman, and another cried gaily, 'O don't look at the drawings—only come & see the view from the window!'[3]

He was still undecided when rumblings of the Franco-Prussian war were heard, and he realised that it would be unwise for him to settle in France. So on the last day of February 1870, he travelled over to San Remo to look at land there. When he had walked along the Corniche five years earlier he had been disappointed with the San Remo scenery, and again he thought it looked bald, with

241

'skimpy meagre' olive trees—but the land was much cheaper there. He stayed for two nights and was introduced to an Englishman called Walter Congreve who lived there—at least there would be one sympathetic soul, he thought. He saw a good piece of land backing onto Congreve's garden with a clear view across to the sea —but he wasn't sure.

Back in Cannes he was told of a house for sale in Corfu; English yachts had begun to call there again and perhaps that would be the place to settle. What, what should he do? Should he settle at all, or should he give up painting altogether and wander away? 'The more I work, the more I feel aware that the defects of hand & eye wh. always made painting so irksome & difficult, but which I used to think time would lessen,—are never to be conquered, but on the contrary increase with age. Whereon, I now speculate,—better perhaps to pass the rest of the years in seeing new places & in living how one can—& not in endeavouring to make good pictures.'[4]

He finished the two paintings of Corsica, and for the first time for fourteen years he sent in for the Academy. With these out of the way he must make up his mind one way or the other. On Friday, March 25th, he went back again to look at San Remo—and the next day he decided to buy. Over the weekend he had discussions with the architect and went into the details of the purchase, and by the time he left on Monday morning the contracts had been exchanged—there was no going back.

But his first thought was that he had made a terrible mistake, and he reached Cannes feeling thoroughly gloomy. 'Disheartened & undecided about San Remo, & dreadfully oppressed & depressed.'[5] But the whole thing—land and house—was costing less than £2,000, which meant that he could keep £1,000 invested. Gradually he felt happier, and he wrote to tell Woolner the news:

'What do you think as I have been & gone & done? I grow so tired of noisy lodgings, & yet am more & more unable to think of ever wintering in England—& so unable to bear the expense of two houses & two journeys annually that I have bought a bit of ground at San Remo & am actually building a house there . . . I shall endeavour to live upon little figs in summertime & on worms in the winter. I shall have 28 olive trees & a small bed of onions: & a stone terrace, with a gray Parrot & 2 hedgehogs to walk up & down on it by day & by night . . .'⁶

At the end of June 1870 he moved across to lodgings in San Remo, but he found it much too hot on the coast and went on up into the mountains near Turin. He found a hotel which had been a Carthusian monastery, La Certosa del Pesio, and there he settled down busily to copy out the words and drawings for a hundred limericks and all the songs and stories he had written in the last few years, so that he could send them to England to be published in time for Christmas: they were to be called *Nonsense Songs, Stories, Botany and Alphabets*. Three of them—'The Owl and the Pussy-cat', 'The Duck and the Kangaroo', and 'The Daddy-longlegs and the Fly'—had already been published earlier in the year in an American magazine called *Young Folks*.

During the summer he had warnings of heart trouble, and the doctor told him that he must take things more easily and not run up hills or climb stairs quickly. Lear wasn't very good at taking things easily, but his father had died of a heart attack and he realised that he must be a little careful, especially when he was exploring around in the mountains.

He didn't like hotel life, and in particular he found the convention of *table d'hôte* unpleasant and trying. But it did give him a chance to see the children who were staying in the hotel, and a little American girl who met him that summer described their meeting. 'One day there appeared at luncheon sitting opposite to us a rosy, grey-bearded, bald-headed, gold-spectacled little old gentleman who captivated my attention. My mother must have met him before, for they greeted each other as friendly acquaintances. Something seemed to bubble and sparkle in his talk and his eyes twinkled benignly behind the shining glasses. I had heard of uncles; mine were in America and I had never seen them. I whispered to my mother that I should like to have that gentleman opposite for an uncle. She smiled and did not keep my secret. The delighted old gentleman, who was no other than Edward Lear, glowed, bubbled and twinkled more than ever; he seemed bathed in kindly effulgence. The adoption took place there and then; he became my sworn relative and devoted friend. He took me for walks in the chestnut forests; we kicked the chestnut burrs before us, "yonghy bonghy bos", as we called them; he sang to me "The Owl and the Pussycat" to a funny little crooning tune of his own composition; he drew pictures for me.

'I still have a complete nonsense alphabet, beautifully drawn in pen and ink and delicately tinted in water-colours, done on odd scraps of paper, backs of letters and discarded manuscript. Every day Arthur and I found a letter of it on our plate at luncheon, and finally a title-page for the collection, with a dedication and a portrait of himself, with his smile and his spectacles, as the "Adopty Duncle".'[7]

This was the alphabet with 'The Absolutely Abstemious Ass, who resided in a Barrel, and only lived on Soda Water and Pickled Cucumbers' which is published in *More Nonsense*.

He so enjoyed being called Uncle Lear that he kept the title. Later the same summer another little girl came to stay at the hotel with her mother and her older sister, who disliked *table d'hôte* as much as Lear did. 'I slipped into my place beside my mother in deep dejection which must have shown in my face; for when I looked up to take stock of our neighbours, I became aware that a

The Absolutely Abstemious Ass

244

dear old gentleman on the opposite side of the long, narrow table was regarding me with benevolent if amused pity. He had a long white beard, and very bright eyes that seemed to be watching a pleasant comedy all the time. After a few minutes he found occasion to offer me some small *table-d'hôte* civility, remarking at the same time: "It *is* rather confusing at first, but you will soon get accustomed to it!"

'I never knew how musical an English voice could sound till that moment. Before the meal was over we were the best of friends, and my new acquaintance, remarking that my small sister Daisy, who sat beside me, was in trouble with her big knife and fork, produced a bit of paper and a pencil, and a few seconds later pushed across to her a delightfully funny drawing, with one of Edward Lear's immortal nonsense rhymes written below! That moment betrayed him to us . . . Never was there a man who could so live into the feelings of a child. Daisy was a turbulent little creature, always getting into trouble of some kind, and from that first day she learnt to take her disasters to "Uncle Lear", as he taught her to call him, to have them turned into joys by his rhymes and pictures. A frightful bump on her forehead was the origin of the "Uncareful Cow", who got a similar one, and was horrified to find it growing into a third horn, which had to be rubbed away with camphor. The strange meats and unmanageable cutlery of the *table d'hôte* inspired the marvellous botanical specimen "Manyforkia Spoonifolia", as well as most of the recipes for "Nonsense Cookery". But Uncle Lear did not always wait to be asked for his rhymes. Day after day Daisy would find on her plate some enchanting, highly coloured sketch with an appropriate poem.'[8]

In later years Lear almost always spent the hot summers in the Italian or Swiss mountains, and after months of winter loneliness he would seek out the children to share the new nonsense songs he was busily writing.

The building progressed slowly whilst he was away, and from his mountain resort he wrote to tell Holman Hunt about the new house:

'My dear Daddy,

'I was very glad to get your letter of April last, & to know you were well & at work;—after all to be hard at work is pretty much the same as being well, at least with me (or at least, vice versa). But I could not answer you at that time, & indeed can only do so meagrely even now,—for as you will hear presently, I have had enough to do in a new turn of this ludicrously whirligig life which one suffers from first & laughs at afterwards.

'You remember how I have always been wanting a real settled painting place—I having always been more or less convinced that I have talent enough to do some good Topographical painting yet, what though I am 58—if only I could attain "North light" & "quiet". The idea of getting permanently rooted in England I gave up totally last year—reluctantly however,—for I could well have liked to live near the Tennysons. But how to pass from October to May shivering & coughing?—& how, if I lived that time abroad,—to pay for 2 dwellings continuously, an attempt I have already broken down in? So therefore, I decided that a permanent Winter place— not summer place, must be found.—Next, for beauty of scenery, Cannes seemed the properest spot—but I, who have tried it for 3 years, judged otherwise. The first year I was there, there also happened to be many of my friends—& so I sold a good many drawings:—but afterwards, the true character of the place became evident,—a haunt of rich or Aristocratic people—all perhaps good— but all *absolutely* idle. All smiles & goodness if they could take up the whole of an artist's time—"We shall be so delighted if you will let us come & sit in your studio while you work!"—said one of many good ladies to me—"we will stay all the day! we should never be tired!"—but on the Artist showing a little notion of independence & self assertion—he was quite thrown by, & other painters— awful daubers!—taken up—or art altogether ignored. So it has come to pass that I have never had *one single commission* to draw or paint the beautiful scenery of Cannes, & only 30£ did I gain from visitors all last season! . . . Thereupon I came to San Remo, a place which while I live must be comparatively quiet (Cannes grows at the rate of 10 new hotels & 200 houses yearly,)—& there I got a bit of land—$\frac{3}{4}$ of an acre—for 400£—& am building—or rather have half built a house, which is to cost me 1200£—rather large— but its being so was requisite for various causes—to give a good chance of reselling etc. Neither too much *in*, nor altogether *out* of the world,—my plan may ultimately succeed, if I can only work hard enough to send to every kind of exhibition in England, for that tack I am now (perforce) going to try . . .'⁹

So he was going to change his way of working again. '. . . private patronage must end in the natural course of things, but eating and drinking and clothing go on disagreeably continually,'¹⁰ he wrote, but now that he no longer had the expense of travel and rent he needed less to live on and could afford to risk painting the kind of pictures that he knew he still had it in him to paint. He could then send them to England to try their luck in the large public exhibitions—the paintings he had sent to the Academy that year had been accepted and one of them had sold almost at once. He would try for election to the Old Water Colour Society so that he would have at least one guaranteed shop window in London: 'I'm sure 8 or 10 of my various subjects would attract more than everlasting Hampstead Heaths,'¹¹ he told Holman Hunt. There wasn't the slightest hope of his being elected to the Academy, and exhibiting there would always be a matter of selection which was bound to be chancy.

But before he settled down to his new system he had a sudden wish to do one final work for a very old patron. In 1869 the 15th Earl of Derby had succeeded to the title. Lear remembered him as a small boy dressed in black velvet whom he had amused with his nonsense, and now he wrote asking if he could paint a picture for him. Back came 'a wonderfully kind & nice letter, wishing for a Corfu—for 100£'.¹² 'So I begin my San Remo life with the same Knowsley patronage I began life with at eighteen years of age,'¹³ he told Fortescue.

Giorgio went back to Corfu for the summer to see his family, so Lear was alone until October and as the months went on he found it trying having to wait so long for the house to be finished. Through the autumn his depression increased, and so did his fear of tying himself to a permanent home. He would sell the house and go and live in America. He would sell the house and just wander. He would never be happy living there. The excitement of his new plans flopped into a long, lonely depression.

247

San Remo

There were two spots of light. One was an order of 500 copies of his new nonsense book from Fields of Boston: the other was the Congreve family. Walter Congreve had been Under-master at Rugby under Tait, and had just been appointed second master at Marlborough when first his wife.and then his eldest son became ill. Their only chance of getting better was to leave England at once, but soon after they arrived both the boy and his mother died, and Congreve was left with two small sons, Hubert and Arnold, to bring up.

Hubert later recalled his first meeting with Lear: 'I ran down the steep path which led up to our house at San Remo to meet my father; I found him accompanied by a tall,[14] heavily-built gentleman, with a large curly beard and wearing well-made but unusually loosely fitting clothes, and what at the time struck me most of all, very large, round spectacles. He at once asked me if I knew who he was, and without waiting for a reply proceeded to tell me a long, nonsense name, compounded of all the languages he knew, and with which he was always quite pat. This completed my discomfiture, and made me feel very awkward and self-conscious. My new acquaintance seemed to perceive this at once, and, laying his hand on my shoulder, said, "I am also the Old Derry Down Derry, who loves to see little folks merry, and I hope we shall be good friends." This was said with a wonderful charm of manner and voice, and accompanied with such a genial, yet quizzical smile, as to put me at my ease at once.'[15]

At the beginning of December copies of *Nonsense Songs, Stories, Botany and Alphabets* arrived—Bush had advised Lear to hold over the limericks for another book the following year. It contained the first of his songs including 'The Owl and the Pussy-cat' and 'The Jumblies'.[16] It was a delightful collection—a real child's book, and Charles Kingsley wrote to Tom Taylor that it 'has more wisdom & genius in it than all that Bain and Herbert Spencer ever wrote'.[17]

But his painting plans weren't going as he had hoped. Two of the three oil paintings which had been in the Academy were unsold, and he arranged for them to go to Foord & Dickenson, who were picture handlers, for sale at £50 each instead of £200. And he hadn't been elected to the Old Water Colour Society. Money was getting tight again, and he wrote to Fortescue: 'Ain't it funny, at nearly 60, and with talents like mine, to be in such a mess.'[18] But he wanted 'to skriggle on without borrowing for the present',[19] and as the house was nearly finished he wouldn't have to pay for rooms for much longer.

On March 20th, 1871, almost exactly a year after he had bought the land, the house was at last finished. It was to be called Villa Emily, after—as he said—his niece in New Zealand. He moved in on the 25th, and wandered delightedly from one room to another. 'I never before had such a painting room,' he told Fortescue, '32 feet by 20—with a light I can work by at all hours, and a clear view south over the sea. Below it is a room of the same size, which I now use as a gallery, and am "at home" in once a week.'[20]

But he had nobody, except for Giorgio, with whom he could share his excitement, '. . . no letters: no friends: no newspapers . . . & I can't think how I shall get through years of it.'[21] But the letters began to arrive, and one of the first was from Fortescue and Lady Waldegrave. 'I have just got your letters, left in my new post box in my new front door, over the old plate that used to be in 15 Stratford Place,' Lear told them. '. . . I took the letters out into "my garden" and read it under one of my own olive trees.'[22]

He was proud of this garden. He had spent a long time arranging the lay-out of trees and shrubs and flowers, and had planted exotic seeds which his sister had sent from New Zealand and others that Professor Bell's family had sent from Selbourne. He planted local species too, and the flowers that he had admired for so long on his travels were soon flowering on his own land.

With so much time to think his thoughts turned back more and more to his early childhood. He didn't, like so many ageing people, romanticise about it, and most of his memories were sad ones. He never mentioned his mother in his diary, but it is impossible to believe that he didn't think of her. He certainly dreamt about the happiness he could dimly remember which had ended so suddenly when she went away, and he put this into his nonsense songs, like 'The Dong':

Happily, happily passed those days!
While the cheerful Jumblies staid;
They danced in circlets all night long,
To the plaintive pipe of the lively Dong,
In moonlight, shine or shade.
For day and night he was always there
By the side of the Jumbly Girl so fair,
With her sky-blue hands, and her sea-green hair.
Till the morning came of that hateful day
When the Jumblies sailed in their sieve away
And the Dong was left on the cruel shore
Gazing—gazing for evermore . . .[23]

The Owl and the Pussy-cat

Only once did Lear see anything but sadness in a sea-shore, and that is at the end of 'The Owl and the Pussy-cat' when they danced by the light of the moon. 'We come no more to the golden shore where we danced in days of old,'[24] he quoted to himself over and over again, but for Lear the days of dancing had been so short that they were nothing but the dimmest of memories, and the golden shore was a place where happiness ended and loneliness began.

He had another cruel memory from his childhood which he had never mentioned before. Early in June his cousin, his mother's sister's child, died in England. His name was Frederick Harding, and when Lear heard of his death he wrote in his diary: 'It is just 50 years since he did me the greatest Evil done to me in life, excepting that done by C:—& which must last now to the end—spite of all reason & effort.'[25] It was Easter Monday, April 8th, 1822, and Frederick Harding, who was nineteen, had just been bought out of his regiment and was staying at Bowman's Lodge. Lear was not quite ten. He never elaborated on this, nor did he say who C was— perhaps it was his brother, Charles[26] but he thought of it often, and for many years afterwards when April 8th came round he would note the day in his diary.

He would often wander over to see the Congreves after dinner, when he sat and talked, 'and delighted us all by singing his "Tennyson Songs", set to music by himself, which he sang with great feeling and expression, and with what must have been at one time a fine tenor voice. He accompanied himself on the piano with spread chords, of which he was very fond. He generally finished up with some humorous songs, sung with great spirit, our favourite being "The Cork Leg".'[27]

But he longed for visits from his old friends, and tried bribing Fortescue to come and see him: '. . . if you come here directly, I can give you 3 figs, and 2 bunches of grapes: but if later, I can only offer you 4 small potatoes, some olives, 5 tomatoes, and a lot of castor oil berries. These, if mashed up with some crickets who have spongetaneously come to life in my cellar, may make a novel, if not nice or nutricious Jam or Jelley. Talking of bosh, I have done another whole book of it: it is to be called 'MORE NONSENSE' and Bush brings it out at Xmas: *it will have a portrait of me outside.* I should have liked to dedicate it to you, but I thought it was not dignified enough for a Cabinet M(inister).'[28] These were the limericks and other nonsense left over from the book of 1871, and this time he was taking no chances about the identity of the author. The book was called *More Nonsense Pictures, Rhymes, Botany &c.*

He began work again on the Tennyson illustrations that he had planned and thought about over the years, and as well as this he filled his 'maggrifficent gallery, with ninety-nine water color drawings, not to speak of five larger oils . . . (In one is a big beech tree, at which all intelligent huming beans say—"Beach!"—when they see it. For all that one forlorn ijiot said—"Is that a *Palm*-tree Sir?"—"No", replied I quietly,—"it is a Peruvian Brocoli".)'[29]

San Remo

'My elth is tolerable, but I am 60 next May, and feel growing old,' he wrote. 'Going up and downstairs worries me, and I think of marrying some domestic henbird and then of building a nest in one of my own olive trees, where I should only descend at remote intervals during the rest of my life.'[30]

Then in September his quiet withdrawal from life was disturbed by an invitation. Lord Northbrook had been appointed Viceroy of India, and he wrote asking Lear if he would like to go out there to live for six months at his expense.

CHAPTER NINETEEN

Coast of Coromandel

1872–75

Lear wasn't sure that he wanted to go to India. He had just settled down for the first time in his life, and it seemed the wrong moment to be on the move again—though he had often predicted that if he ever did settle he would leave the next day for Tobago.

When he went across to Cannes at the end of March 1872 to see Northbrook who was on his way out to India, the invitation was put to him again. It was a difficult decision for Lear to make— 'with all my attachment to the whole lot, there is something antagonistic to my nature in travelling as part of a suite; and indeed, though I am not in the strongest sense of the word Bohemian, I have just so much of that nature as it is perhaps impossible the artistic and poetic beast can be born without. Always accustomed from a boy to go my own ways uncontrolled, I cannot help fearing that I should run rusty and sulky by reason of retinues and routines. This impression it is which keeps me turning over and over in what I please to call my mind what I had best do. Sometimes I think I will cut away to Bombay, with my old servant, and writing thence to Northbrook, do parts of India as I can, and ask him to let me take out some money in drawings. On the other hand, I hate the thought of being ungracious or wanting in friendliness. The Himalayas, Darjeeling, Delhi, Ceylon, etc. etc. are what I have always wished to see: but, all' opposto, here I have a new house, and to flee away from it as soon as it is well finished seems a kind of giddiness which it rather humiliates me to think of practising.'[1]

But he thought he would spend the summer of 1872 in England, really to see if he could get commissions for work in India if he should go. During the winter he had bought himself a cat called Potiphar, but Potiphar could go with Giorgio to Corfu. In England he could see his friends, for not many of them were likely to come and visit him:

> But the longer I live on this Crumpetty Tree
> The plainer than ever it seems to me
> That very few people come this way
> And that life on the whole is far from gay![2]

he wrote just before he left San Remo. For the Quangle Wangle, of course, things turned out all right, and quantities of the kindest, most sympathetic creatures arrived to join him, like the Fimble Fowl with a corkscrew leg, and the small Olympian bear, the Dong with the luminous nose, and the Blue Baboon who played the flute, and the Atery Squash, and the Bisky Bat—

> And at night by the light of the Mulberry moon
> They danced to the Flute of the Blue Baboon,
> On the broad green leaves of the Crumpetty Tree,
> And all were as happy as happy could be,
> With the Quangle Wangle Quee.

The Quangle Wangle's Hat

When he reached England at the end of June he had decided that he would see only a few friends—'I will never again commence the ineffable worry of distant hurried journeys to country houses, at a serious expense, and to almost no purpose as to seeing the friends whom nominally I go to see. The conditions and positions of life of most of those I knew in earlier years are so altered,

that although they, (happily,) the friends themselves, are quite
unaltered—no personal communication can now be had with them
worth such sacrifices as must be made to obtain it . . . I do not much
suppose that we shall ever talk as of old, until we come to sit as
cherubs on rails—if any rails there be,—in Paradise.'[3]

But despite his resolution he spent a busy time in England, for
at the back of his mind was the thought that he might not return
again. He saw Holman Hunt who had just come back from Jerusalem. 'He is little changed,—as he was indeed unlikely to be. We
talked—naturally—incessantly.'[4] This was what Lear needed
more than anything.

Strawberry Hill was ghastly. Last time he had stayed there he
had been given a room facing the stables; this time he had a tiny
room looking onto a wall, and he left the next morning at seven
o'clock, promising himself never to go there again.

He moved from one country house to another leaving his 'fare-
well testimonials'—and collecting commissions. But all the travelling had an alarming effect on him: '. . . rattling about so much as
I have lately done, is fast destroying the small amount of intellect
yet left me, and I am constantly on the point of believing in my
proximate metamorphosis into a Railway whistle or a Boiler about
to Bust.'[5]

At the beginning of September he heard again from Northbrook, who this time enclosed a cheque for £50 for a drawing of
Cairo which he wanted Lear to do on his way out to India. During
the summer he had collected nearly £1,000 worth of commissions
for paintings of India, and he realised that he must go—he just
hoped that his Vice-regal friends would realise that he was 'not
a swell full of tin but a hard working painter'.[6]

Just before he left England he fell and knocked his right temple.
The fall made him feel rather unsteady, and it increased his
anxiety about the hazards of the trip. But he had made up his mind,
and he left London for San Remo to collect his luggage and close
the house for the winter.

Lear picked up Giorgio in Corfu, and together they went on to
Suez. In Egypt they heard that the boats were very full, and it was

difficult to get berths. He was still feeling unwell from his fall and was in no mood to dally around, so when a French boat came in a few days later he decided to take a cabin on this rather than risk being left behind altogether. Some of his baggage was delivered to the quayside and the rest put onto a barge ready to go out to the boat, then they waited for customs clearance. When the official arrived he told Lear that the bags already on the barge must be transferred to another before he would examine them. Lear was already afraid that he was going to miss the boat, and he saw no point in moving his things from one barge to another: he started to argue with the official who then refused to examine anything, but mounted his horse and left.

The noise and the delay and the uncertainty of the voyage had already upset Lear. Now he was thoroughly angry, and he ordered that all his luggage was to be taken straight to the station. By seven that evening he and Giorgio were on the train to Alexandria, '& the Indian bubble is burst'.[7]

When he began to think of what he had done he was worried. He had always been frightened that the constant epileptic attacks might one day damage his brain—could it be that giving up his journey in a sudden fit of pique meant his mind was going awry?

It was ridiculous—he had lost nearly £1,000 in commissions which were rare enough nowadays, and his paints and canvases were already on their way out to India. He couldn't just throw the whole thing up. Within two days he had begun to make new plans for the trip, but it was too late in the season for him to go now and he would have to settle down again in San Remo and try again the following autumn.

Potiphar had disappeared during his summer in Corfu, so Lear bought another kitten and he called him Foss. One morning Foss was discovered tearing the letters to shreds, and was banished to the kitchen: 'Pity,' wrote Lear, 'for he was a sort of companion;— yet being very literally & really alone—it is perhaps as well to have no sham substitute for society.'[8] But Foss crept back onto the hearthrug and became a much loved cat, 'a good addition to one's lonely lonely life'.[9]

Lear and Foss

To pass the winter he settled down to read nine volumes of Horace Walpole's letters, then went on to eight more of Thomas Moore's diaries: he had built up a large library of books to which he was constantly adding and which he lent out to other English residents and visitors. As well as reading he launched into a batch of 120 new Tyrants, but as he was painting he felt that his right eye wasn't working properly and he was finding difficulty in seeing what he was doing.

As the months went by the tension of waiting began to sap his energy. One moment he would be planning the trip, the next it was all off—he wasn't going. He was cheered by a mention of his work in a Commons debate, when William Vernon-Harcourt said that a friend of his—an admirable artist, had published a *Book of Nonsense*. 'But Parliament published every year a much more celebrated "Book of Nonsense", called the Statute Book. (Laughter.) . . .' 'Sich is phame,'[10] Lear wrote in his diary.

San Remo

In April he was taken ill, and spent several days in bed, a thing he rarely allowed himself to do. 'One thing . . . is certain,' he wrote to Fortescue, 'a sedentary life, after moving about as I have done since I was twenty-four years old, will infallibly finish me off *suddingly*. And although I may be finished off equally suddingly if I move about, yet I incline to think a thorough change will affect me for better rather than for wusse. *Whereby I shall go either to Sardinia, or India, or Jumsibojigglequack this winter as ever is . . .'*[11]

In May his face swelled up painfully, and he wondered again if he should call the Indian trip off: '. . . sometimes it seems to me utterly ridiculous & impossible—at others, the real & only thing I have to look forward to.'[12] That month he wrote a new nonsense song—'The Pobble who has no Toes', and in July he composed an Indian absurdity about the Ahkond of Swat, 'of whom one has read in the papers, and some one wrote to me to ask, "who or what is he"—to which I sent this reply . . .

1. Why, or when, or which, or what
   Or who, or where, is the Ahkond of Swat—oh WHAT
   Is the Ahkond of Swat?

2. Is he tall or short, or dark or fair?
   Does he sit on a throne, or a sofa, or chair,—or SQUAT?
   The Ahkond of Swat!

8. Do his people like him extremely well,
   Or do they whenever they can, rebel,—or PLOT?
   At the Ahkond of Swat!

11. Does he study the wants of his own dominion
    Or doesn't he care for public opinion—a JOT?
    The Ahkond of Swat!

17. Does he like to sit by the calm blue wave?
    Or sleep and snore in a dark green cave,—or a GROT?
    The Ahkond of Swat!'[13]

Then in September came news which a few years earlier would have been a bitter shock, and even now distressed him. During the summer Lord Westbury had died and, free now from any obligations to her parents, Gussie had decided to marry. She was marrying a man called Adamson Parker who was much older than she, and an invalid. Lear had so often wondered if she could have been happy sharing his strange kind of life: instead she had chosen for herself a life which was going to be much more demanding.

It had been years since he had decided that he could never marry Gussie—yet Lear greeted the news dramatically: 'There is now no hope of any but a dark & lonely life. I must leave this place,'[14] he wrote. But it did remove his doubts about going to India, and a few days later he wrote a fanciful letter to Fortescue: 'I wrote you a long letter from San Remo on September 18, but at that time I do not think I had finally decided on India. Presently afterwards a circumstance happened that threw another weight into the "yes" scale—to wit, Gussie Bethell's engaging herself—on her father's death—to one who is disapproved of as her husband by all the family . . . but not as I could have wished to myself. You know now how I have always had the dream—ie—from a good many years now—and just as the time came when I meant to let the decision of my proposal yes or no determine my plan as to India—the question suddenly resolved itself without my having pains of a refusal, which is so far a good feature in the cause. *Please say nothing of this except to Mi Lady*—who with you knows of the matter. So altogether I consider that to go to India for eighteen months would be really my best course, as a change of scene may do me good, and besides, living as I do from hand to mouth by my art, I dare not throw away the many commissions for painting and drawings I already have for Indian subjects.'[15] The last sentence was more to the point.

He spent some weeks sorting his possessions and papers in case he shouldn't return. He had three 'chestfuls or chestsfull' of letters, and as he looked through them he thought firstly that 'every created human being capable of writing ever since the invention of letters must have written to me, with a few exceptions perhaps, such as the prophet Ezekiel, Mary Queen of Scots, and the Venerable Bede. 2ndly. That either all my friends must be fools or mad; or, on the contrary, if they are not so, there must be more good qualities about this child than he ever gives or has given himself credit for possessing—else so vast and long continued a mass of kindness in all sorts of shapes could never have happened to him.

Seriously it is one of the greatest puzzles to me, who am sure I am one of the most selfish and cantankerous brutes ever born, that heaps and heaps of letters—and these letters only the visible signs of endless acts of kindness, from such varieties of persons could have ever been written to me! Out of all I kept some specimens of each writer more or less interesting—four hundred and forty-four individuals in all.'[16]

Why was Lear so extraordinarily popular? He was perhaps ugly, certainly badly dressed and socially his background was very shaky; he was often depressed and irritable, and when pressed upon by 'heaps of small botherations'[17] might fly off at his friends, a thing he always deeply regretted afterwards. Yet after his death Lushington could say of him that the love of his friends was 'the best and sweetest of garlands that can in spirit be laid on his tomb'.[18] Perhaps it was because he was a man who had known, and who never ceased to know, the meaning of grief. Sadness—especially sadness in childhood—which can destroy a personality, can also evolve into the richness of compassion. Lear cared about his fellow men, and he was uninhibited enough to show it—indifference he thought the worst of all human characteristics. He was also very good company—he had proved that in the days at Knowsley—and as he was alone in the world he valued his friends enough to work at friendship. He was never afraid of placing himself in debt to them, nor of acknowledging their help at every turn.

When he had tied the letters into bundles he wrote to Fortescue: 'I cannot help thinking that my life, letters and diaries would be as interesting . . . as many that are now published: and I half think I will leave all those papers to you, with a short record of the principal data of my ridiculous life, which however has been a hardworking one, and also one that has given much of various sorts of stuff to others, though the liver has often had a sad time of it.'[19] It is a shame that he didn't go through with this half-thought, for all the letters he wrote to Fortescue have been carefully preserved. As a final act in clearing his affairs he wrote a new will leaving any money realised from the sale of his house and pictures to his great niece, Emily Gillies.

Now he was ready to leave for India, and he sent Giorgio to

Corfu to see his family whilst he 'shut and sealed and screwed up all the Villa Emily: and doddled about the Portofino coast some time'.[20] Then he boarded the boat going via Corfu to Suez. It was delayed for a day before it left Genoa and, almost unbelievably, Lear became so angry that he ordered his bags off the boat—the journey was off. The small cases were actually delivered back to his hotel, but the porters waited for confirmation before heaving the big ones off as well, and this gave him time to cool his anger, and he asked for the small bags to be delivered back on board again. The boat sailed from Genoa on October 25th, and Lear was at last on his way to India.

It was a long, slow voyage, enlivened a little by the eccentricities of the other travellers like the sad German Pessimist:

'P. You vear spegtakles always?
E.L. Yes.
P. They vill all grak in India: von pair is no use.
E.L. But I have many.
P. How many?
E.L. Twenty or thirty.
P. It is no good:—they vill all grak:—You should have got of silver.
E.L. But I have several of silver.
P. Dat is no use:—they will rust. You might got gold.
E.L. But I have some of gold.
P. Dat is more worse: Gold is always stealing'.[21]

They docked at Bombay on November 22nd, and at once he felt 'nearly mad from sheer beauty and wonder of foliage! O new palms! O flowers! O creatures! O beasts! Anything more overpoweringly amazing cannot be conceived. Colours and costumes and myriadism of impossible picturesqueness. These hours are worth what you will.'[22]

From Bombay they went north-east by train through Jabalpur to Lucknow, where he joined the Vice-regal party and delighted in seeing Lord Northbrook and Evelyn Baring, who as Northbrook's secretary had made all the arrangements for his trip. But his

Lucknow, December 8th, 1873

luggage hadn't arrived and Lear found himself without the proper clothes, which was unfortunate for Anglo-Indians took the formalities of life very seriously. Perhaps it was because they were so far from home and in a country whose own culture wouldn't be conquered, that they lived in such an exaggeratedly Anglicised way. They attended matins in their neo-Gothic churches and played bridge at the Club, and when the evening came they would change, despite the tremendous sultry heat, into starched collars and nipping stays and dine on roast meat and cabinet pudding. They taught the Indians to read Shakespeare and play cricket, and though they weren't particularly interested in the eastern mystics the English did learn to play polo. It could be a hard life too: for men posted to remote stations it was a lonely country, the weather was merciless and many died from sudden, swift diseases or returned home permanently sick and weakened. It was less than twenty years since the Indian Mutiny when rebels had reinstated a Mogul Emperor in Delhi, and a great many lives had been lost before the Indians were finally defeated and the India Act of 1858 transferred the authority of administration from the East India Company to the British Crown. Resentments were still strongly felt on both sides, the Indians generally loathing their English rulers and the English regarding the Indians, almost without exception, with complete disdain.

Lear found that he had to attend their glittering dinners, and he went in a procession through the streets of Lucknow riding in a carriage with Northbrook's daughter. He didn't enjoy it, 'they are so blessed viceregal',[23] he grunted, wanting to get away to see India.

During the next thirteen months he travelled from Bombay to Calcutta, from Simla to Ceylon, spending days in trains and bumpy garries in oppressive, overwhelming tropical heat and bitterly cold Himalayan winds. Giorgio was with him to push him up muddy banks made slippery by torrential rains, to sew on buttons and carry his sketch books. He lived in Vice-regal houses and slept in railway waiting-rooms, he ate enormously and drank more than was good for him, and when he wasn't working or travelling he was fretting about the time that he had to waste on social pleasanteries, or waiting for the monsoons to ease enough for him to get on again.

Travelling was exhausting, for they had to cover such large distances and this meant being on the move for days at a time, tiring work for a man of nearly sixty-two with a troublesome heart. He loathed the 'frightful fuss-ticket-baggage-bother and tumult'[24] so much that he wrote, 'I am half wild when I think of my folly in coming to India at all. The only thing now is to make the best of a miserable mistake.'[25]

But when they stopped at Benares, the holy city of the Hindus which climbs in tiers from the sacred Ganges sliced by ghats down which the pilgrims climb into the water, Lear thought it 'one of the most abundantly.*bruyant*, and startlingly radiant of places full of bustle and movement'.[26]

Calcutta, which they reached on December 21st, was a complete contrast. He stayed for three weeks in the Governor's house, and the whole place seemed permeated with the British. There was 'no rest in Hustlefussabad',[27] and he was glad to leave and travel north towards the Himalayan mountains and Tibet. His changes

Benares

of mood were rapid and complete—one moment he was bewitched
with the colour and the beauty of the country, and the next he
was horrified that he had ever agreed to come: it was all hurry,
hurry, move, move. They stayed in hotels and private houses, but
Lear was happier when he could sleep in one of the Dak bungalows.
There they could look after themselves, get up early and go to bed
when they liked, and not waste endless hours in chatting to hosts
or waiting for meals. Giorgio looked after him splendidly, though
it was soon pointed out to him that it was most unusual for an
Englishman to travel with a European servant. Lear was dependent
on him and he didn't want to take on a man who knew nothing
about the way he liked things done.

They travelled up to Darjeeling by garry, stopping frequently to
change horses, but as the roads were bumpy and Lear's sketching
stool had broken beneath him a few days earlier, he found the
journey very uncomfortable. He had four commissions to paint the
mountain of Kinchinjunga from Darjeeling, and as they came near
the view became 'continually more and more lovely'.[28] But it was
very high and so bitterly cold that he found it difficult to hold a
pencil, and Giorgio piled coats and blankets onto him to try and

keep him warm. 'Kinchinjunga is not, so it seems to me, a sympathetic mountain,' he wrote; 'it is so far off, so very god-like and stupendous, and all that great world of dark opal valleys full of misty, hardly to be imagined, forms; besides the all but impossibility of expressing the whole as a scene, make up a rather distracting and repelling whole.'[29]

But the mountain at sunrise was 'a glory not to be forgotten',[30] and he was up whilst it was still dark, and bitterly, bitterly cold so that he could be out in time to draw at dawn. It was difficult, for he wasn't used to this kind of massive scenery and he thought that he had seen lovelier mountain views in Greece. The vegetation was beautiful, but there was a strange lack of animal life; there were birds—and he knew many of these from the work he had done on Gould's book of Himalayan birds—but they didn't sing and it was strangely quiet.

When he had finished the drawings he went south again, and travelled along the Ganges to Alahabad where he found a letter waiting, telling him that his sister Sarah had died in New Zealand. 'We live and live and live on and perhaps so living from day to day through long years, feel these losses less,'[31] he wrote, but he felt them no little bit less. In fact, as he travelled over India he had constantly to remind himself that looking back and thinking of the people and the places that he would never see again could only bring unhappiness. What was cheerful was that his poetry had come to India: 'While drawing birds for the landlord's little girl before dinner, another little girl just as I was drawing an owl, called out, "O please draw a pussy cat too! because you know they went to sea in a boat, with plenty of honey and money wrapped up in a £5 note!" On enquiry, I found that she and all the school she went to had been taught that remarkable poem!'[32]

In mid-February 1874, travelling on west, he came to Agra and the Taj Mahal: '. . . descriptions of this wonderfully lovely place are simply silly, as no words can describe it at all. What a garden! What flowers! . . . effects of colour absolutely astonishing, the great centre of the picture being ever the vast glittering ivory-white Taj Mahal, and the accompaniment and contrasts of the dark green of cypresses, with the rich yellow green trees of all sorts! And then the effect of the innumerable flights of bright green parrots flitting across like live emeralds; and of the scarlet poinciannas and countless other flowers beaming bright off the dark green! The tinker or tinpot bird ever at work; pigeons, hoopoes and, I think, a new sort of mynah, pale dove colour and gray; also squirrels, and all tame, and endlessly numerous. Poinsettias are in huge crimson masses, and the purple flowered bougainvillaea runs

Sholapur. Lotus plants, July 19th, 1874

up the cypress trees. Aloes also, and some new sort of fern or palm, I don't know which. The garden is indescribable. Below the Taj Mahal is a scene of pilgrim-washing and shrines, altogether Indian and lovely. What can I do here? Certainly not the architecture, which I naturally shall not attempt, except perhaps a slight sketch of one or two direct garden views. Henceforth, let the inhabitants of the world be divided into two classes—them as has seen the Taj Mahal; and them as hasn't.'[33]

He stayed for ten days in Delhi, 'making Delhineations of the Dehlicate architecture as is all impressed on my mind as inDehlibly as the Dehliterious quality of the water of that city'.[34] But it was ruined by British military barracks and iron railings, 'and other hideous British utilities'.

When he reached Simla he heard that Villa Emily had been broken into, and he wrote philosophically: 'Perhaps it is a good thing to be reminded that nothing on earth is permanent—which one might fancy was the case were nothing to go wrong, to one's harm . . .'[35]

But there was good news as well, for Fortescue, who had lost his seat in the 1874 election, had been given a peerage as Lord Carlingford. Lear wrote happily to congratulate him:

> O! Chichester, my Carlingford!
> O! Parkinson, my Sam!
> O! SPQ, my Fortescue!
>   How awful glad I am!

> For now you'll do no more hard work
> Because by sudden pleasing-jerk
>   You're all at once a peer,—
> Whereby I cry, God bless the Queen!
> As was, and is, and still has been,
>   Yours ever, Edward Lear.[36]

Leaving the Himalayas behind him he hurried down to Poona to get there before the monsoons began. '. . . like Tennyson's rivulet once goes on forever and forever,'[37] he wrote as he packed his things to dash south. Giorgio, on the whole, was coping well with the extraordinary conditions of travel: '. . . how very many of his best qualities only come out now in this hard Indian journey!' Lear wrote. 'His quiet, content, and unmurmuring patience, and his constant attention to me, his often wrong-doing master!'[38] But at times he became silent and sullen and would refuse to talk to Lear, who realised that he was tired of travelling and that Indian melancholy engulfed him.

They had to stay in Poona for two months, longing to get on

but quite unable to begin until the rains had eased. He had some
tin cases made whilst he was there, and packed his drawings into
them—500 drawings of Bengal, the North-west Provinces and the
Punjab, the product of six months' hard work.

Waiting in Poona he wrote The Cummerbund, and for this he
went back to the ditty—'She sits upon her Bulbul'—that he had
written as he sailed from Corfu with Evelyn Baring in 1864.

> She sat upon her Dobie,
> To watch the Evening Star,
> And all the Punkahs as they passed,
> Cried, 'My! how fair you are!'
> Around her bower, with quivering leaves,
> The tall Kamsamahs grew,
> And Kitmutgars in wild festoons
> Hung down from Tchokis blue. . .
>
> Beware, ye Fair! Ye Fair, beware!
> Nor sit out late at night,—
> Lest horrid Cummerbunds should come,
> And swollow you outright.[39]

which is rather like a poem that had appeared two years earlier:

> Beware the Jabberwock, my son!
> The jaws that bite, the claws that catch!
> Beware the Jubjub bird, and shun
> The frumious Bandersnatch![40]

for the Cummerbund was a kind of cheerful Jabberwock. The poem
was published in the *Bombay Times* in July.

At last, in mid-July, the weather was good enough for them to
get away south on the journey to Madras and Ceylon. At Hyderabad
the Residency was in a fuss and bother for they were expecting the
Nizan, the local ruler. Lear kept getting in the way, so he went out
and sat with a sympathetic lizard. To help pass the time he read
Plato's *Phaedo*, and this set him on a stream of thought: 'The
[   ] [and] misery of some 55 or 56 years of past life ever before
me—& ever I have to turn away from too much thought of it, by

Lord Northbrook,
Viceroy of India

a decision that it was no fault of my making, but inevitable and
[growing] always from my 6th or 7th year—year by year,[41] he
wrote in his journal, an entry which was heavily inked out by
Lushington when he read the journal after Lear's death.

From Hyderabad he went on south to Madras on the Coromandel
coast. They were coming into tropical jungle and it was oppressively
hot and humid. At Mamallapuram he saw the ancient temples and
the 'Seven Pagodas' with their fine Pallavan sculpture, and he
visited the temples of Conjeeveram, but the heat was beginning to
get him down. Giorgio too was exhausted, and a little disagreement
between them suddenly burst into an unhappy row. 'If I have been,
as he says, a bad master to him, we ought to part,' wrote Lear
afterwards, 'if not, still we ought to part, because such accusations
are unjust, and the relations of master and servant should not so go
on. Therefore, I think it best he should go back, and so it must be.'[42]
But within a few days the angry words had been forgotten.

It was cooler in Ootacamund—'Ooty'—the English summer
home in the hills, but he didn't like it there. It reminded him of
Leatherhead, and he wanted to find the Indian-ness of India, not
escape from it.

By mid-October they had reached the Malabar coast and Calicut, but it was so hot and heavy that he decided in a rush to go on to Ceylon. Here Giorgio developed dysentery and for several days he was really ill. Lear tended him as he had done on Mount Athos, and when he was a little better they went on to Colombo and crossed back to the mainland.

Within a few days Lear had strained his back and soon it was so stiff he couldn't move. He knew that he could go no further.

From Calicut they went straight up the west coast to Bombay, where a letter was waiting with the news that Giorgio's wife had died in Corfu—it was an appalling ending to the trip.

Yet as they sailed from India on January 12th, 1875, Lear was already planning to come back to see the places that he had missed.

CHAPTER TWENTY

The Cruel Shore

1875–80

The return was depressing. Giorgio of course went straight back to Corfu and Lear reached San Remo alone. The house had been turned upside down by the burglary though little apart from winter clothes seemed to be missing.

After the bustle and colour and the movement of India, quietness and loneliness closed round him in a 'solitary weariness'.[1] He couldn't settle to anything: the change of climate had given him '42 thousand 875 colds in my head',[2] and his right eye was worrying him. In the end he decided to go to England for the summer: he would get some new glasses, and he might even come back with more commissions for Indian paintings. He was feeling rather worried about his one remaining sister Ellen too: she was 75 now and almost completely blind and deaf, and it was nearly three years since he had seen her.

He arranged that whilst he was away he would have a new carriageway built and add some more servants' rooms, for although—with eight rooms on each floor—it was already amply big enough for him and Giorgio, he might one day want to sell it and the bigger and better planned it was the more readily it would sell. The garden certainly looked wonderful: it had filled out and matured, and in the early summer flowers began to spill over it in giddy abundance; in the evening their heavy scent would fill the warm air and after dinner he would sit out on the terrace and look over to the darkening sea: it was 'very much like Paradise—only Adam hath no Eve'.[3]

He left for London in the middle of June 1875, but his friends all seemed to have gone into the country—though scarcely to escape the heat of the city for it was chilly and damp. There

271

weren't the usual rounds of dinner parties, and he told a friend, 'I intend to purchase a leg of mutton and eat it on one of the smaller trees in the Park by degrees daily.'⁴ But he did sell a number of paintings, and Louisa, Lady Ashburton, who had bought the 'Cedars', commissioned him to make a large painting of Kinchinjunga.

Giorgio was in San Remo to greet him when he arrived, and they settled back into the quiet routine that had been interrupted by the trip to India. Lear shied away from San Remo society—he was too old to make real friends and he didn't enjoy collecting acquaintances: '. . . my idea of happiness in life, such as we can get, growing more distinct as I grow older . . . and more remote from noise and fuss. At the very door of St Peter of the Keys, I shall stipulate that I will only go into Heaven on condition that I am never in a room with more than ten people.'⁵ But in the spring old friends began to visit him and dispel the quiet loneliness of his life. Frank Lushington stayed for a fortnight; Lord Northbrook, who had resigned as Viceroy in January 1876, stopped in San Remo on his way back from India—there would be no second trip there for Lear; Lord Aberdare and his children came, and in July Charles Church stayed for a week, so there was 'a plethora of friendship all in a lump',⁶ visits which were a source of real happiness to Lear.

In the autumn he worked on 120 Tyrants to fill his large ground floor gallery so that he could open it again once a week, and in December Bush brought out *Laughable Lyrics*—Lear had wanted to call it 'Learical Lyrics and Puffles of Prose'—the last nonsense book to be published in his lifetime. This contained songs from the final phase of his nonsense writing, like 'The Dong with the Luminous Nose', 'The Courtship of the Yonghy-Bonghy-Bò' and 'The Pobble who has no Toes'.

The critics on the whole gave the book a good reception, though most of them admitted that they preferred the earlier songs. The *Standard* critic, on the other hand, had this to say: 'We should not like to be condemned to read much of this kind of literature. Fortunately, in the present volume there is not much of it. The author must have supposed what he calls his lyrics to be laughable, since he gives them that title. If there is any man or woman whose

Giorgio Kokali,
Lear's Suliot servant

Hubert Congreve

features would curl, as novelists might express it, on reading them, we are certain it would not be with a smile.'[7]

Since his return from India Lear's feelings for Hubert Congreve had been gradually deepening. He had been a child when Lear came to San Remo, but now he had become 'a wonderfully delightful lad—free from all priggishness & vanity & yet full of knowledge'.[8] When Hubert came to visit him the day brightened, and he came frequently for drawing lessons. 'I was frequently with him in his studio,' wrote Hubert later, 'and we also went sketching expeditions together, Lear plodding slowly along, old George following behind, laden with lunch and drawing materials. When we came to a good subject, Lear would sit down, and taking his block from George, would lift his spectacles, and gaze for several minutes at the scene through a monocular glass he always carried; then, laying down the glass, and adjusting his spectacles, he would put on paper the view before us, mountain range, villages and foreground, with a rapidity and accuracy that inspired me with awe-struck admiration.'[9] Lear began to hope that the boy would become an artist, and he even conceived the idea of Hubert coming to live with him so that he could teach him to paint. Lear was at the end

273

of his life, Hubert was just beginning his, and Lear dreamt of seeing fulfilled in him some of the things that he himself had missed. In fact, he began to place on Hubert all his affections—he was Lushington and Fortescue and Northbrook, only he was in San Remo and they were not. He longed for companionship, and in Hubert he found both this and a charming, youthful enthusiasm. All his life he had craved spiritual involvement, and after years of utter loneliness he thought that he could find it in this boy.

When 1877 began badly he asked Hubert for his help. Giorgio, though he seemed much better, hadn't really recovered from his illness and the shock of so many deaths in his family, and in February he told Lear that he wanted to go back to Corfu to be with his three remaining children. He couldn't make the journey on his own, so Lear decided to go with him and he asked Hubert to come and take charge of the money and the tickets. In bitterly cold winter weather the three men set out for Brindisi, and when they got there a gale was blowing and it was snowing hard. It was a responsibility for Hubert to have two elderly, unfit men to look after, and he became thoroughly alarmed about Lear. 'I shall never forget the night we spent there,' he wrote many years later. 'It was cold and wretched in the extreme, and Lear was thoroughly dejected; and though a fowl we had for dinner—roasted, boiled, and then browned over, and which collapsed on being touched— roused him to make some jokes about the effect of snow on hens, all his fun vanished when we got into beds with a single thin blanket each in a room with the fine snow drifting in through the badly fitting windows, and he spent the night tossing about and moaning, thoroughly upset by the long journey and his anxiety about his old servant.

'Next day the gale had increased in force, and I became very anxious about my old friend's state, so I encouraged his disinclination to face the sea voyage, for I knew that he was a bad sailor. Finally it was decided that George and his son should go on to Corfu by themselves, and that we should go to Naples and Rome. So after seeing George off we started for Naples, which we reached early next morning in warm and brilliant sunshine, and Lear at once began to revive.

The Cruel Shore 1875-80

'At the station I had to leave him for a few minutes to look after our luggage. I found him again outside the station, surrounded by a crowd of outporters, all struggling to get hold of his bag, Lear hitting out right and left and shouting "*Via, via pellandroni*", the scamps all enjoying the, to them, good fun. The scene was so irresistibly funny that I was helpless with laughter, and before I could intervene my old friend had tumbled into the wrong 'bus, out of which nothing would move him, and so we were driven off to an hotel at which we had had no intention of staying, Lear, on the way there, giving me a long lecture on the care I must take while we were in Naples, as the Neopolitans were the greatest scoundrels he had ever met!

'We spent two days at Naples, visiting Baiae, Pompeii &c., Lear pointing out every object, each point of view, and dwelling on the historical or other associations with eager interest in my un-restrained delight at all we saw.

'We then went on to Rome, and the week we were there was one of the fullest and happiest we ever spent together. No one knew his Rome better than Lear, and in a week he had shown me more of the wonders and beauties of the old city and its surroundings than most people see in three months. We spent a Sunday at Tivoli, where the changed conditions due to the union with Italy struck him very much. "Why! last time I was here," he said, as we strolled up the main street of the old town, "I saw two men stabbed, and had to fly for fear of being dragged in as witness, and that, my boy, was almost as bad as being a criminal! . . ."

'We met in the evening in our hotel an old lady who greatly attracted Lear, and they had a long conversation on poetry and music; after dinner she mentioned Tennyson's song, "Home They Brought her Warrior Dead". Lear at once went to the piano and sang his own setting of the words in a voice hollow with age, but with great style and deep feeling and accompanied with his favour-ite open chords, and he brought tears into the old lady's eyes. "Why!" she exclaimed, "that is the setting I referred to; do please tell me whose it is." "It is mine," replied Lear, and seeing the old lady's evident pleasure he sat down again and sang several of the Tennyson songs he had set to music, and the room filled with

275

attentive listeners. As soon as he became aware of their presence he got up, and with an abrupt "Good-night" retired. A sudden change of feeling and manner to casual acquaintances was one of his characteristics. . . .'[10]

When they reached San Remo Lear knew that he must settle into long months of solitude; for twenty-one years Giorgio had organised his house, and latterly he had become a companion as well. Now Lear moved into the hotel next door where he slept and ate his breakfast and dinner, and each day he went up to the villa to work, taking with him a cold lunch which he and Foss shared. 'As yet—all this kind of life simply stupifies me, & the cruel loneliness of every day drives me wild,' he wrote in his diary. 'All I can do is to try hard to work off what has to be done—before I decide on any plan of life for what short time remains.'[11]

He thought he would go back to England for the summer of 1877 as he had to deliver two large paintings, and whilst he was there he would take some rooms for three months and exhibit some of his work.

He paid a happy visit to the Tennysons. Emily looked well and the poet had lost much of his cantankerousness and seemed almost gentle. He went to see poor Ellen once or twice: she rambled on and on, reminiscing about the past, and he found it difficult to stay awake—but she was so pitifully blind and deaf that she didn't notice.

Then at the end of June came news that shattered Lear: Hubert was leaving Italy and coming to London to go to King's College in the Strand. Lear's dreams of companionship, of seeing the boy grow under him as an artist, were suddenly exploded. Time and again he had told himself that he must not care for anyone new, and now he had grown to love the boy. Rationally, of course, it was a foolish thing for Lear to have done, but he wasn't rational about this.

During August he came nearer to a mental breakdown than he had ever done. It was like the black winter in Corfu in 1855, and as then he was fighting to suppress his homosexual love and aching with the grief of his loneliness. Then there had been a future, but now he knew there was nothing in front of him. 'Tears, idle tears—

always,' he wrote in his diary on August 2nd. 'In vain I resolve & re-resolve:—gloom contracts & convulses me. But I am gradually getting to see that the past must be past, & buried:—yet I can by no means think of anything to put forward as the future. Meanwhile the present is a fearful blank—cutting of heart strings the only serious order of the day . . In vain I work for an hour—tears blind me. In vain I play on the Piano,—I get convulsed: in vain I pace the large room—or try to sleep. True, all these symptoms happened also in 1855—but then there was not the finality there is now:—then—there were unreal glimpses of light—: now—back returns the dark, "with *no more* hope of light". God help me. I was never nearer to utter & total madness than now. Yet, I don't mean to give way, I shall stave off worse things, if I can.'[12]

Is it better to have loved and lost than never to have loved at all? If only he could have loved a little less, or where there was some hope of its being returned, but compared with this his affection for Gussie had been nothing. He was a man who couldn't exist in an emotional vacuum, but the sorrows of his childhood and the secret of his epilepsy had destined him to a solitary life.

At the end of the summer he heard that Giorgio was worse, and he decided to go to Corfu to see him. It was eleven years since he had been there, and the beauty and memories of the island overwhelmed him. His old servant was better than he had expected, though he still looked thin and ill. There were two things now that Giorgio could do: either come back with Lear to live in San Remo, or stay on in Corfu with his sons, but if he remained there he would need better rooms than the dreadful ones in which Lear had found him. He decided to stay, and Lear found a flat where the whole family could live: it wasn't marvellous, but it was better than their present home. He made all the arrangements and paid the rent, then he helped them to move in. As soon as this was done he left the island.

But Giorgio preyed on his mind. It had shocked him to see the conditions in which he had been living after all the faithful service he had given, and he brooded on his lack of thought in taking him away from his family and expecting him to travel so far. It was going to be difficult to find money for the new rooms in Corfu, but it would help to quieten his conscience.

Giorgio stayed in Corfu throughout the winter and spring; then in the early summer a letter arrived from his doctor saying that he was much better and could do with a complete change of air. Immediately Lear cabled to him to come, and he went down to Genoa to meet the boat. Together they travelled up to Monte Generoso in Switzerland, and for six weeks soaked in the mountain air. It did Giorgio an immense amount of good, and when they left in August he was fit enough to carry Lear's folio along the shores of Lake Como—it was like the days of old. Lambi, one of his sons, came from Corfu to help with the heavy work, and life at Villa Emily was ordered again.

Then one day in the early autumn Lear realised that there was activity on the piece of land that separated his house from the sea. Back in 1873 he had wanted to buy this and had offered £800, but the owner was bound by contract not to sell whilst the adjoining villa was let. When he had had the chance to buy two years later

Lear's house in San Remo

he no longer had enough money, though they did draw up a written agreement that nothing would be built there without Lear being told, and then only two-storey villas. Now the olive trees were being felled and the land cleared, and it was rumoured that a huge hotel was going up—still he had the agreement, so he need not worry too much.

By now his Indian commissions had come to an end, and he turned again to the Tennyson illustrations. 'Ah the Tennyson illustrations!' wrote Holman Hunt, 'how they take one back—twenty seven years by Jupiter! when we neither had a gray hair—and there seemed plenty of time for regenerating oneself and the world by display of powers yet unknown. I feel that I might have got nearer than I did—to speak of my own part only but there were the heavy weights to drag me back all the while my life had spring in it, and so the impossibility of thinking of anything but how to get my next quarter's rent. I often wonder that when a young man has done something to prove the possession of talent some of the many people who have more money than they know how to have with satisfaction do not endow him with a hundred or two per annum to give him a better chance of doing his best with his short life. It used to strike me as very preposterous that while I met scores of millionaires—male and female who rightly or wrongly glorified my works as a sort of revelation from Heaven I was at the time wearing away my powers in doing miserable pot boilers sitting up half the night scraping glittering copper to illustrate some rubbishing book.'[13] How Lear must have agreed!

His mind was still on money when he wrote to tell Fortescue some sad news. 'The Ahkond of Swat would have left me all his ppproppprty, but he thought I was dead; so didn't,' he wrote. 'The mistake arose from someone officiously pointing out to him that King Lear died seven centuries ago, and that the poem referred to one of the Ahkond's predecessors.'[14]

On the whole Lear saw little of the people in San Remo, but there was a new family there that winter to whom he took a liking. Their name was Bevan, and one day in April Miss Bevan and Lear joined forces to write a new poem:

San Remo

How pleasant to know Mr Lear!
Who has written such volumes of stuff!
Some think him ill-tempered and queer,
But a few think him pleasant enough.

His mind is concrete and fastidious,
His nose is remarkably big;
His visage is more or less hideous,
His beard it resembles a wig.

He has ears, and two eyes, and ten fingers,
Leastways if you reckon two thumbs;
Long ago he was one of the singers,
But now he is one of the dumbs.

He sits in a beautiful parlour,
With hundreds of books on the wall;
He drinks a great deal of Marsala,
But never gets tipsy at all.

He has many friends, laymen and clerical;
Old Foss is the name of his cat;
His body is perfectly spherical.
He weareth a runcible hat.

When he walks in a waterproof white,
The children run after him so!
Calling out, 'He's come out in his night-
Gown, that crazy old Englishman, oh!'

He weeps by the side of the ocean,
He weeps on the top of the hill;
He purchases pancakes and lotion,
And chocolate shrimps from the mill.

He reads but he cannot speak Spanish,
He cannot abide ginger-beer:
Ere the days of his pilgrimage vanish,
How pleasant to know Mr Lear![15]

The Cruel Shore 1875–80

When Lear called on the family one afternoon he found the children having tea, so he sat down at the piano to entertain them with some of his nonsense songs. He sang 'The Owl and the Pussy-cat', and then the 'Yonghy-Bonghy-Bò'—but half-way through he broke down in tears.

Throughout the spring of 1879 the activity on the land next door had increased, and Lear discovered that indeed a huge, four-storey hotel was to be built there. This would completely block his view to the sea, and wreck his studio light—to him the most important feature of the house. Not only had the agreement been broken, but the transaction had been kept a secret until it was too late for him to do anything about it. Moreover, the hotel was being built by a German, a race whom Lear had always loathed, and San Remo would become even more 'bescattered with horrid Germen, Gerwomen, and Gerchildren.'[16]

But for Lear it was a far greater tragedy than a vanished view or a ruined studio light. All his life he had been wary of encumbering himself with a house which experience told him could only lead to unhappiness, and now he knew that he had been right. He felt it as a personal attack and gradually it acquired a huge dimension in his mind.

In fact, it was a disaster in every way. Ever since he had been a young man he had saved carefully to safeguard himself financially against the very real possibility of his sight going, and to make sure that he would avoid the financial collapse and misery that his parents had known. Most of his money had gone into the house and the improvements, and now its value had been cut away behind his back.

In July he got away from the building and went up to Monte Generoso for his usual summer stay. On the way he stopped in Varese, and in the papers for Monday, July 7th, he saw that Fortescue had a far greater tragedy to bear—for Lady Waldegrave was dead. Lear knew how devotedly Fortescue had loved her, and how terrible he must be feeling now, and he sat down at once and wrote him a heart-felt little note:

San Remo

I have just seen the London and Paris papers of Monday, and know—to my great sorrow—what has happened.

At present I only write to say that I am thinking of you and grieving for you.

> God bless you.
> Yours affectionately,
> Edward Lear[17]

By the time he reached Monte Generoso he had worked out ways that Fortescue could travel out to be with him. He suggested routes, where he could meet him, what he should bring to wear in the cold mountain air . . . almost as soon as one letter was posted he began on another with different, better suggestions. For the first time in years he felt that he might really be needed: he had always been Fortescue's confidant, and he was in a better position than anyone to help him now. Somewhere in his mind was probably the thought, too, that he could reclaim Fortescue's friendship which had been mortgaged since his marriage.

But though Lear always moved on when his life became unbearably saddened, Fortescue preferred to stay near the places that his wife had known. He blamed himself entirely for her death: she had had a chill and congestion had moved slowly into her lungs. Nobody had realised how ill she was until it was too late: if only he, her husband, had watched her she need never have died. He lived for another twenty years and never ceased to blame himself for what he saw as his terrible negligence.

It was as well that he didn't come, for Lear wouldn't have been good company just then. Samuel Butler met him that summer and found no gaiety in the old man. Marianne North was luckier, for he made a real effort to be a bright companion for her. She was on her way back from India so they had a lot to talk about, and Lear travelled down to Lake Como to see her. They decided to have a day out, and went by rail up to Monza to visit a new hotel at Monte Civita still undiscovered by the English. Marianne had been ill, and the 'laughing and sunshine did more than any doctor's physic'.[18]

But when she saw him in San Remo a month later he was no

longer able to make the effort. 'The laughing humour was over, and he was very grave, but had promised to avoid his great grievance if I came, and did so, showing me all his wonderful sketches of India, making me eat pellucid periwinkle soup, mulberry jam, and every other luxury only Mr Lear could think of, till at last, as the train was moving off, he looked in at the window and moaned out lugubriously, "Hasn't someone been good not to mention the Enemy all day"? '[19]

The Enemy had grown whilst he had been away, and he was heart-broken to see the size of it. Not only did it completely block his view to the sea, but it had been painted white so that the dazzling sun and sea light were reflected in glaring brilliance into his studio. Wilkie Collins had been asking him to finish the story of Mr and Mrs Discobbolos, and it was now that he wrote the second part:

> Suddenly Mr Discobbolos
> Slid from the top of the wall;
> And beneath it he dug a dreadful trench,
> And filled it with dynamite, gunpowder gench,
> And aloud he began to call—
> 'Let the wild bee sing,
> 'And the blue bird hum!
> 'For the end of your lives has certainly come!'
> And Mrs Discobbolos said,
> 'O, W! X! Y! Z!
> 'We shall presently all be dead,
> 'On this ancient runcible wall,
> 'Terrible Mr Discobbolos.'

> Pensively, Mr Discobbolos
> Sat with his back to the wall;
> He lighted a match, and fired the train,
> And the mortified mountain echoed again
> To the sound of an awful fall!
> And all the Discobbolos family flew
> In thousands of bits to the sky so blue,

San Remo

And no one was left to have said,
'O, W! X! Y! Z!
'Has it come into anyone's head
'That the end has happened to all
'Of the whole of the Clan Discobbolos?'[20]

He sent a copy of the poem to Mr Fields of Boston, who had published his nonsense songs in *Young Folks*, and to it he attached a fictitious newspaper cutting reminiscent of excerpts from the *Nonsense Gazette*, only this time there was no nonsense and it showed, all too pathetically, what he was feeling:

'We regret to learn that a serious misfortune has happened to the well known Artist & Author, Edward Lear, whose various works have for years been favourably noticed by the Press. Millions of English-speaking people have laughed over Mr Lear's "Books of Nonsense"; many have read his "Journals of a Landscape Painter" in Italy, Albania, & Corsica: & not a few delight in his Landscapes in numerous houses throughout England. A considerable portion of the Public therefore, cannot but be interested in what affects a man who has been the cause of instruction & of infinite amusement to so many.

'Some 10 years back Mr Lear bought a piece of ground at Sanremo, on which he built a house, trusting to pass the rest of his life in quiet there, and to carry out a long-ago commenced series of Landscape Illustrations of the Laureate's Poems. But,— through the unworthy intrigues of a few heartless persons the land immediately below that of Mr Lear has suddenly been sold;—and, —notwithstanding the written promise of its owner that no such outrage would be committed, an immense Hotel has been erected, which not only shuts out every particle of sea view and condemns the Garden of the unfortunate Artist to sunlessness in winter,— but—what is of far greater importance,—wholly destroys the Light of his Studio by the vast mass of glaring reflection thrown from the enormous whitewashed building opposite.

'Unable any longer to use his house for Artistic purposes, we hear that Mr Lear is preparing to abandon the place he had made so pleasant, and is about to leave Europe for New Zealand. It is sad

that a person so well known & to whose talents so many are be-
holden should be thus cruelly treated. His departure from Sanremo
will be greatly regretted; nor are the Sanremesi at all reticent in
their remarks on the parties whose intrigues are about to cause
it.'[21]

He thought seriously of going to New Zealand to live with
Sarah's son, Charles Street, but he knew that he couldn't bear
never to see his friends again. He did tell Mr Fields about another
idea he had had though, 'that I should stump all Europe & America
& wherever the English Language is spoken, as the Writer of the
Book of Nonsense, with a view to collect innumerable sixpences so as

to raise 7 or 8 Thousand Pounds to buy new land & build another
house!!—So look out for me & my cat some fine day—by a Boston
steamer, on my way to San Francisco.'[22]

In England his friends were worrying about him. At Knowsley
Lord Derby and Lord Northbrook discussed how they could best
help him— '(How extremely queer),' wrote Lear, '(2 Earls talking
over this d——d Landscape painter's affairs!)'[23]—and in October
Northbrook wrote offering him an interest-free loan of £2,000
towards building another house. 'I cannot understand how such
an asinine beetle as myself could ever have made such friends as
I have,'[24] Lear thought.

He must decide now if he would start again with a new piece
of land and a new house. At the end of December, 1879, whilst
he was still uncertain what he should do and completely preoccupied with the whole affair, he heard that Fortescue was coming

to the south of France for the wedding of Constance, Lady Walde-grave's niece, and that afterwards he wanted to come on to San Remo to stay with Lear. It would be the first time he had been there, and Lear dreaded the visit. He was in no mood for it himself, and he heard that Fortescue had recovered very little from the shock of his wife's death.

He arrived on January 24th, 1880, and found his old friend inturned on his troubles: they were two isolated men filled with thoughts of their own. Still, he stayed for two months and felt happier than he had done since Lady Waldegrave's death. Before Fortescue left Lear found a new piece of land, and this time he was making sure that no one would spoil it for him.

CHAPTER TWENTY-ONE

Villa Tennyson

1880–83

'My new land has only the road and the Railway between it & the sea, so unless the Fishes begin to build, or Noah's Ark comes to an Anchor below the site, the new Villa Eduardo cannot be spoiled,'[1] Lear told Emily Tennyson.

Buying the land meant that until he had sold Villa Emily he would have to live on £100 a year, plus anything extra from the sale of his paintings. Since he had come to San Remo ten years before it had become an accessible and profitable resort, and he was going to have to pay a lot more for his new house than he had done for the old. Of course, he should get a good price for Villa Emily with its additions and improvements, and he was advised to ask as much as £7,000 for it—in a dreadful way he was going to re-enact the mistake he had made when he priced the 'Cedars of Lebanon'.

Northbrook's loan was only a beginning. He had to rely on other friends—Lord Derby, Lord Aberdare, Fortescue, Clowes and Cross— to lend him the rest of the money to bridge the gap. He would repay them when Villa Emily was sold, and Lord Derby's money was an advance for commissions. For his part he began to sort through his thousands of drawings so that he could send boxes of them to London to be sold off. It was a sad task choosing the first four hundred, and as he turned over his old drawings of Rome and Greece and Corfu and Palestine he felt that he was parting with something of himself. Whilst he was sorting and arranging them in packing cases Northbrook arrived to visit him: he was horrified at the thought of Lear selling off his work like this for quick money, and at once offered to buy the first fifty for £500. But Lear needed still more money, and he arranged to go once more to London.

Lushington had invited him to stay at his house in Norfolk Square, and to exhibit his work there.

Lear was in London by the end of April 1880 and his exhibition opened a month later. It went well, but London was bewildering: '. . . in the interval between possible ruin or prosperity and present worry and work, I walk daily in this mucilagenous metropolis, handed over the streets by polite policemen in mercy to my blindness—but horribly exasperated by the quantity of respirators and refrigerators and percolators and perambulators and whatever those vehicles are called that bump your legs with babies' heads. There are also distressing bicycles, and altogether the noise and confusion so bewilder me that I have little knowledge of my personal identity left . . .'[2]

He saw Hubert Congreve, and went to the end-of-year prize giving at Kings. He wasn't sure how well he would cope, so he sat at the back of the hall and almost wept with pleasure and pride at Hubert's success. He recorded the occasion like an anxious, protective and unbearably proud parent: 'Hubert called up 11 times: great applause for him & some others—most to him: (He was the only one who "backed" properly.) Well for me I was a good way off as it was no slight task to keep nerves straight.'[3]

He saw the Tennysons, and Holman Hunt who was working on his painting of the 'Flight into Egypt' which Lear thought 'very unlovely';[4] he went down to Dudbrook to see the tablet that Fortescue had put up for Lady Waldegrave in the church, and he stayed with the Northbrooks; he saw Evelyn Baring and made twenty drawings of coloured birds for his small son who was having difficulty in learning his colours, and he had dinner with Gussie and her husband. 'Adamson Parker's gentleness under complete privation is beautiful,' he wrote in his diary, '& so is Gussie's constant care of him. What would not life have been with that woman!!'[5]

In June Bush went bankrupt, so there would be no more editions of the nonsense from him, nor any of the money he owed Lear. Worse than this, he had lost all the blocks of the last three nonsense books, and if Lear wanted more editions he would have to do all the drawings again.

The Light Green bird. One of a series of drawings done by Lear to help a small child to learn the different colours

He stayed in London for four months, and before he left he made a final visit into the past. One evening he took Hubert to have dinner at the Zoological Gardens. ' "You are just beginning the battle of life," he said, "and we will spend the evening where I began it." It was a beautiful evening in July and we dined in the open and sat under the trees till the gardens closed, he telling me all the story of his boyhood and early struggles, and of the meeting with Lord Derby in those gardens, and the outcome of that meeting —the now famous book, *The Knowsley Menagerie*. I never spent a more enjoyable evening with him, and Lear—when at his best, was the most inspiring and delightful of companions. He was then absolutely natural and we were like youths together, despite the forty and more years that lay between us.'[6]

How one longs for a record of that evening's conversation. But would all the queries and doubts surrounding the first twenty-five years of Lear's life be sorted out? Did he really tell Hubert what had happened in those early years, or did he tell him his own version of it, for no one else—not even Lushington—really knew? One wonders, for it was Hubert whom he told about his Danish grandfather.

Lear left London at the end of August 1880. It was his last visit to England.

'The new house he go on like one Tortoise',[7] Giorgio had written, and it was only up to the second floor when Lear got back.

San Remo

It was still unpleasantly hot in San Remo, so he left the building and went up to Mendrisio for a few weeks. Hubert Congreve joined him there and they spent a week together. The Congreves had moved now from San Remo, and when they parted for the last time Lear broke down and wept.

In San Remo he began to plan his winter's work, and decided to begin on a group of three hundred Tennyson drawings. 'Painting is silent poetry; poetry is painting that speaks', wrote Simonides of Ceos, and this thought of ancient Greece was built into Lear's whole approach to painting, particularly now as he settled into his final, self-appointed task. Nothing made him happier than being described as 'the Painter of Poetical Topography'[8] or, as Lady Waldegrave had once put it, told that his father was a poet and his mother a photographer.[9]

'I suppose no "dirty Landscape painter" ever got together so curiously diversified a collection of Topographical illustrations,' he wrote to Hallam Tennyson, 'tho' many have illustrated particular places more betterer,—for I don't pretend to be a painter in the ordinary sense of the word. Very few painting coves,—however superior to this child as artists, could illustrate the Landscape allusions in your Father's poems with such variety and perhaps accuracy.'[10] The Tennyson illustrations were to be his Liber Studiorum,[11] and reproduced and published as a set they would represent his life's work as a painter.

But by now his eyesight had become horribly bad. His right eye was virtually useless, and he had to lay in heavy outlines so that he could see where he was working. This spoilt the quality of the work, and the project could never have been anything but a grandly conceived failure. Yet he could still dream of its eventual success: 'When the 300 drawings are done, I shall sell them for £18,000: with which I shall buy a chocolate coloured carriage speckled with gold, and driven by a coachman in green vestments and silver spectacles—wherein, sitting on a lofty cushion composed of muffins and volumes of the Apochryfa I shall desport myself all about the London parks, to the general satisfaction of all pious people.'[12]

By June the new villa was finished. He named it Villa Tennyson, and this time he couldn't claim that he was calling it after a relation in New Zealand: the names of his two houses complemented one another to make up all that was most beautiful in a home. To make the move as easy as possible the new house had been built as an exact replica of the old, but as he moved in it struck him as rather ridiculous to be beginning again at nearly seventy. From Balmoral, Fortescue wrote to wish him well: 'I write a line to send you at once my best and warmest wishes for the Villa Tennyson, and for your prosperity and happiness—at all events for your peace, within its walls,'[13] he said, realistically.

Lear went as usual into the Swiss mountains for the summer months, and on August 8th he wrote in his diary: 'I am obliged to add that I have not felt so well or so cheery for a long long time. O! the difficulty of dovetailing the charm of early artist life, with the formality of later days! The calm & brightness of the view, & the lovely sweetness of the air, bring back infinite days & years of outdoor delight;—& I am thankful for this blessing,—though it can only last a few minutes.'[14]

He came back after two months with one hundred and fifty Tennyson drawings, and the idea of an immense new oil painting of Enoch Arden's island into which he would put all the exotic trees and flowers that he had drawn in India. His study of nature and his world of fantasy were converging, and as his drawings had been part of his nonsense, now something of fantasy was coming into his painting.

He continued to work hard when he got back to San Remo for he wanted to fill the walls of his new gallery ready for his open days, but he was pulled up suddenly by a frightening attack of giddiness, and Giorgio told him that he was working too hard and drinking too much. He had been warned about over-drinking the summer he had stayed with Fortescue in Ireland, but now it had become a more chronic state and he was drinking a good deal of Marsala and water, though by his own account he 'never gets tipsy at all'.[15] As for working too hard—the alternative was for him to settle into a brooding gloom which would have been much worse for him. He did think though that he should perhaps cut down on the number of letters he had to write, and he told Hubert

*Study of lianas in India, used in Lear's painting of Enoch
Arden's island, one of his illustrations to Tennyson's poems*

Congreve, 'I am about to make a new arrangement at the end of
1881, i.e., to correspond only with those I have been in the habit
of writing to since 1850.'[16] But this was an impossible threat, for
his correspondence was such a joy to him. 'He really *lived* upon the
letters of his distant friends more than any man I have ever
known,'[17] Lushington wrote after his death.

So he carried on with both his letters and his work, and by the
end of November his gallery was ready. Constance Strachey, Lady
Waldegrave's niece, later recalled Lear on his open days: 'He was
by way of showing his studio on one afternoon in the week,' she
wrote. 'On this day he sometimes sent his servant out and opened
the door himself. This procedure was resorted to in order that he
might keep out Germans, whose presence, for some unknown
reason filled him with dread. If he did not like the appearance of a
visitor, with a long face and woe in his voice he would explain that
he never showed his pictures now, being much too ill. He would
then shut the door, and his cheerfulness would return.'[18] But
generally the visitors were allowed in, in fact his Wednesdays were
usually very busy, but though his picture prices were modest

enough—£9, £12 and £14 for the drawings and 40 and 50 guineas for the oil paintings—he sold very little. One person who did buy a drawing was Mrs Stuart Wortley who was in San Remo with her two daughters, and for them he wandered into fairy-land, mixing the excursion with a sizeable portion of nonsense.

'My dear Mrs Stuart Wortley,

'. . . I thought it so kind of you to have purchased the Mte. Generoso drawing, that I wanted you to have two scraps to remind you of "Simla" & "Ravenna forest". Which two I enclose, hoping you may think them worth a corner in some Album. I also send two still smaller—one for each of the Young Ladies. These are of singular—I may say bingular value,—as they were done in the Moon, to which I lately went one night, returning next morning on a Moonbeam. As the Signorina Blanche and Katherine appreciate nonsense, I will add some few notes concerning the 2 subjects which I got with great rapidity during my visit, nothing being easier in that wonderful country than to travel thousands of miles in a minute. And these journeys are all done by means of Moonbeams, which, far from being mere portions of light, are in reality living creatures, endowed with considerable sogassity, & a long nose like the trunk of Nelliphant, tho' this is quite imperceptible to the naked eye. You have only to whisper to the Moonbeam what you wish to see, & you are there in a moment, & its nose or trunk being placed round your body, you cannot by any possibility fall. The first view is of the Jizzdoddle rocks, with 2 of the very remarkable planets which surround the moon rising or riz in the distance. These orange coloured & pea green orbs leaving a profound impression of sensational surprise on the mind of the speckletator who first beholds them. The second view represents the Rumbytumby ravine, with the crimson planet Buzz and its 5 Satanites on the horizon. In the foreground on the right is a Blompopp tree, so called from the Blompopp, a gigantic and gorgeous bird which builds on its summit. On the left are the tall Vizzikilly trees, the most common vegetation of the lunar hemisphere. These trees grow to an immense height, and bloom only once in 15 years, when they produce a large crop of immemorial soapbubbles, submarine suckingpigs, songs of sunrise and silver sixpences—which last are ground into powder by the lunar population, and drunk in warm water without any sugar.

'So little is known of the inhabitants of the moon, that a few descriptive but accurate notes relating to them may be interesting. They do not in the least resemble the people of our world,—as for instance they are all much broader than they are high; they have no hair on their heads,—but on the contrary a beautiful crest of yellow feathers which they can raise or depress at will, like that of an ordinary Cockatoo. And from the tip of their nose, depends an elegant and affecting bunch of hair, sometimes extending to as much as 20 miles in length, and as it is considered sacriligious to cut it, it is gradually wound round a silver-gilt post firmly placed in the ground, but removable at pleasure. The faces of the more educated classes have a positively perverse and placid expression—not unlike the countenance of an oyster, while frequently a delicately doubleminded semi visual obliquity adds a pathos to their pungent physiognomy.

'These remarkable people, so unlike ourselves, pass 18 months of their year (which consists of 22) in the strictest seclusion,—suspended with their heads downwards, and tied carefully in crimson silk bags,—which are severely and suddenly shaken from time to time by select servants. Thus, exempt from the futile and fluctuating fatuity of fashion, these estimable creatures pass an indigenous life of indefinite duration surrounded by their admiring ancestors, and despised by their incipient posterity. The servants are not natives of the moon, but are brought at great expense from a negative although nutritious star at a remote distance, and are wholly of a different species from the Lunar population, having 8 arms and 8 legs each, but no head whatever;—only a chin in the middle of which are their eyes,—their mouths (of which each individual possesses 8) being one in each little toe, and with these they discourse with an overpowering volubility and with an indiscriminatory alacrity surprising to contemplate. The conduct of these singular domestics is usually virtuous & voluminous, and their general aspic highly mucilagenous and meritorious.

'I have no time at present to dilate further on other particulars of Lunar Natural History;—the prevalence of two sorts of Gales,

gales of wind and Nightingales;—the general inebriety of the Atmosphere, or the devotional functions of the inhabitants, consisting chiefly in the immense consumption of Ambleboff pies.

'Hoping that I may see you and the 2 Young Ladies &c, Wednesday,

Believe me,
Yours sincerely,
Edward Lear'[19]

That spring Queen Victoria came to stay at Mentone, and it was rumoured that she was coming over into Italy to see Lear. In fact, word went round San Remo that Giorgio had been working for two days and nights making quantities of maccaroons for 'it is known that the Queen of England eats maccaroon cakes continually, and

Part of a page from Lear's diary for July 31st, 1882

30. Then shewed Ly R & Miss L. the A subjects, & then read, slept, & penned out No. 1 of the A lot, till 5. The day is lovely = glorious – all beautiful without – within depression & vexation. Opposed to my being so utterly at sea mentally & morally, my better health contrasts most curiously. I suppose the ever=presence of the Demon since I was 7 years old would have prevented happiness under any sort of circumstances. It is a most merciful blessing that I have kept up as I have, & have not gone utterly to the bad mad & sad. When I have done the last of these penned out A Autotype boshes, shall I go in for doing some in a similar way, but large? – Or shall I go for 10 days or so about Switzerland? – or to Sanremo? – II

At 5 went down to Castelletto, & read somewhat: Nicola came up, but nothing more had been said by Giorgio.

Adml Sir R. Robinson

Lady Robinson — Miss Louis.

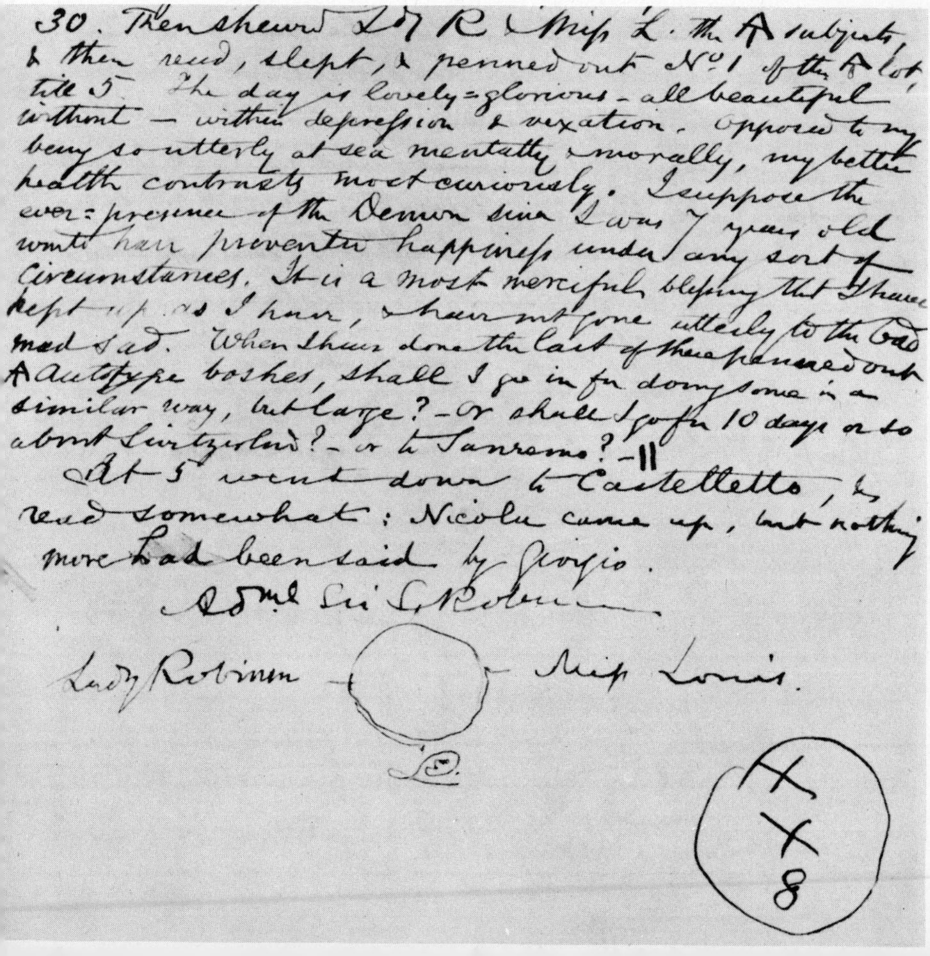

also insists on her suite doing the same. And there is no one in all Sanremo who can make maccaroon cakes except Signor Giorgio Cocali,'[20] they said. Lord Spencer, the President of the Council, came over to lunch, and then more than a hundred people gathered outside the gate hoping that the Queen, too, would come. She did not because of the protocol involved in crossing the frontier. But she had not forgotten her one-time drawing master.

He spent the summer of 1882 working on the Tennyson drawings. So far he had done them in water colour, but as he wanted to publish them and there were then no methods of reproducing delicate water-colour drawings, he was having to begin again this time working in brown monochrome so that they could be printed in autotype.

As usual he disliked the hotel life with its noise and bother:

> The Octopeds and Reptiles,
> They dine at 6 o'clock,
> And having dined rush wildly out
> Like an electric shock.
> They hang about the bannisters
> The corridors they block
> And gabbling bothering
> A most unpleasant flock.
> They hang about the bannisters
> Upon the stairs they flock
> And howly-gabbling all the while
> The corridors they block.[21]

Sitting at dinner one evening he noticed a little woman peering at him through the dining-room door. Eventually, the tall man beside her pushed open the door and walked over to him. 'My wife wishes to know if you are Mr Lear, and she would be glad to make your acquaintance again—the Princess Royal of England,'[22] he said. It delighted Lear to know that both the Queen and her daughter still remembered him.

Villa Tennyson 1880–83

In September he went back to San Remo, his pockets crammed with Alpine plant roots—it was as well that he wore such loosely fitting clothes. 'I was glad to get home again,' he wrote to Laura Coombe, '& to have the fun of gardening once more, which is really the only unchangeable pleasure now left in life.'[23] His new garden was almost as splendid as his old one had been.

> And this is certain; if so be
> You could just now my garden see,
> The aspic of my flowers so bright
> Would make you shudder with delight.
>
> And if you voz to see my roziz
> As is a boon to all men's noziz,—
> You'd fall upon your back and scream—
> 'O Lawk! O criky! it's a dream!'[24]

But fewer people were going to have the opportunity of seeing them now, for he had decided to stop having his open days. Practically nothing was bought, and the interminable chatter thoroughly bewildered him. Instead, he arranged with Foord and Dickenson in Wardour Street to take over all the exhibition and sale of his work. As always, though he had plenty to send them, he wanted new work to be on show as well, so he went on to finish a task he had begun years before of making a complete water-colour record of Corsica.

In January Lord Derby wrote saying: 'Come over this spring and bring a room full of work with you. There is space still at Knowsley for a few more of your drawings, though I have a pretty good stock already.'[25] But Lear felt too old to take up this offer from a family that had never allowed him to be forgotten.

Then in the spring of 1883 Gussie arrived in San Remo. Her husband had died a few months earlier and she was free again. 'What will now happen, who can tell,'[26] Lear had pondered when he heard the news—would he, even now, think of marrying her? He had talked about it often enough, and with a home of his own he was in a better position than before to offer marriage. She came to the Villa Tennyson every day during her stay, but he didn't propose. On the morning she left he went into his garden and picked three nosegays—one for Gussie, and one for each of her nieces who were travelling with her, and he took them up to the hotel. Whilst he was with them he was composed: as he left he wept.

CHAPTER TWENTY-TWO

The End

1883–85

One by one Giorgio's sons had moved into Villa Tennyson. Lambi had come first to help his father with the heavy work, then thirteen-year-old Dmitri joined him, and soon Nicola, who found himself a job in the local trattoria, became part of the household as well. Now that Giorgio was with his family Lear was seeing a different, much less attractive, man and there were frequent noisy rows which Lear—who hated quarrels—was called in to umpire. Then Giorgio began to turn against him, and early in 1882 Lear realised that his old servant was drinking heavily. One day in June he disappeared, and was found, days later, wandering on the hills above Toulon: he had lost his memory and was in a pitiable state; all that Lear could discover was that Giorgio had cabled to Lushington that he needed money, and was apparently on his way to England. Nicola went to collect him, and together they travelled up to Monte Generoso so that Giorgio could rest in the mountains. 'I scout the notion of treating domestics less kindly than horses or dogs,' wrote Lear, 'and even when they are ever so much in fault I think it is wiser to try and keep them from total ruin, than to be indifferent to their welfare. And if I am laughed at for these ideas and acts,—I don't care for that the 999th part of a spider's nose.'[1] He had always been an unusually thoughtful master—within the convention of those days when servants were regarded as personal chattels. He had let Giorgio go home to see his children when they were ill, and had sent him back to Corfu each summer to be with his family; he had taught him to read and write, and had taken responsibility for his children after his wife had died. But all along he had worried that he was keeping him too much away from home, though he had grown to be so dependent upon Giorgio that he did not want to let him go. Now he wanted to try and make this up to him, but it was not easy, for when he followed Giorgio and Nicola to Monte Generoso the unpleasantness began again and he was thoroughly relieved when they went back to San Remo.

As the summer of 1883 came on there was more trouble, for Lambi was discovered stealing wine. Then it came out that he had a wife and two children in Corfu. Lear was annoyed—not at the marriage, for after all Giorgio had been with him for years before Lear had known about his wife and children—but because he had invited Lambi into his home thinking that he was alone in Corfu after his mother's death. Lambi was told to go, and Giorgio backed Lear's decision, though the fuss did him no good and his health became gradually worse. He had had bronchitis, and this sapped what little physical resistance he still had. In June Lear sent him to Monte Generoso hoping that the air would make him well again, but when he followed in July he saw that Giorgio was really ill. For a month he watched his old servant becoming tireder and weaker, and he could do nothing to help: as he weakened his belligerence disappeared, and he became as Lear had always known him.

Early on the morning of August 8th, 1883, he died quietly. Lear wrote at once to Fortescue:

'This is to say, my dear good servant and friend George died, quite calmly, an hour ago.

'He is to be buried at Mendrisio, by the Milan English Protestant chaplain.

'Please write to me.'[2]

> 'I hold it truth with him who says
> To one clear harp in divers tones
> That men may rise on stepping stones
> Of their dead selves to higher things'

he wrote to Emily Tennyson, misquoting from *In Memoriam*. 'It is well for foolish people to say,—how can a mere servant be such a stepping stone?—but to me who for 30 years knew George's constant fidelity, activity, humility, goodness of disposition,—endless cheerfulness—honesty—patience, & untold other virtues, it is plain since his death, that as a 'stepping stone' he is ever of more value to my life now than in all the 30 years of his unbroken kindness & service. I wish that I could think that I had merited such a friend, & that I had never been hasty or cross; but if *anything* is known to those separated from us, then *all* may be known, & more allowance may be made for faults than self accusing memory can imagine.'[3]

The idea that friends who had died could be stepping stones into his own eternity appealed to Lear as his thoughts turned more and more to the purpose of life and death. It was positive, a continuing act of human kindness, and he made lists of the people who had become his stepping stones, from Ann to Giuseppe, his little gardener who had died of fever after working on in the cold rain.

As soon as Giorgio had been buried he wanted to be on the move again. 'I feel that the only thing that can mitigate this sorrow, & give a thorough change to the direction of my thoughts, will be to try the novelty of some place hitherto unvisited, say Madeira, or S. America, or Japan, or Java. But neither my 72 years nor my general health would allow of this relief.'[4] Instead, with little Dmitri to carry his folio as Giorgio had always done, he walked through Florence and Perugia, Spezia and Genoa and reached San Remo in September.

The first thing he did there was to choose a site for his own grave, and then he arranged for a stone to be placed alongside to commemorate his old servant. He thought a great deal about death that winter. 'The longer I live the more I think I perceive the spaces of this life to be inexpressibly trivial and small, and that, if there be a life beyond this, our present existence is merely a trifle in comparison with what may be beyond,' he told Fortescue. 'And that there *is* a life beyond this it seems to me the greatest of absurdities to deny, or even to doubt of.'[5] 'I do not know what your views of future states of material-annihilation may be—but probably similar to mine—hating dogma about what we really *know* nothing about,—yet willing to hope dimly. . . .'[6]

As a young man Lear had been a practising Christian, but he had come to loathe aspects of the church's teaching. The thing he found most abhorrent was the Athanasian Creed with its 'exclusion clauses', and he simply wouldn't believe that 'the Almighty damns the greater part of His creatures.'[7] 'I begin to be vastly weary of hearing people talk nonsense—unanswered,—not because they are unanswerable, but because they talk in pulpits,' he once wrote. 'Are not the priests of the age blind indeed not to discern that, though from the unassailable vantage ground of custom they may oppress the human intellect for a long long while, yet that some day the hour will come for them to go the way of all other priesthoods? . . .

Lear and Foss in San Remo

A broader creed,—a better form of worship—the cessation of nonsense and curses—and the recognition of a new state of matters brought about by centuries, science, destiny or what not—will assuredly be demanded and come to pass whether Bishops and priests welcome the changes or resist them. Not those who believe that God the Creator is greater than a Book, and that millions unborn are to look up to higher thoughts than those stereotyped by ancient legends, gross ignorance, and hideous bigotry—not those are the Infidels,—but those same screamy ganders of the church, who put darkness forward and insist that it is light.'[8]

He spent some time sorting through his possessions and deciding what he would leave to each of his friends, but he couldn't finally settle his affairs until the Villa Emily was sold. The previous autumn it had been let to two women as a school for young ladies, but they had disappeared without paying the rent and now he had bills for insurance and tax and repairs for more than £100: '. . . you will perceive,' he wrote to Fortescue, who like some of his other friends was getting a little tired of hearing about Villa Emily and the hotel, 'that *"the Hotel"* is not a mere bugbear, but a matter that will eventually drive me mad, and which in the meanwhile prevents my working and makes me ill.'[9] He had dropped the price from £7,000 to £3,000 which was more realistic, but now in desperation he was prepared to take whatever he could get. In February—at last—the house was sold for £1,600, £400 less than he had paid for it fourteen years before, but he was rid of it and freed from the preoccupying worry.

Then suddenly he developed pleurisy. For several days he was really ill, and he recovered only slowly. As he lay in bed his thoughts were of the past and of the people he had known, and reading through his old diaries he marvelled that he should have made and kept so many dear friends.

As the hot weather came on he left San Remo to convalesce. He had sworn not to return to Monte Generoso after Giorgio's death, so he rented a villa in Recaoro—but it was a failure. He needed clear, dry air for his lungs and it poured with rain, and when crowds of pilgrims massed in on the village for a *festa* he couldn't bear it. He and Dmitri moved on to Abetone for the rest of the summer, and just as soon as it was cool enough he was back in San Remo in the 'Paradise quietness' of his home.

In London his work hadn't been selling, and in desperation for ready money he told Foord & Dickenson to cut the price of the Corsican pictures by half—but paintings aren't like strips of carpet and cutting their price makes them even less attractive than before. Then they tried advertising them for 'wedding or birthday presents . . . of most sizes and prices,' but still no one wanted them.

That winter saw the final unhappy break-up of Giorgio's family. In October little Dmitri too began to steal. It was hard for Lear to see this happening, for he had looked after the boy for five years and had taught him to read and write. But he was dismissed and sent back to Corfu—and now there was just Nicola, and he was dying of consumption. As the winter went on he became weaker, and by February he was more or less confined to his room. He was the last person to whom Lear could repay his debt to Giorgio, and he spent a good deal of time with him. Nicola wanted to talk, but what he had to say wasn't happy. He looked back to his childhood in Corfu: each summer, when Lear had gone back to England and Giorgio had gone home, they had dreaded his coming; he drank and kept another woman, he gave his wife practically no money and he bullied them all. Nicola probably exaggerated what had happened but, unpleasant as it must have been for Lear to see this picture of his old servant, perhaps it did help to settle his worried conscience.

Nicola died on March 4th, 1885, aged 34, and less than a fortnight later Ellen died at her home in Leatherhead. This was the final break with his immediate family—now there were just nephews and nieces in New Zealand and North America. 'The "stage" is indeed fast becoming vacant,'[11] he wrote sadly.

Yet, in spite of everything, he continued to work hard. In January he finished 70 new Tyrants in thirty-two days, and in April Foord & Dickenson mounted an exhibition of Egyptian water-colour drawings which he was offering at only £5 each. The exhibition was reviewed in the *Academy Magazine* by Amelia Edwards, who had recently published an account of her journeys up the Nile. This set Lear thinking, and he got out his own unpublished journals and wrote asking her if she could advise him about placing them with a publisher. She offered to give him an introduction to Harpers, but then he seems to have decided that they weren't good enough and as he wasn't up to re-working them the whole idea was dropped and, sadly, they have remained unpublished.

He spent the summer of 1885 in Brianza, a beautiful place of blues and greens, and found a sympathetic family called Mundella staying in his hotel. When he packed to return to San Remo he expressed to them in verse the difficulties of his life:

The End 1883–85

When leaving this beautiful, blessed Brianza
My trunks were all corded and locked except one;
But that was unfilled, through a dismal Mancanza,
Nor could I determine on what should be done.

For out of three volumes (all equally bulky),
Which—travelling, I constantly carry about,—
There was room but for two;—so though angry and sulky,
I had to decide as to which to leave out.

A Bible! A Shakespeare! A Tennyson!—stuffing
And stamping and squeezing were wholly in vain!
A Tennyson! A Shakespeare! a Bible—All puffing
Was useless, and one of the three must remain.

And this was the end,—and it's truth and no libel,—
A-weary with thinking I settled my doubt,—
As I packed and sent off both the Shakespeare and Bible,
And finally left only Tennyson out.[12]

He was still working on and off at the Tennyson drawings, 'vainly hitherto seeking a method of doing them by which I can eventually multiply my 200 designs by photograph or autograph, or sneezigraph or any other graph.'[13] The autotype reproductions hadn't been successful, and he was thinking now of using lithography. He employed a local artist to transfer the drawings onto the plates, but they had none of his crispness of line and were woolly and useless. In 1863 a young artist called Underhill had helped him with the lithographs for the Ionian Islands book, and Lear wrote asking him to come out to San Remo to help him again. He had just made arrangements for his visit when Fortescue wrote to say that he would like to come out to stay. In 1881 he had been appointed Lord Privy Seal in Gladstone's administration, but now they were out of office he had decided to have a holiday. For months Lear had been trying to inveigle him to come and stay again, offering him a bedroom 'looking out on the sounding syllabub sea and the obvious octagonal ocean,'[14] but he felt that he couldn't cope

and someone pacing there alone', one of the Tennyson drawings

with both Underhill and Fortescue, so he booked him in at the Hotel de Londres.

Both men were shocked at how the other had aged. Fortescue was still overwhelmed with his responsibility for his wife's death, and after a hard term of office he was feeling tired and low. One evening, about a week after his arrival, he sat out on the prom-enade watching the sun go down, and when he got back to the hotel he was thoroughly cold and shivery. He couldn't get himself warm, and within a few hours he had a high temperature. It was the first time he had broken down since his wife's death, and he succumbed completely. For several days he was almost unconscious, and then he began to make a tortuous recovery. Perhaps it would be unfair to say that Lear resented his friend's illness, but possibly it would be true. Certainly he was in no state to be much help. They dined together on Christmas evening, and Fortescue wrote in his diary: '. . . he came at 6, & has just gone at 9. He had felt very unwell, & said he wd. not have come for anyone else "except Frank Lushington". Last night he said he felt as if he were dying. He was better for his dinner, & we had a great deal of talk.'[15]

Within a few days Lear was bedridden with bronchitis; he too was thoroughly weary and ready to give up the fight. Sitting in bed he completed his obituary which he had begun when he was ill with pleurisy in 1884, and he copied it out and sent it to his closest friends: it was called 'Incidents in the Life of my Uncle Arly'. He described his youth when he lived by teaching, and 'by selling Propter's Nicodemus Pills'—his 'uncommon little shop sketches'. Then came his introduction into society, which gave him his 'First Class Railway ticket'. And the pea-green cricket

> 'Clinging as a constant treasure,—
> Chirping with a cheerious measure,—
> Wholly to my uncle's pleasure,—'

Was this his nonsense, his real means of self-expression? Then he wandered for 'three-and-forty winters'—from 1827 when Bowman's Lodge was sold until 1870 when he bought Villa Emily—'sometimes silent;—sometimes yelling'—

> 'Till he came to Borley-Melling,
> Near his old ancestral dwelling;—
> (But his shoes were far too tight.)'

What a strange phrase—and he had written on it before:

> 'O dear! how disgusting is life!
> To improve it O what can we do?
> Most disgusting is hustle & strife,
> & of all things an ill fitting shoe—
>   shoe,
> O bother an ill fitting shoe!'[16]

Is he talking about the constraints that he felt had crippled his life—the epilepsy, the homosexuality, the deep, inexpressible realisation of the sadness of life that had grown from the depths of his own unhappiness? Yet, perhaps even he knew that from this very perception of sadness had grown a compassion, an understanding and a pity for man's suffering, and it was this compassion that made him the loved and loving man he was. It was from this too that Lear's humour had come—as Carlyle said, 'The essence of humour is sensibility, warm tender fellow feeling with all forms of existence'.[17]

This was the last piece of nonsense he wrote: Prospero's wand was broken. But as he snapped it, he knew that it had been worthwhile, for in February 1886 Ruskin wrote in the *Pall Mall Magazine*: 'I don't know of any author to whom I am half so grateful for my idle self as Edward Lear. I shall put him first of my hundred authors.'[18] It was a moment of rare pride for Lear—and he made one more copy of 'Uncle Arly' and sent it to Ruskin.

Fortescue left in February, but it wasn't until April that Lear was well enough to be out of bed again. He had been ill for four months, and he never really picked up. It was a boost to his morale that he was able to settle the final payment of his debt to Northbrook in March, but it was six years since he had borrowed the money and now that he was straight again he was old and ill and tired.

He tried Brianza once more for the summer, but it was too hot and he went on to Mendrisio. He came home through Lucerne in September, and was taken ill there. He managed to finish the journey home, but now, for the first time in his life, he had no work planned. His right side was useless through rheumatism and he had completely lost the sight in his right eye: but the real trouble was that he had lost the will to work. Underhill's lithographs had been failures, and in February he had sent some more drawings to be autotyped, but when he reached San Remo that autumn he heard that these had been useless as well. There was just no point in going on.

Lushington came to stay in November, and from San Remo he wrote to Hallam Tennyson:

'I won't leave this place without sending you an account of my dear old Lear. He is much better than he was in the summer, and his Dr (Hassell) who at Lucerne thought very ill indeed of his chances of recovery, now says that he may be considered as having "taken out a new lease" subject to various conditions which always make his life more or less precarious. But he is really sadly aged and feeble—very crippled at times with rheumatism—totters about within the house—hardly goes out at all even on his terrace just outside the windows—has to be dressed and undressed by his manservant Luigi—and goes to bed by 6 o'clock. A great deal of the day he passes on the sofa—and all that he does do is only done by short fits and starts. He still occupies himself mainly with his series of illustrations of your father's poems—always trying some new schemes for getting them properly reproduced in autotype with a view to publication. I am afraid it will turn out an expensive hobby to him, even if it is successfully done—I doubt if he is likely ever to do much more work as a painter—and it is a grievous pity to see the large picture of Mount Athos which has been for so many years on the verge of completion & which I have always thought one of his finest subjects, standing on its easel with the foreground incomplete and with (as I fear) no chance of its completion. The only point in which he is quite his old self is his intense interest in all his friends and his pleasure in hearing from them . . . If you do write to him, tell him in which room at Aldworth his picture of the "someone pacing there alone" is hung—as he is always interested in realising the habitat of the pictures he cares for. He is grown considerably more deaf—which always throws a man in upon himself—and he leads a horribly solitary life here . . . It is but a melancholy account to read to you of my dear old friend—but he is so infinitely attached to you and yours . . .'[19]

> He only said, 'I'm very weary,
> The rheumatiz he said,
> He said, it's awful dull & dreary,
> I think I'll go to bed,'[20]

wrote Lear in his diary on December 10th.

In the spring he thought he felt better and tried again to work through a full day, but by the evening he had collapsed.

And then in March he wrote to Gussie asking her to come out to San Remo. She stayed in the hotel, and each day she sat with him, talking and looking over his drawings, or occasionally reading to him—and on April 4th he wondered 'more or less perplexed as to if I shall or shall not ask Gussie to marry me. Once or twice the crisis nearly came off, yet she went at 5 & nothing occurred beyond her very decidedly showing me how much she cared for me . . . This I think was the day of the death of all hope.'[21] And so at seventy-four, when he was almost a complete invalid, he had come nearer to proposing to her than he had ever done. The fears he had had about marriage were unimportant now, and if she had accepted him he would have been nursed lovingly out of life.

His friends didn't forget him, and a few weeks after Gussie left the Northbrooks came to stay. In England Lushington was arranging the purchase of his oil painting of Argos by members of Trinity College, Cambridge, and the Tennysons were thinking of him too, for in April Hallam wrote to say that an American publisher called Estes was bringing out a new edition of his father's poems, and would like to see Lear's drawings. 'The work will never be what I intended it to be,' Lear wrote apologetically to Hallam when he heard this, 'for I did not set out properly at the first to make the drawings purely fit for reproduction; but at that time I had not the experience I now have as to the immense difficulty in the way of photography, Autotype, or any of the many "graphies". I have tried with so much patience—such great expense—and such continual failure . . .'[22]

Mr Estes arrived on May 7th, 1887, and later told Hallam: '. . . upon enquiry for Villa Tennyson I was warned not to visit it unless I was a friend of its inmate. I found Mr Lear sitting up for the first time for several weeks, and he insisted upon showing Mrs Estes & I not only all the Tennyson drawings but all his other drawings and paintings one of the latter of which I bought to his evident satisfaction. He assured us that our call had enlivened him and done him a world of good. The 200 drawings *are* very interesting, and would add greatly to the interest of our proposed edition, but some portions are unfinished in details, and would require *very artistic treatment* at the hand of an engraver or etcher. It is very evident that their reproduction & publication are the dearest wish of this old gentleman's heart, but that he almost despairs of this result. . . . I fear a sensation of pleasure is a rare thing to him in his sad old age.'[23]

But the idea came to nothing, and it was only after Lear's death that a small book was published, limited to one hundred copies signed by Tennyson, containing three poems—'The Daisy', 'The Princess', and 'The House of Art'—and using some of his two hundred illustrations.

And so he sat, sometimes reading the Greek Testament or *In*

The last photo of Lear taken in 1887.
Foss had just jumped off his lap

Memoriam, sometimes just looking out of the window. The terrace was 'one complete bower of full blown roses, little cluster flowers',[24] and eleven pigeons, nurtured by the cook, had hatched and fluttered busily around outside. 'No bird is more beautiful than a pigeon,'[25] he wrote as he watched them, and he was ending where he had begun.

He managed to get to Adorno in the mountains for the three summer months, and he was back in San Remo in September. A few days later Foss, his last faithful companion, died.[26] As the winter progressed he grew gradually weaker. Each day he lay on the sofa and took occasional walks on the terrace, but by the beginning of January he no longer tried to get out of bed. One day he seemed a little better, but all at once he became really ill. 'For a month and a half he was never tired of talking of his nearest and dearest, his good friends,' his servant Giuseppe Orsini wrote to Lushington. 'But on the 29th, half an hour after midnight, with the greatest grief I act as interpreter of his last words—they are these precise and holy words—"My good Giuseppe, I feel that I am dying. You will render me a sacred service in telling my friends and relations that my last thought was for them, especially the Judge and Lord Northbrook and Lord Carlingford. I cannot find words sufficient to thank my good friends for the good they have always done me. I did not answer their letters because I could not write, as no sooner did I take a pen in my hand than I felt as if I were dying." '[27]

At about 2.20 a.m. on the morning of Sunday, January 29th, 1888, Lear died peacefully.

'We went of course to the funeral. I have never forgotten it, it was all so sad, so lonely. After such a life as Mr Lear's had been and the immense number of friends he had, there was not one of them able to be with him at the end.'[28]

> On a little heap of Barley
> Died my agèd uncle Arly,
>   And they buried him one night;—
> Close beside the leafy thicket;—
> There,—his hat and Railway-Ticket;—
> There,—his ever faithful Cricket;—
>   (But his shoes were far too tight.)[29]

CHRONOLOGICAL TABLE

NOTES TO THE TEXT

NOTES TO THE ILLUSTRATIONS

BIBLIOGRAPHY

ACKNOWLEDGMENTS

INDEX

A BRIEF CHRONOLOGICAL TABLE
OF LEAR'S TRAVELS

1831   or 1832. Amsterdam, Rotterdam, Berne, Berlin.

1835   *July–August*, Ireland.

1836   *August–October*, Lake District.

1837   *June–July*, Devon and Cornwall. *July–December*, Belgium, Luxembourg, Germany, Switzerland, Italy, Rome.

1838   Rome. Bay of Naples.

1839   Rome. Walking tour towards Florence.

1840   Rome. Subiaco.

1841   Rome. England. *September*, Scotland.

1842   Rome. *April–May*, Sicily.

1843   Rome. *July–October*, Abruzzi.

1844   Rome. *September–October*, Abruzzi.

1845   Rome. *May*, England.

1846   England. *December*, Rome.

1847   Rome. *May–June*, Sicily. *July–October*, Southern Calabria and the Kingdom of Naples.

1848   Rome. *April–June*, via Malta to Corfu, Ionian Islands. *June*, Greece: Athens, Marathon, Thermopylae, Thebes. *August*, Constantinople. *September–December*, tour of Greece and Albania. *December*, Malta.

1849   *January–February*, Cairo, Suez, Sinai. *February*, Malta. *March–June*, tour of southern Greece, Yannina, Vale of Tempe, Mount Olympus. *July*, England.

1850   London, Royal Academy Schools.

1851   London, Royal Academy Schools. *July–August*, Devon.

1852   London. *July–December*, Hastings.

1853   *January–February*, Hastings, London. *December*, Egypt.

1854   *January–March*, Egypt. *April*, Malta, Marseilles, England. *September–October*, Switzerland, England.

1855   England. *October*, Corfu.

1856   Corfu. *August–October*, Greece, Mount Athos, Dardanelles, Troy, Corfu.

1857   Corfu. *May*, via Venice to London. *November*, Corfu.

1858   Corfu. *March*, Alexandria, Jaffa, Jerusalem. *April*, Bethlehem, Hebron, Petra, Dead Sea. *May*, Beirut. *June*, Corfu. *August*, to England. *November*, Rome.

1859   Rome. *May*, England. *July–November*, St Leonards. *December*, Rome.

Chronological Table

1860   Rome. *May*, Bay of Spezia, England. *October–December*, Weybridge.

1861   Weybridge, *January*, London. *May–August*, Florence, Switzerland, England. *November*, Corfu.

1862   Corfu. *May*, via Malta to England. *November*, Corfu.

1863   Corfu. *April–May*, Ionian Islands. *June*, via Italy to England.

1864   *January*, Corfu. *April*, Athens, Crete. *June*, England. *November*, Nice. *December*, Corniche walk.

1865   Nice. *April*, England. *November*, Venice. *December*, Malta.

1866   Malta. *April*, via Corfu, Dalmatian coast, Trieste to England. *December*, Egypt.

1867   Egypt. *April*, Palestine. *May*, northern Italy. *June*, England. *November*, Cannes.

1868   Cannes. *May–June*, Corsica, England. *December*, Cannes.

1869   Cannes. *June*, Paris. *July*, London. *December*, Cannes.

1870   Cannes. *March*, San Remo (briefly). *June*, San Remo. *Summer*, Certosa del Pesio.

1871   *March*, moves into VILLA EMILY, San Remo. *Autumn*, Genoa, Rome, Frascati, Bologna, Padua.

1872   Villa Emily. *June–October*, England. *October*, sets out to India, but turns back at Suez.

1873   Villa Emily. *October*, to India. *November*, arrives Bombay.

1874   India. *November*, Ceylon. *December*, leaves for San Remo.

1875   Villa Emily. *June–September*, England.

1876   Villa Emily.

1877   Villa Emily. *February*, Brindisi, Rome. *May–September*, England. *September*, Corfu, San Remo.

1878   Villa Emily. *Summer*, Monte Generoso, Switzerland.

1879   Villa Emily. *Summer*, Monte Generoso.

1880   Villa Emily. *April–August*, England. *September–October*, Varese, Monte Generoso.

1881   Villa Emily. *May*, moves out of Villa Emily. *Summer*, Monte Generoso. *October*, moves into VILLA TENNYSON, San Remo.

1882   Villa Tennyson. *Summer*, Monte Generoso.

1883   Villa Tennyson. *Summer*, Monte Generoso. *September*, Perugia, Florence, Pisa, Spezia, Genoa.

1884   Villa Tennyson. *Summer*, Recoaro, Milan.

1885   Villa Tennyson. *Summer*, Brianza.

1886   Villa Tennyson. *Summer*, Brianza.

1887   Villa Tennyson. *Summer*, Andorno.

1888   Dies on January 29th at Villa Tennyson.

NOTES TO THE TEXT

ABBREVIATIONS USED IN THE NOTES

EL   Edward Lear.

d   Edward Lear's diary. These are all in the Houghton Library, Harvard.

Ann   Transcriptions of the letters which Lear wrote to his sister Ann in the possession of Mr Michell.

F   Chichester Fortescue.

Ly.W   Lady Waldegrave.

ET   Emily Tennyson. All the letters referred to here both to and from the Tennyson family are preserved in the Tennyson Research Centre, Lincoln.

HH   Holman Hunt. Letters from Lear to Holman Hunt are mostly in private ownership. A collection from Holman Hunt to Lear is in the John Rylands Library, Manchester.

LEL   *The Letters of Edward Lear*

LLEL   *The Later Letters of Edward Lear.*

G & A   *The Journal of a Landscape Painter in Greece and Albania.*

Carl. ms.   Carlingford manuscripts deposited by Lord Strachie in the Somerset Record Office, Taunton. This collection includes the letters which passed between Lear and both Chichester Fortescue and Lady Waldegrave, as well as a few volumes of Fortescue's diaries.

IJ   The *Indian Journal* at the Houghton Library, Harvard. An edited edition of this was published in 1953.

CN   *The Complete Nonsense of Edward Lear*, ed. Holbrook Jackson. Faber & Faber, 1947.

OF   William B. Osgood Field—*Edward Lear on my Shelves.*

AD   *Edward Lear*, by Angus Davidson.

BP   By way of Preface, *Nonsense Songs and Stories*, Sixth Edition.

NOTES TO THE TEXT

CHAPTER 1

1. EL–Hubert Congreve, 31.12.82, quoted LLEL 18.
2. The statements about Lear's ancestors have been built up from the following documents:
   a. the wills of George Lear, 1745; Henry Lear, 1763 (administration); Margaret Lear, 1795 and

CHAPTER 1 (*cont'd*)

Florence Brignell Usher, 1802; all in Somerset House;
b. London Directories from 1763;
c. the records of the Corporation of London in the Guildhall Library;
d. the records of the Chamberlain's Office in the Guildhall;
e. the parish records of St. Mary's,

THE LEARE/LEAR FAMILY

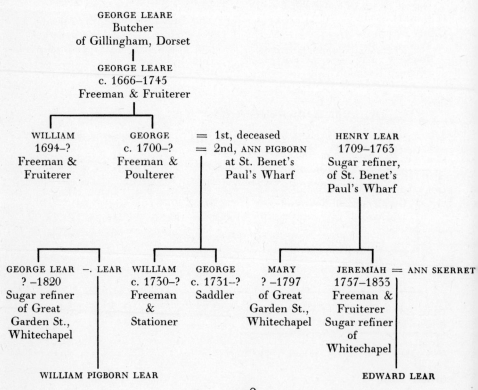

GEORGE LEARE
Butcher
of Gillingham, Dorset

GEORGE LEARE
c. 1666–1745
Freeman & Fruiterer

WILLIAM
1694–?
Freeman &
Fruiterer

GEORGE
c. 1700–?
Freeman &
Poulterer

= 1st, deceased
= 2nd, ANN PIGBORN
at St. Benet's
Paul's Wharf

HENRY LEAR
1709–1763
Sugar refiner,
of St. Benet's
Paul's Wharf

GEORGE LEAR –. LEAR
? –1820
Sugar refiner
of Great
Garden St.,
Whitechapel

WILLIAM
c. 1730–?
Freeman
&
Stationer

GEORGE
c. 1731–?
Saddler

MARY
? –1797
of Great
Garden St.,
Whitechapel

JEREMIAH = ANN SKERRET
1757–1833
Freeman &
Fruiterer
Sugar refiner
of
Whitechapel

WILLIAM PIGBORN LEAR

EDWARD LEAR

Notes to the Text

CHAPTER 1 (cont'd)

Whitechapel in County Hall, Westminster;

f. Boyd's Marriage Register, and the parish records of All Hallow's, London Wall, in the Guildhall Library. Despite a search of all the possible relevant documents other than these, I have been unable to trace Henry Lear's parentage: he may have been a son of George Leare who, like Jeremiah, was a Freeman of the City of London and a Livery Member of the Fruiterers' Company. There are sufficient circumstantial linkages to show that they were members of the same family, but whether Henry was of direct or collateral descent from George Leare I do not know (*see previous page*).

3. Wanstead Parish Church Marriage Register. The banns of marriage between Jeremiah Lear, bachelor,

CHAPTER 1 (cont'd)

and Ann Clark Skerrett, spinster, were published on July 27th, August 3rd and August 10th, 1788. 'Jeremiah Lear of this Parish, bachelor, and Ann Clark Skerratt of this parish, spinster, married in this church by Banns this 24 day of August, 1788 by me, Thomas Lyttetton, Curate. This marriage was solemnized between us Jeremiah Lear

    Ann Clarke Skerrett

in the presence of

    Emma Lawrence

    Thomas Barker (parish clerk)'

4. (*See below.*) Lear spoke of his gt.gt.gt.gt.gt.gt. grandfather Usher as Irish and a bishop, e.g. EL-F, 6.9.63. LEL 290.

5. The Fruiterers' Company Minute Book, 1764–91, ms. 5401/2 in the Guildhall Library. 'At the Dolphin Inn, Bishopsgate St. on 12 April 1790, Mr Jeremiah Lear of Pinners

---

THE BRIGNALL/BRIGNELL FAMILY (Edward's mother)

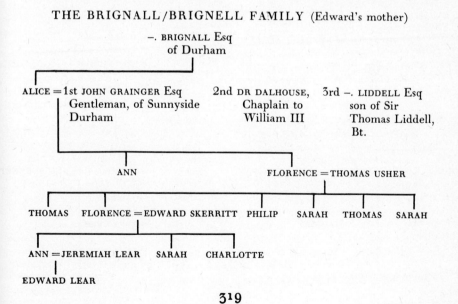

—. BRIGNALL Esq
of Durham

ALICE = 1st JOHN GRAINGER Esq   2nd DR DALHOUSE,   3rd —. LIDDELL Esq
    Gentleman, of Sunnyside   Chaplain to   son of Sir
    Durham   William III   Thomas Liddell, Bt.

ANN   FLORENCE = THOMAS USHER

THOMAS   FLORENCE = EDWARD SKERRITT   PHILIP   SARAH   THOMAS   SARAH

ANN = JEREMIAH LEAR   SARAH   CHARLOTTE

EDWARD LEAR

Notes to the Text

CHAPTER 1 (*cont'd*)

Court Broad Street, Sugar Refiner was admitted into the Freedom of this company (by Purchase) & took the oath for that purpose Prescribed and paid his ffees—at the same time the said Jeremiah Lear took upon himself the Livery or Cloathing of this company and paid his ffine and the usual fees.'

He was admitted to the Freedom of the City of London on April 27th, 1790, by redemption in the Fruiterers' Company. (Records in the Chamberlain's Court, Guildhall.)

6. The Fruiterers' Company Minute Book, 1764–91:
January 25th, 1797—Jeremiah Lear elected Renter Warden;
January 25th, 1798—Jeremiah Lear elected Upper Warden;
January 25th, 1799—Jeremiah Lear elected Master, a post that he held for two years as his successor was unable to take up his post.

Records of the Corporation of London, Guildhall—'Jeremiah Lear of 21 Hermes Street, Pentonville, and later of Pinners Court, Old Broad Street, was admitted and sworn a broker on 12th March, 1799.'

7. List of Proprietors of the New Stock-Exchange anno 1801 in the Guildhall Library. Certificate in the possession of the Stock Exchange for one share.

8. Islington Rate Books Poor L–D to Michaelmas 1806, Upper Side, in the Central Library, Islington. The house was empty for the Midsummer Quarter: Jeremiah Lear began to pay in the Michaelmas Quarter. He paid £80 rent for the house and £20 for an adjoining piece of land.

CHAPTER 1 (*cont'd*)

9. The Lear family tree lent to me by Mr Michell.

10. Death registered in St James's district of Dover, Kent, on May 31st, 1844, and recorded at Somerset House.

11. Records of the Official Assignees Office, Stock Exchange, London— Register of Defaulters. Jeremiah Lear was a defaulter to £2,150.11.1. His account was settled for him by William Smith Jr @ 2s. 6d. in the £—£269.5.5.

12. AD 4. This was based on written family tradition in a collection of papers formerly in the possession of the late Mrs Bowen, the greatgranddaughter of Lear's sister, Sarah Street. Since Mrs Bowen's death in 1939 the papers, which included all the ms. letters from Edward Lear to Ann, seem to have disappeared.

13. The Fruiterers' Company Minute Book 1764–91 in the Guildhall Library. Jeremiah Lear remained on the livery of the company until his death so that it is doubtful if he ever went to prison at all, but in his diary on 27.4.81 Edward Lear wrote of an old acquaintance: '. . . her memory being wonderful, & her gossipry odious, she was more or less particularly disagreeable. "Your Father lived in a large square House called Bowman's Lodge"—(& no doubt she equally well remembered that he was imprisoned for fraud & debt, & that 2 of my Brothers suffered for deserting the Army & for Forgery . . .)'.

Jeremiah Lear's name is not to be found in the surviving records of all the debtors' prisons preserved in the Public Records Office, Chancery Lane, though the

Notes to the Text

CHAPTER 1 (*cont'd*)

records of the Clink, Milbank, and the New Gaol, Southwark, have not survived. He was definitely not bankrupt: his name does not appear on the list of bankrupts published by the *London Gazette* throughout all the years of his business life. In fact, the whole thing is odd, as there is no break in his membership of the Stock Exchange from 1799 until 1828 as there should have been when he became a defaulter—but there is no doubt at all that he was a defaulter.

14. IJ, 13.1.74.
15. CN 248.
16. EL–Ann, 10.2.56. 'Lady Hunter's husband, Sir Paul H.—is the son of that Sir Claudius Hunter you were in love with so many years ago; so you see, that had you married Sir Claudius, this baronet might have been my nephew; but he is not, because you did not, or would not, marry his papa.'
17. Edward's recorded memories of Highgate jump from 1815 to 1819 or 1820. The Islington Rate Books give Jeremiah or J. Lear's name throughout these years. It is interesting to note that in the entry for 1819–20 Jeremiah Lear's name is given as Jh. Lear. In the next entry this becomes Josiah Lear until 1825 when Josiah Lear is crossed out and Jeremiah written over the top. This could mean that the house was taken by a relative during this time: but I believe that it was a clerk's error in substituting Josiah for Jh. as the family was certainly at Bowman's Lodge during the years the entry reads Josiah.
18. d, 27.9.62. OF 17.
19. d, 24.3.77.

CHAPTER 1 (*cont'd*)

20. d, 24.2.72, d. 21.8.73.
21. d, 14.2.80, '... it is wonderful that these fits have never been discovered—except that partly apprehending them beforehand, I go to my room.' Also d, 21.8.73.
22. d, 17.2.87, '... reappearance of the Demon, after several weeks absence, a longer period than for years past. As yet it seems, the "self-control" is not worth much.' d, 12.4.87, 'X—it does not seem that "self control" has much to do with the matter.' See also d, 13.5.59, and 25.5.59, and Chapter 19, note 41.
23. d, 15.8.66.
24. *Sandition*, Jane Austen, p. 25.
25. EL–Ann, 9.9.48.
26. EL–F, 2.9.59, LEL, 148.
27. d, 18.9.61. No explanation is given of where '——' was.
28. Preserved at the Houghton Library, Harvard, and in the National Library of Scotland, Edinburgh.
29. AD 5. This is part of the same family tradition which has disappeared.
30. *Pickwick Papers*. 'See Mr Blackmore Engages an Office Boy' by Wm. J. Carlton, in *The Dickensian*, vol. 48, The Dickensian Fellowship, 1952.
31. EL–Fanny Coombe, about July 15th, 1832. Houghton Library.
32. EL–C. Empson, 1.10.31. Pierpont Morgan Library, New York.
33. Both these poems are in the Houghton Library, Harvard.
34. Sussex County Magazine, January 1936, p. 69. This poem is dated 12.12.1829.
35. Talk of these introductions is found in Lear's diaries, e.g. 11.8.73, and in letters, e.g. EL–F, 12.6.74, LLEL 174.

Notes to the Text

CHAPTER 1 (*cont'd*)

36. Sir Edward Strachey's Introduction to *Nonsense Songs and Stories*, where he talks of Lear having heard Turner sing at a party, and d, 28.4.71. At this party, in Hullmandel's studio, the only occasion Lear mentions of having been with Turner, Lear heard Turner sing 'And the world goes round a-bound, a-bound.'

CHAPTER 2

1. Uncle Arly. CN 275.
2. BP. p. 6. Quoted LEL xxvii.
3. EL–F, 21.1.62, LEL 222—this was Charles Edward Luard, R.E., whose father Major Robert Luard Selby, R.A., married for a second time Lewis Marianne, the eldest daughter of Prideaux John Selby. Several plates—e.g. CXLVII and CXLIX (1835) are signed by Lear.
4. BP. p. 6. Quoted LEL xxviii. There is nothing to support the idea that Lear was employed by the Zoological Society—he himself says that he was employed *at* the Zoological Society and he probably meant this in the sense that he worked at the Zoological Society.
5. Minutes of the meeting of the Zoological Society for June 16th, 1830.
6. Page 125. See *Edward Lear's Parrots* by Brian Reade, p. 10. I am indebted to Brian Reade for his book, from which a number of points made in this chapter have been culled.
7. The Houghton Library possess a splendid collection of drawings, water colour drawings and lithographs, and there is a further

CHAPTER 2 (*cont'd*)

collection in the Wood Library of McGill University, Montreal.

8. Lear was proposed for Associateship on November 2nd, 1830, and elected on January 18th, 1831.
9. EL–C. Empson, 1.10.31. Pierpont Morgan Library.
10. ibid.
11. W. Swainson–EL, 26.11.31. OF 117. Houghton Library.
12. EL–W. Jardine, 23.1.34. Houghton Library.
    On January 16th, 1834, John Gould wrote to Sir William Jardine: 'Mr. Lear's Parrots stopped at the 12th number. I have purchased from him the whole of his stock so that if you are not complete as far as published I can make them so—I have some idea of finishing them myself.'
13. The copy given by Lear to Ann is inscribed 'Ann Lear with the sincere regards of her brother E. Lear. April 15th, 1832. 61 Albany St., Regent's Park.' This copy is in the Houghton Library.
14. EL–C. Empson, 1.10.31. Pierpont Morgan Library.
15. d, 20.2.85, 'considering that I myself in 1833 had every sort of syphilitic disease, who am I to blame others, who have had less education and more temptation.' In d, 8.8.81 Lear wrote on the death of an old friend, Henry Greening, 'I fear dear good Bern HH will feel this. *What* days (& *what* nights) we used to share so long ago as 1830 or even earlier. Harry Greening was in those times the life of all our parties, albeit through him partly I got into bad ways.'
16. National Library of Scotland. Published in *Poetry Review*,

Notes to the Text

CHAPTER 2 (*cont'd*)

London, April 1950. This is subscribed *Bury Hill, E. L. Novr. 1829.*

17. The Pelican Chorus. CN 234.
18. National Library of Scotland. Published in *Poetry Review*, London, April 1950. This is subscribed *E. Lear, December 3rd, 1829.*
19. These drawings are ascribed to Mrs Gould but Lear almost certainly helped her. The drawings by Lear in the Transactions of the Zoological Society are all animals.
20. Vol. XIX *Pigeons*, and vol. XVIII *Parrots.*
21. See for example *Birds of Europe—* Barn Owl and Cinerous Vulture, both in vol. I. It is worth noting that Lear spoke of assisting Mrs Gould 'in all her drawings of *foregrounds*' (BP. p. 6. Quoted LEL xxviii) and not *backgrounds.*
22. d, 7.2.81. This date is not 1880 as stated in OF 116.

CHAPTER 3

1. Uncle Arly. CN 276.
2. *Creevey Papers*, vol. II, p. 57.
3. *The Diary of Frances, Lady Shelley, 1787–1817*, p. 13.
4. See AD 15.
5. EL–C. Empson, 1.10.31. Pierpont Morgan Library.
6. LEL xix.
7. AD 17. EL–Miss Coombe. I have been unable to trace this letter.
8. Introduction to *More Nonsense.*
9. ibid.
10. LEL xix.
11. One of Lear's fellow students was William Frith.
12. EL–Gould, 31.10.36. Houghton Library.
13. AD 14.

CHAPTER 4

1. EL–Ann, 3.11.37.
2. ibid.
3. ibid.
4. EL–Ann, 14.12.37.
5. EL–Ann, 3.11.37.
6. EL–Ann, 14.12.37.
7. ibid.
8. ibid.
9. ibid.
10. EL–Ann, 27.1.38.
11. EL–Ann, 28.5.38.
12. EL–Ann, 10.6.38.
13. EL–Ann, 26.9.38.
14. ibid.
15. EL–John Gould, 17.10.39. Houghton Library.
16. ibid.
17. EL–John Gould, 27.2.41. Houghton Library.
18. ibid.
19. EL–Ann, 29.10.38.
20. EL–Gould, 28.8.41.
21. *Illustrated Excursions in Italy*, vol. I, 27.7.43.
22. ibid., 28.7.43.
23. EL–Ann, 27.8.44.
24. *Illustrated Excursions in Italy*, vol. I, 26.9.44.
25. Carlingford diary, 1.5.45, quoted LEL xxiii.
26. ibid., n.d., quoted LEL xxv.
27. ibid., Sunday, quoted LEL xxv.

CHAPTER 5

1. For material in this paragraph I am indebted to Muriel Jaeger for her book *Before Victoria*, Chapter V, 'The Model Child'.
2. *The Butterfly's Ball* started a spate of similar books, and during 1807 and 1808 appeared *The Peacock at Home, The Lion's Masquerade, The Lioness's Ball, The Elephant's Ball, The Jackdaw at Home, The*

Notes to the Text

CHAPTER 5 (*cont'd*)

Fishes' Grand Gala,. and *The Water-King's Levee.* There is a suggestion of these in 'The Quangle Wangle's Hat' and 'Calico Pie'.

3. Lear himself probably never used the word 'limerick' and preferred to call the rhymes 'nonsenses'. All kinds of explanations have been put forward for the origin of the word, most of them quite unconvincing. However, amongst the letters printed in *The Observer* on Sunday, December 24th, 1967, was the following:

   'Limericks.
   Sir,
   ...'It is surely more than a coincidence that the poetic school— Fili na Maighe—which flourished in Co. Limerick a half-century before the birth of Edward Lear should have made extensive use of this verse form. The following translation, which preserves the metre of the Irish original (c. 1765), is addressed to the chief poet of the school, the erudite Sean O Tuama (died 1775), by his fellow poet Aindrias Mac Craith:—
   O Tuomy! you boast yourself handy
   At selling good ale and bright brandy,
   But the fact is, good liquor
   Makes everyone sicker,
   I tell you that, I your friend Andy. etc.
   E. T. Hanrahan, M.E., PhD. Dublin.'

4. *A Diplomat's Wife in Many Lands,* vol. II, Chapter XX.

5. Brian Reade has pointed out that 'the illustration to the written Nonsenses are often clichés of a skilled draughtsman, not much interested in human figures as

CHAPTER 5 (*cont'd*)

such, but with considerable experience in drawing birds and animals—birds especially. When his hand was left to itself it seems to have sought the lines of least resistance in the forms of amiable harpies, sometimes with birds' legs, and usually with vestigial wings functioning as arms.' (*Edward Lear's Parrots,* p. 30.)
Lear himself said that Madame de Bunsen 'would never allow her grandchildren to look at my books, inasmuch as their distorted figures would injure the children's sense of the beautiful.'

6. An edited transcript of Queen Victoria's diary preserved in the Royal Archives.

7. EL–F, 29.12.61, LEL 214.

8. LEL xx. Introduction written by Lady Strachey.

9. EL–Ann, 31.12.46.

10. EL–Ann, 6.2.47. In August 1846, Queen Victoria and Prince Albert visited Mount Edgcumbe, and the Queen wrote: 'We walked about the garden near the house and then drove to the "Kiosk", by beautiful stone pines and pinasters, which interested Albert very much, and put me so much in mind of Mr Lear's drawings.' (*Leaves from the Journal of our Life in the Highlands,* Smith, Elder and Co., 1868, p. 286.)

11. EL–Ann, 6.2.47.

12. ibid.

13. EL–Ann, 8.1.47.

14. Cicero. *Against Verres,* II. IV.

15. EL–Ann, 11.7.47.

16. EL–Ann, 17.6.47.

17. EL–Ann, 24.7.47.

18. See AD, p. 47. I have been unable to trace this story.

19. *Journal of a Landscape Painter in Southern Calabria,* 31.7.47.

Notes to the Text

CHAPTER 5 (cont'd)
20. ibid., 20.8.47.
21. ibid., 16.8.47.
22. ibid., 1.9.47.
23. ibid., 2.9.47.
24. ibid., 5.9.47.
25. EL–Ann, 16.10.47.
26. EL–F, 12.2.48, LEL 8-9
27. ibid., LEL 6.

CHAPTER 6

1. EL–Ann, 19.4.48.
2. EL–Ann, 14.5.48.
3. EL–Ann, 19.4.48.
4. EL–Ann, 3.6.48.
5. ibid.
6. EL–Ann, 19.7.48. The length of his letters to Ann is truly remarkable. At the end of days of travelling he would settle down to write pages describing in detail the places he had visited and the things that had happened to him. He asked Ann to keep his letters and he used them when he wrote up his journals for publication.
7. EL–F, 19.7.48, LEL 10.
8. EL–Ann, 19.7.48.
9. EL–Ann, 12.8.48.
10. EL–F, 25.8.48, LEL 12–13.
11. ibid., LEL 13.
12. ibid., quoted LEL 12.
13. EL–Ann, 27.8.48.
14. G & A, 13.9.48.
15. G & A, 19.9.48.
16. EL–Ann, 21.10.48.
17. G & A, 22.10.48.
18. ibid.

CHAPTER 7

1. EL–F, 26.8.48.
2. EL–Ann, 8.3.49.
3. Joint Compositions—A Rural Ride.
4. ibid.—Swing.

CHAPTER 7 (cont'd)
5. EL–Ann, 21.4.49.
6. d, 29.1.62.
7. d, 1.6.70.
8. d, 10.5.62.

CHAPTER 8

1. EL–F, 1.8.49, LEL 16.
2. ibid., LEL 15.
3. EL–F, 20.1.50, LEL 23–25.
4. EL–Henry Catt, 11.4.51. Houghton Library.
5. Household Words, 15.6.50.
6. d, 14.3.68.
7. Early Victorian England, Oxford University Press, 1934, vol. 1, p. 177.
8. EL–F, 26.8.51, LEL 21.
9. Pre-Raphaelitism and the Pre-Raphaelite Brotherhood by William Holman Hunt, vol. 1, p. 239
10. ibid., vol. 1, p. 241.
11. Hunt–F. G. Stephens. Bodleian Library, MS. Don. e. 66, fol. 10v. Later during that stay Hunt told Stephens: 'I shall be glad when I can get back to town—everything tries my patience here, even good natured Lear who, being older than myself, I am obliged to humour.' (fol. 16v.)
12. EL–ET, 12.10.52.
13. HH–EL, 24 April n.y.
14. d, 27.5.65.
15. EL–HH, 19.12.52. The painting of Reggio hangs now in the Tate Gallery.
16. EL–F, 23.1.53, LEL 29–30.
17. Recollections of a Happy Life, Marianne North, vol. I, p. 29.
18. See Alfred Tennyson by Sir Charles Tennyson, p. 441.
19. EL–F, 9.12.82, LLEL 279.
20. John Everett Millais by John Guille Millais, vol. 2, p. 142.

Notes to the Text

CHAPTER 8 (cont'd)

21. EL–ET, 18.11.52.
22. EL–HH, 9.2.53.
23. F. G. Stephens–T. Woolner, 21.4.53, quoted in *Thomas Woolner R.A.*, by Amy Woolner, pp. 58–9.
24. EL–HH, [June 1853].
25. EL–HH, 11.7.53.
26. EL–ET, 8.10.53.
27. HH–EL, 8.12.52. John Rylands Library.
28. EL–ET, n.d.
29. d, 8.12.60.
30. EL–F, 12.2.82, LLEL 257.

CHAPTER 9

1. EL–Ann, 7.12.53.
2. EL–Ann, 19.12.53.
3. Thomas Seddon to his brother, 30.12.53, quoted in *Thomas Seddon* by his brother, p. 32.
4. EL–Ann, 21.12.53.
5. EL–Ann, 23.12.53.
6. EL–Ann, 4.1.54.
7. EL–Ann, 17.1.54.
8. EL–Ann, 7.2.54.
9. EL–George William Curtis, 1.1.81. Houghton Library.
10. EL–Ann, 17.3.54.
11. EL–HH, 7.7.54.
12. EL–HH, 11.9.54.
13. EL–Mrs Ford, 19 February, n.y. Houghton Library.
14. Carlingford diary, 18.3.55. Carl. ms.
15. EL–AT, 9.6.55.
16. ibid.
17. *Alfred Tennyson* by Sir Charles Tennyson, Macmillan, p. 286.
18. EL–ET, 27.7.55.
19. ET–EL, 17.8.55.
20. ET–EL, 30.8.55.
21. ET–EL, 7.9.55. This is a stanza from the much criticised Maud.
22. ET–EL, n.d. [Sept 1855].
23. ET–EL, 27.10.[55?].

CHAPTER 9 (cont'd)

24. EL–ET, 28.10.55.
25. Carl. diary, 16.9.55. Carl. ms.

CHAPTER 10

1. EL–Ann, 29.11.55.
2. Lear had been painting large canvasses as far back as 1844 when he was working on one 6 feet long. See EL–Ann, 24.9.44.
3. When he lived in Rome Lear had apparently been in love with a Danish painter called Wilhelm Marstrand to whom he refers later in his diary. On October 18th, 1873, Lear wrote: 'Wilhelm Marstrand died 2 months ago. He was the F.L. of those days & I cannot dare to think of them.' See also, d, 7.10.61. He doesn't mention Marstrand's name in any papers which have survived from the time he was in Rome, but the drawing of Lear in Rome reproduced in chapter 4 is by Marstrand.
4. EL–Ann, 13.12.55.
5. EL–Ann, 26.1.56.
6. Quoted in F–EL, 17.9.56, LEL 37.
7. EL–Ann, 19.6.56.
8. EL–F, 8.2.63, LEL 270.
9. EL–Ann, 3.4.56.
10. EL–Ann, 27.4.56.
11. EL–ET, 9.10.56.
12. EL–HH, 11.5.56.
13. EL–Ann, 8.10.56.
14. EL–Ann, 31.5.56.
15. EL–Ann, 21.8.56.
16. EL–Ann, 23.8.56.
17. 'The Story of the Four Little Children who went round the World.' CN 100.
18. I am indebted to that most enjoyable book, *Mount Athos* by John Julius Norwich, Reresby Sitwell and A. Costa, for many of

Notes to the Text

CHAPTER 10 (cont'd)
the facts about Mount Athos contained in this chapter.
19. EL–Ann, 8.10.56.
20. ibid.
21. ibid.
22. ibid.
23. ibid.
24. EL–F, 9.10.56, LEL 41-2.
25. EL–F, 11.1.57, LEL 49.
26. EL–F, 9.10.56, LEL 38.
27. EL–F, 11.1.57, LEL 45.
28. EL–ET, 9.10.56.
29. EL–Ann, 15.12.56.
30. EL–HH, 7.2.57. Houghton Library.
31. EL–Ann, 15.12.56.
32. EL–Ann, 25.12.56.
33. EL–Ann, 22.3.57.
34. EL–Ann, 15.3.57.
35. EL–F, 1.5.57, LEL 49.
36. EL–Ann, n.d.

CHAPTER 11

1. Thomas Woolner–ET, 25.6.57. Quoted in *Thomas Woolner* by Amy Woolner.
2. Lady Waldegrave retained this name after her third and fourth marriages. Lady Waldegrave's first husband, John, was illegitimate, so that she was legally able to marry her deceased husband's brother.
3. Carl. diary, 8.8.57. Carl. ms.
4. Carl. diary, 9.8.57. Carl. ms.
5. ET–EL, 17.11.57.
6. EL–F, 6.12.57, LEL 65–8.
7. d, 28.2.58.
8. EL–Ann, 1.1.58.
9. EL–F, 9.3.58, LEL 92–3.
10. EL–Ann, 29.3.58.
11. ibid.
12. EL–Ann, 30.3.58.
13. d, 28.3.58.
14. d, 29.3.58.
15. 'The Journey to Petra—A Leaf

CHAPTER 11 (cont'd)
from the Journals of a Landscape Painter.' First published in *Macmillans Magazine* in April 1897, and subsequently in *Edward Lear's Journals*, ed. Herbert Van Thal, Arthur Baker, 1952, p. 236. 10.4.58.
16. ibid., 13.4.58, pp. 244–5.
17. ibid., 14.4.58, p. 253.
18. EL–Ly.W, 27.5.58, LEL 106–7.
19. ibid., LEL 110.

CHAPTER 12

1. d, 21.6.58.
2. EL–F, 5.7.58, LEL 112.
3. d, 22.10.58.
4. d, 1.10.58.
5. d, 12.10.58.
6. EL–F, 10.11.[58?].
7. EL–F, 13.12.58, LEL 123.
8. EL–F, 5.1.59, LEL 124.
9. EL–F, 13.12.58, LEL 123.
10. EL–Ann, 1.1.59.
11. EL–Ann, 20.1.59.
12. EL–ET [Rome, 1859].
13. It was Lear's habit, when he had been to a dinner party, to draw a plan of the seating at the table that night in his diary.
14. EL–ET (Rome, 1859).
15. d, 29.3.59.
16. d, 7.6.59.
17. EL–F, 12.6.59, LEL 138.
18. d, 8.6.59.
19. EL–F, 12.6.59, LEL 139.
20. EL–F, 7.9.59, LEL 151-2.
21. EL–F, 31.7.59, LEL 145–6.
22. d, 13.10.59.
23. EL–F, 4.11.59, LEL 155–6.
24. EL–HH, 9.12.59.
25. On the channel steamer Lear met Thackeray, and he told Fortescue: 'The great man was very amiable & gave me No. 1 of his new magazine, *The Cornhill*.'

Notes to the Text

CHAPTER 12 (cont'd)

26. d, 27.12.59.
27. d, 29.1.60.
28. EL–Ann, 16.2.60.
29. EL–F, 29.4.60.
30. EL–F, 1.5.59, LEL 135–6.
31. EL–F, July 1859, LEL 141.

CHAPTER 13

1. d, 13.2.61.
2. d, 16.6.60.
3. d, 17.6.60.
4. Ly.W–EL, 26.5.59. LEL 143.
5. EL–F, 9.7. [60], LEL 143. This is wrongly dated in LEL.
6. EL–ET, 19.7.60.
7. *Saturday Review*, p. 770, 15.12.60.
8. EL–F, 30.9.60, LEL 175.
9. ibid.
10. d, 30.9.60.
11. EL–F, 30.9.60. LEL 175.
12. EL–Ly.W, 23.10.60, LEL 180.
13. EL–ET, 30.12.60.
14. EL–Ly.W, 8.5.61.
15. EL–ET, 6.3.61.
16. EL–F, 7.3.61, LEL 183.
17. d, 9.3.61.
18. d, 10.3.61.
19. d, 11.3.61.
20. EL–F, 11.3.61.
21. d, 17.1.65.
22. ET–EL, 15.3.61.
23. d, 22.4.61.
24. EL–F, 25.6.61.
25. d, 27.5.61.
26. EL–HH, June 1861.
27. EL–F, June 1861.
28. EL–F, 29.8.61, LEL 189.
29. EL–F, 5.9.61, LEL 194.
30. EL–HH, [1861].
31. Reproduced in *Queery Leary Nonsense*, p. 6.
32. EL–F, 21.1.62, LEL 222.
33. *Saturday Review*, 21.12.61.
34. EL–F, 21.1.62, LEL 219 and 222.

CHAPTER 13 (cont'd)

35. EL–F, 17.12.61, LEL 212.
36. EL–F, 20.4.62, LEL 234–6.
37. EL–F, 20.4.62.
38. In his diary, 10.7.62, Lear noted for tax that his average annual income was £250—about £1,250 by present-day standards.
39. EL–HH, 22.10.62.
40. EL–F, 4.10.62, LEL 249–250.
41. EL–Ly.W, 4.11.62, LEL 255.
42. EL–F, 22.8.68, LLEL 105.
43. EL–F, 23.3.63, LEL 280.
44. d, 7.11.62.
45. d, 10.1.63.
46. EL–Ly.W, 1.1.63, LEL 261.
47. d, 31.12.62.
48. d, 31.1.63.
49. EL–Ly.W, 1.1.63.
50. EL–F, 5.9.61, LEL 193.
51. EL–F, 17.10.62, LEL 250.
52. EL–F, 26.5.72. LLEL 150.
53. EL–F, 1.3.63, LEL 274.
54. d, 13.4.62.
55. d, 15.1.63.
56. d, 6.3.63.
57. d, 30.3.63.
58. EL–F, 14.9.63.
59. EL–F, 9.8.63.
60. ibid., LEL 284.
61. d, 4.9.63.
62. EL–F, 14.9.63.
63. d, 10.9.63.
64. EL–F, 31.3.64, LEL 304.
65. d, 17.12.63.
66. d, 22.12.63.
67. EL–F, 1.1.64, LEL 296.

CHAPTER 14

1. EL–F, 6.9.63, LEL 289.
2. EL–F, 31.3.64, LEL 308.
3. d, 4.4.64.
4. ibid.
5. d, 10.4.64.
6. Homer, *The Odyssey*, Book XIX.
7. d, 15.4.64.

Notes to the Text

CHAPTER 14 (*cont'd*)
8. d, 22.4.64.
9. d, 18.4.64.
10. d, 15.5.64.
11. d, 15.6.64.
12. d, 26.7.64.
13. EL–HH, 2.10.64.
14. d, 24.1.65.
15. d, 11.12.64.
16. EL–HH, January 1865.
17. d, 11.2.65.
18. EL–F, 24.2.65, LLEL 59.
19. EL–HH, January 1865.
20. EL–F, 21.4.65. LLEL 61.
21. EL–ET, 10.5.65.
22. ibid.
23. d, 8 & 9.7.65.
24. d, 10.7.65.
25. d, 23.9.65.
26. d, 11.1.66.
27. EL–Ly.W, 24.11.65, LLEL 63–4.
28. EL–F, 13.4.66, LLEL 77.
29. ibid.
30. EL–Ly.W, 13.2.66, LLEL 69.
31. d, 18.4.66.

CHAPTER 15

1. d, 29.5.66.
2. d, 1.6.66.
3. d, 2.6.66.
4. 'The Courtship of the Yonghy-Bonghy-Bò', CN 238. Gussie too was a writer of children's books, including *Echoes of an Old Bell, and other tales of fairy-lore* (1865), and *Stories from the Realms of Fancy* (1874).
5. EL–Gussie Bethell, 7.8.66. Trinity College, Cambridge.
6. EL–Ly.W, 17.10.66, LLEL 78–9.
7. EL–Gussie Bethell, 7.8.66.
8. EL–F, 11.12.66, LLEL 81.
9. 'Once-a-Week', 5.1.67.
10. d, 17.12.66.
11. d, 23.12.66.
12. d, 25.12.66.

CHAPTER 15 (*cont'd*)
13. d, 16.1.67.
14. d, 9.1.67.
15. d, 5.1.67.
16. 'The Pelican Chorus', CN 232.
17. d, 30.1.67.
18. d, 8.2.67.
19. d, 24.1.67.
20. EL–Ly.W, 9.3.67, LLEL 83.
21. d, 7.2.67.
22. d, 8.2.67.
23. EL–ET, 22.3.67.
24. d, 25.3.67.
25. d, 14.4.67.
26. EL–F, 9.8.67, LLEL 86.
27. d, 22.7.67.
28. d, 22.8.67.
29. d, 26.7.67.
30. d, 2.11.67.
31. d, 5.11.67. The objections were almost certainly social ones, for though they liked Lear and enjoyed his company the family didn't approve of Gussie marrying an artist.
32. EL–ET, 10.5.65.
33. EL–F, 26.8.51, LEL 20.
34. 'The Story of the Four Little Children who went round the World', CN 91.
35. 'The Courtship of the Yonghy-Bonghy-Bò', CN 240.

CHAPTER 16

1. EL–F, 26.12.67, LLEL 89.
2. d, 10.12.67.
3. 'Eclogue', CN 277–8.
4. d, 18.9.60. The *nonsense songs* such as 'The Owl and the Pussy-cat' are distinct from the *limericks* or *nonsenses* which Lear was writing from the time he was at Knowsley, and the *nonsense stories* which he wrote in prose.
5. EL–F, 4.10.66. This need not, of course, have referred to nonsense.

Notes to the Text

CHAPTER 16 (*cont'd*)

If not it doesn't relate to anything that he did eventually publish.

6. Published in *Teapots and Quails*, ed. Philip Hofer and Angus Davidson, pp. 50–4.

7. I am indebted to Elizabeth Sewell for her thought-provoking book, *The Field of Nonsense*, the most extensive and convincing book I have seen on this subject.

8. 'How Pleasant to know Mr Lear', CN vii.

9. The dates of publication of Lear's and Carroll's relevant nonsense works are:

    1865 *Alice in Wonderland*
    1871 *Nonsense Songs, Stories, Botany and Alphabets*
    1872 *Through the Looking Glass*
    1876 *The Hunting of the Snark.*
    1877 *Laughable Lyrics*

10. Charles Dodgson from Canon Dodgson, quoted in *Lewis Carroll* by Derek Hudson, p. 24.

11. EL–F, September, 1863, LEL 295.

12. Perhaps this is why, as has often been observed, nonsense writing and drawing go so closely hand in hand.

13. 'The Daddy Long-legs and the Fly', CN 69.

14. 'The Pelican Chorus', CN 234. There is a feeling here of separation by death—seeing so many of his brothers and sisters die must have had a profound effect on Lear as a child and a young man and probably contributed to his exaggerated fear of separation.

15. 'The Dong with the Luminous Nose', CN 225.

16. d, 1.11.62. The friends were the Prescotts, relations of Jeremiah Lear's bankers, Prescott, Grote and Prescott.

CHAPTER 16 (*cont'd*)

17. d, 28.11.67.
18. EL–F, 26.12.67, LLEL 88.

CHAPTER 17

1. EL–Ly.W, 9.1.68, LLEL 91.
2. *Journal of a Landscape Painter in Corsica*, 10.4.68.
3. EL–Ly.W, 6.5.68, LLEL 104.
4. *Journal of a Landscape Painter in Corsica*, 3.5.68.
5. ibid., 28.4.68.
6. ibid., 28 and 29.4.68.
7. d, 11.7.68.
8. EL–F, 22.8.68, LLEL 105.
9. d, 10.12.68.
10. d, 22.12.68.
11. d, 11.2.69.
12. EL–HH, 6.7.69.
13. d, 17.11.70.
14. EL–F, 11.1.57, LEL 44.
15. EL–F, 16.8.69, LLEL 106–7.
16. d, 18.8.69.
17. d, 27.9.69.
18. d, 11.7.65. Lord Westbury also found Lear's facetiousness trying, and on October 21st, 1862, Lear told Fortescue of a conversation he had had with the Lord Chancellor. 'He—speaking of "undique sequaces"—"sequax",—and saying "let us remember the line and go and look for the translation", quoth the Landscape painter in a fit of absurdity;

    "My Lord I can remember it easily by thinking of wild ducks".

    "How of wild ducks Lear?" said the Lord C.—"Because they are *sea-quacks*" said I.

    "Lear", said his Lordship, "I abominate the forcible introduction of ridiculous images calculated to distract the mind from what it is contemplating." ' LEL 253.

Notes to the Text

CHAPTER 17 (*cont'd*)
19. 'The Poet's Mind.'
20. *Tennyson*, by F. L. Lucas, p. 24.
21. d, 11.7.65.
22. d, 17.10.64.

CHAPTER 18

1. d, 29.3.68.
2. EL–F, 1.1.70.
3. d, 8.2.70.
4. d, 18.3.70.
5. d, 4.4.70.
6. EL–Thomas Woolner, 1.5.70, quoted in *Thomas Woolner, R.A.*, by Amy Woolner, p. 284.
7. *Roman Spring*, by Mrs Winthrop Chanler, pp. 29–30.
8. *A Diplomat's Wife in Many Lands*, by Mrs Hugh Fraser, vol. II, ch. XX, p. 333. In his introduction to *Edward Lear's Indian Journal*, Ray Murphy pointed out the similarity between Lear's nonsense botany and one of the drawings in the medieval book *Ortus Sanitatis*, a copy of which is in the library at Knowsley.

THE UNCAREFUL COW

The Uncareful cow, she walked about,
But took no care at all;
And so she bumped her silly head
Against a hard stone wall.
And when the Bump began to grow
Into a Horn, they said—
'There goes the Uncareful Cow,— who has
Three Horns upon her head!'

And when the Bumpy Horn grew large,
'Uncareful Cow!'—they said—
'Here, take and hang the Camphor bottle

CHAPTER 18 (*cont'd*)
Upon your bumpy head!—
And with the Camphor rub the bump
Two hundred times a day,!'—
And so she did—till bit by bit
She rubbed the Horn away.
8.9.70. Houghton Library.

9. EL–HH, 7.7.70.
10. EL–Ly.W, 6.7.70, LLEL 117.
11. EL–HH, 7.7.70.
12. d, 26.7.70.
13. EL–F, 31.7.70, LLEL 124.
14. Some people remember Lear as a small man, but the people who knew him best recall a tall, large man. He himself said in 1880 that he weighed 13 stone 4¼ lbs., and Holman Hunt spoke of him as 'a man of nearly six feet, with shoulders in width as of Odysseus'. (*Pre-Raphaelitism and the Pre-Raphaelite Brotherhood* vol. 1, p. 241.)
15. Preface to LLEL, p. 17–18.
16. It is strange that Lear, with his musical sense, should have left a line out of verse V of 'The Jumblies'.
17. Charles Kingsley–Tom Taylor, 16.3.71.
18. EL–F, 21.12.70.
19. EL–Ly.W, 22.1.71, LLEL 129.
20. EL–F & Ly.W, 24.4.71, LLEL 133.
21. d, 7.4.71.
22. EL–F & Ly.W, 24.4.74, LLEL 131.
23. 'The Dong with the Luminous Nose', CN 226–7.
24. These lines come from the verse:
'On through the storm and the summer warm,
On through the winter cold,
For we come no more to the golden shore
Where we danced in days of old.'

Notes to the Text

CHAPTER 18 (cont'd)

25. d, 19.6.71. Lear tells us no more of this incident which was probably a homosexual advance which he later saw as the origin of his own homosexual inclinations.
26. This reference to Charles may have referred to an introduction to masturbation.
27. Preface to LLEL by Hubert Congreve, LLEL 19–20. The 'Cork Leg' was probably the 'Quangle Wangle's Hat', where one of the characters is The Fimble Fowl with a Corkscrew Leg.
28. EL–F, 13.9.71, LLEL 139.
29. EL–F, 28.2.72, LLEL 145.
30. EL–F & Ly.W, 25.12.71.

CHAPTER 19

1. EL–F, 26.5.72, LLEL 149.
2. 'The Quangle Wangle's Hat', CN 253.
3. EL–F, 26.5.72, LLEL 147–8 and 150.
4. d, 14.7.72.
5. EL–Sir Edward Strachey, 25.8.72, Carl. mss.
6. EL–Baring (Lord Aberdare), 4.9.72.
7. d, 21.10.72.
8. d, 31.1.73. Had Lear not turned back from India he would not have bought the famous Foss.
9. d, 23.2.73.
10. d, 17.2.73.
11. EL–Ly.W, 6.7.73, LLEL 153–4.
12. d, 16.6.73.
13. EL–F, 12.9.73, LLEL 161–3. This differs slightly from the version published in *Laughable Lyrics*, CN 257.
14. d, 20.9.73.
15. EL–F, 15.10.73.
16. EL–F, 12.9.73, LLEL 155–6.

CHAPTER 19 (cont'd)

17. EL–F, 19.10.64, LLEL 46.
18. Lushington–Hallam Tennyson, 4.2.88.
19. EL–F, 12.9.73, LLEL 156–7. During the summer of 1886 Lear drafted a few notes about his life. The page is headed hopefully Sheet 1, but the notes take only one side of the page:
1837–1866.
Highgate
    & sisters
Bad cousin & brothers
Began art. Sister Ann
1837. Rome.
Rome—& hills
1849–1850. AT.
    [Alfred Tennyson]
1852. WHH Painting
    cousins etc etc
Knowsley Hornbys etc.
1856–7 Sinai
Albania—Greece
F.L. Egypt
1854 Topography
1855–6 Campagna
1870 Jerusalem
1875—Ditto new house
1876 Syria
    India.
It's interesting to see the points he chose from his childhood—what, I wonder, had he in mind for the gap which precedes '& sisters'?

The Houghton Library, Harvard, have thirty manuscript diaries from 1858 to 1887. Lear himself destroyed the diaries he had kept during the Knowsley years, but he recalls later in life looking back over volumes between then and 1858, so it seems that Lushington either lost or destroyed some of the earlier volumes after Lear's death —and these would have included the years when Lear met and fell in love with him. The journals

Notes to the Text

CHAPTER 19 (cont'd)

describing Lear's Indian travels, now also in the Houghton Library, have been censored either by Lushington or Lord Northbrook to whom Lushington sent them, and any parts which could conceivably be compromising—generally the epileptic Xs whose meaning he probably didn't understand but guessed at, and Lear's reference to Plato's *Phaedo*—have been heavily inked out.

Lushington asked some of Lear's correspondents if they would like their letters returned, and this is how those from Emily Tennyson and Fortescue have been preserved. Either he or his descendants must have destroyed all the letters which passed between him and Lear, so there is no record of their friendship apart from what we find in Lear's diaries after 1857.

In 1929 the Lushington family put the surviving Lear papers still in their possession onto the market. In March that year a London book-seller bought 30 volumes of Lear's manuscript diaries in auction at Sotheby's for just £32, 110 original pen and ink drawings for *More Nonsense* for £39, 200 sepia Tennyson drawings for £32, a collection of original drawings and proofs for *A Book of Nonsense* for £31, and a nonsense alphabet for £31. The following November the same firm bought 12 original water-colour drawings for the *Parrots* for £32, and a copy each of the *Parrots* and the *Gleanings* bound together with A.L.s for £19. Much of this is now in the collection at the Houghton Library and was given by William B. Osgood Field, an American collector, who in 1933 published *Edward*

CHAPTER 19 (cont'd)

Lear on my Shelves in which he described his magnificent Lear collection.

20. EL–F, 15.10.73, LLEL 166.
21. IJ 1.11.73.
22. IJ 22.11.73.
23. IJ 4.12.73.
24. IJ 11.12.73.
25. IJ 12.12.73.
26. IJ 14.12.73.
27. IJ 2.1.74.
28. IJ 17.1.74.
29. IJ 18.1.74.
30. IJ 19.1.74.
31. IJ 10.2.74.
32. IJ 13.2.74.
33. IJ 16.2.74.
34. EL–F, 24.4.74, LLEL 171.
35. IJ 20.4.74.
36. EL–F, 24.4.74, LLEL 170.
37. IJ 28.4.74.
38. IJ 6.2.74.
39. 'The Cummerbund'. An Indian Poem. CN 255.
40. 'Jabberwocky', from *Through the Looking Glass* by Lewis Carroll.
41. d, 1.8.74. This entry in Lear's Journal has been heavily inked out. Reading of the Platonic ideals of love Lear pondered on his own sexuality. He struggled to keep this bricked up behind a wall of suppression—except for the masturbation and I believe that this is what he is referring to here. See Chapter 1, note 22, and Chapter 18, notes 25 and 26.
42. IJ 25.8.74.

CHAPTER 20

1. d, 23.3.75.
2. EL–F, 28.3.75.
3. d, 6.6.75.
4. EL–Mrs Scrivens, 27.7.75.
5. EL–F, 7.5.76, LLEL 195–6.

Notes to the Text

CHAPTER 20 (cont'd)
6. ibid., LLEL 195.
7. The Standard, 14.12.76.
8. d, 17.12.76.
9. Introduction to LLEL by Hubert Congreve, LLEL 23.
10. ibid., LLEL 28–31.
11. d, 27.3.77.
12. d, 2.8.77.
13. HH–EL, 22.8.78. John Rylands Library.
14. EL–F, 28.10.78, LLEL 213.
15. CN vii and viii.
16. EL–F, 12.9.73, LLEL 159.
17. EL–F, 9.7.79, LLEL 218.
18. Recollections of a Happy Life, by Marianne North, vol. II, p. 83.
19. ibid., p. 85.
20. CN 250.
21. EL–Mr Fields, 15.10.79. Henry E. Huntington Library and Art Museum, San Marino.
22. ibid.
23. d, 30.10.79.
24. EL–F, 25.3.84, LLEL 307.

CHAPTER 21

1. EL–ET, 16.2.80.
2. EL–F, 19.5.80.
3. d, 3.7.80.
4. d, 19.7.80.
5. d, 12 and 26.6.80.
6. Preface to LLEL by Hubert Congreve, LLEL 35–6.
7. Quoted in EL–F, 27.6.80.
8. Arthur Stanley to Lear. Quoted EL–F, 22.8.81. LLEL 245.
9. d, 28.10.65. This was not then the insult that unhappily most artists would consider it to be today.
10. EL–HT, 16.9.80.
11. EL–F, 31.8.82. Northbrook had recently given Lear a copy of Turner's Liber Studiorum in auto-type. Lear had himself bought a

CHAPTER 21 (cont'd)
copy in facsimile in July 1863 and in August 1867 he had studied Claude Lorrain's Liber Veritatis.
12. EL–F, 24.10.80.
13. EL–F, 7.6.81, LLEL 241.
14. d, 8.8.81.
15. 'How Pleasant to Know Mr Lear', CN vii.
16. EL–Hubert Congreve, 28.9.81, LLEL 34.
17. Franklin Lushington–Hallam Tennyson, 7.3.88.
18. Introduction to LEL by Constance Strachey, LEL xxxiii.
19. EL–Mrs Stuart Wortley, 26.2.82.
20. EL–F, 10.4.82, LLEL 262.
21. September 1882, OF 95.
22. d, 2.8.82.
23. EL–Laura Coombe, 22.10.82, Victoria & Albert Museum.
24. EL–F, 30.4.85, LLEL 336.
25. d, 31.1.83, OF 96.
26. d, 5.8.82.

CHAPTER 22

1. EL–F, 21.12.84, LLEL 325.
2. EL–F, 8.8.83, LLEL 288.
3. EL–ET, 18.8.83.
4. d, 12.8.83.
5. EL–F, 21.1.84, LLEL 299.
6. EL–F, 5.12.75, LLEL 190.
7. EL–F, 21.10.62.
8. EL–F, 15.3.63, LEL 276–7.
9. EL–F, 27.1.84.
10. EL–Miss Grant, 4.1.85. Houghton Library.
11. d, 28.2.87.
12. EL–Hallam Tennyson, 8.9.85.
13. EL–Hubert Congreve, 1883, LLEL 25.
14. EL–F, 21.1.84, LLEL 298.
15. Carl. diary, 25.12.85. Carl. ms.
16. d, 3.1.79.
17. Carlyle. Richter.
18. Pall Mall Magazine, 15.2.86.

Notes to the Text

CHAPTER 22 (*cont'd*)

19. Franklin Lushington–Hallam Tennyson, 14.11.86.
20. EL–F, 10.12.86.
21. d, 4.4.87.
22. EL–Hallam Tennyson, 27.4.87.
23. Mr Este–Hallam Tennyson, 8.5.87.
24. EL–F, 22.5.87.
25. ibid.
26. Lear buried Foss in his garden and put up a stone claiming that the

CHAPTER 22 (*cont'd*)

cat was 31 years old—in fact he had bought him as a kitten in 1872.
27. Franklin Lushington–Fortescue, 6.2.88. quoted LLEL 362. Lear spoke these last words in Italian.
28. Madame Philipp, widow of Dr Hassall who had attended Lear—. Lady Strachey, 21.1.1911, LLEL 361.
29. Uncle Arly. CN 276.

NOTES TO THE ILLUSTRATIONS

Notes to the Illustrations

Notes to the Illustrations

Notes to the Illustrations

Notes to the Illustrations

BIBLIOGRAPHY

I Works by Edward Lear published in his own lifetime

NONSENSE

A Book of Nonsense, by Derry Down Derry (Edward Lear). Thomas Maclean, 1846.
A Book of Nonsense. Routledge, Warne and Routledge. Second and enlarged edition, 1861.
Nonsense Songs, Stories, Botany and Alphabets. Robert John Bush, 1871.
More Nonsense, Pictures, Rhymes, Botany etc. Robert John Bush, 1872.
Laughable Lyrics. Robert John Bush, 1877.

NATURAL HISTORY

Illustrations of the Family of Psittacidae, or Parrots. Pub. R. Ackermann and E. Lear, 1832.
Gleanings from the Menagerie and Aviary at Knowsley Hall, Knowsley. Privately printed, 1846.
Tortoises, Terrapins and Turtles, drawn from Life by James de Carle Sowerby FLS and Edward Lear. Henry Sotheran, Joseph Baer & Co., 1872.

TOPOGRAPHY & TRAVEL

Views in Rome and its Environs. Thomas Maclean, 1841.
Illustrated Excursions in Italy. First series. Thomas Maclean, 1846.
Illustrated Excursions in Italy. vol. II. Thomas Maclean, 1846.
Journals of a Landscape Painter in Albania &c. Richard Bentley, 1851.
Journals of a Landscape Painter in Southern Calabria, &c. Richard Bentley, 1852.
Views in the Seven Ionian Islands. Pub. Edward Lear, 1863.
Journal of a Landscape Painter in Corsica. Robert John Bush, 1870.

NATURAL HISTORY books to which Lear contributed

Illustrations of British Ornithology, Sir William Jardine, Bt., and Prideaux John Selby. vols. III and IV. 1834.
The Gardens and Menagerie of the Zological Society Delineated, ed. E. T. Bennett. vol. II. 1831.
A Century of Birds from the Himalayan Mountains, J. Gould. 1831.

Bibliography

A Monograph of the Ramphastidae, or Family of Toucans, J. Gould. 1834.
The Transactions of the Zoological Society, vol. I. 1835.
Birds of Europe, J. Gould. 5 vols. 1837.
The Zoology of Captain Beechey's Voyage. 1839.
The Zoology of the Voyage of HMS Beagle, ed. Charles Darwin. 1841.
The Naturalists Library, ed. Sir William Jardine, Bt. vol. IX, Pigeons, and vol. XVIII, Parrots. Henry G. Bohn, 1843.
The Genera of Birds, G. R. Gray, vol. II. 1849.

II Works by Edward Lear published posthumously

MISCELLANEOUS

Poems of Alfred Tennyson, illus. Edward Lear. Boussod, Valadon & Co., 1889.
Lear in Sicily, intro. Granville Proby. Duckworth, 1938.

NONSENSE

Nonsense Songs and Stories, intro. Sir Edward Strachey. Frederick Warne, 1894.
Queery Leary Nonsense, ed. Lady Strachey. Mills & Boon, 1911.
The Lear Coloured Bird Book for Children, foreward J. St. Loe Strachey. Mills & Boon, 1912.
The Complete Nonsense of Edward Lear, ed. Holbrook Jackson. Faber and Faber, 1947.
A Nonsense Alphabet. H.M.S.O., 1952.
Teapots and Quails, ed. Angus Davidson and Philip Hofer. John Murray, 1953.
ABC. Constable Young Books, 1965.

LETTERS

Letters of Edward Lear, ed. Lady Strachey. T. Fisher Unwin, 1907.
Later Letters of Edward Lear, ed. Lady Strachey. T. Fisher Unwin, 1911.

TOPOGRAPHY & TRAVEL

Edward Lear's Journals: A Selection, ed. H. Van Thal. Arthur Barker, 1952.
Edward Lear's Indian Journal, ed. Ray Murphy. Jarrolds, 1953.
Edward Lear in Southern Italy, intro. Peter Quennell. William Kimber, 1964.
Edward Lear in Greece. William Kimber, 1965.
Edward Lear in Corsica. William Kimber, 1966.
Lear's Corfu, intro. Lawrence Durrell. Corfu Travel, Corfu, 1965.

Bibliography

III Books about Edward Lear

OSGOOD FIELD, William B. *Edward Lear on my Shelves.* Privately printed, 1933.

DAVIDSON, Angus. *Edward Lear: Landscape Painter and Nonsense Poet.* John Murray, 1938.

READE, Brian. *Edward Lear's Parrots.* Duckworth, 1949.

HOFER, Philip. *Edward Lear as Landscape Draughtsman.* Oxford University Press, 1968.

IV Selected list for further reference

BARING, Maurice. *Punch and Judy and other Essays.* Heinemann, 1924.

BOWRA, Sir Maurice. *The Romantic Imagination.* Oxford University Press, 1950.

BUTLER, Samuel. *Alps & Sanctuaries of Piedmont and the Canton Ticino.* David Bogne, 1882.

CARROLL, Lewis. *Alice in Wonderland.* 1865.
Alice Through the Looking Glass. 1872.
The Hunting of the Snark. 1876.
Useful and Instructive Poetry. Geoffrey Bles, 1954.

CAMMAERTS, Emile. *The Poetry of Nonsense.* Routledge, 1925.

CHANLER, Mrs Winthrop. *Roman Spring.* Little, Brown & Co., Boston, 1934.

CHARNWOOD, Lady. *An Autograph Collection.* Benn, 1930.
Call Back Yesterday. Eyre and Spottiswoode, 1937

CHESTERTON, G. K. *A Handful of Authors.* Sheed & Ward, 1953.

CREEVEY, T. *The Creevey Papers.* John Murray, 1903.

CROFT-COOKE, Rupert. *Feasting with Panthers.* W. H. Allen, 1967.

DURRELL, Lawrence. *Prospero's Cell.* Faber, 1945.

FRANCILLON, R. E., *Mid-Victorian Memories.* Hodder & Stoughton, 1914.

FRASER, Mrs Hugh. *A Diplomat's Wife in Many Lands.* Hutchinson, 1911.

FRITH, W. *My Autobiography and Reminiscences.* R. Bentley & Son, 1887.

GROSSKURTH, Phyllis. *John Addington Symonds.* Longmans, 1964.

HEWETT, Osbert Wyndham. *Strawberry Fair.* Murray, 1956.
. . . *and Mr. Fortescue*, Murray. 1958.

HUDSON, Derek. *Lewis Carroll.* Constable, 1954.

HUNT, William Holman. *Pre-Raphaelitism and the Pre-Raphaelite Brotherhood.* Macmillan, 1905.

JAEGER, Muriel. *Before Victoria.* Chatto & Windus, 1956.

JONES, Henry Festing. *Samuel Butler.* Macmillan, 1917.

Bibliography

LAMB, Sir Walter R. M. *The Royal Academy*. G. Bell, 1935.

LENNON, Florence Becker. *The Life of Lewis Carroll*. Cassell, 1947.

LENNOX, W. G. *Epilepsy*. Harper, 1941.

LEWIS, S. Jnr. *The History and Topography of the Parish of St. Mary Islington*. J. H. Jackson, 1842.

LONGFORD, Elizabeth. *Victoria R.I.* Weidenfeld & Nicolson, 1966.

LUCAS, F. L. *Tennyson*. The British Council and The National Book League, Longman's Green, 1957.

LUSHINGTON, F. *Wagers of Battle, 1854–1899*. Macmillan, 1900.

LUSHINGTON, H. & F., *Joint Compositions*. 1840(?).
Points of War. Macmillan, Cambridge, 1954.
Two Battle Pieces. Macmillan, Cambridge, 1855.

MAGNALL, R. *Questions*. 1818.

MALLET, B. *Thomas George, Earl of Northbrook*. Longmans Green & Co., 1908.

MALCOLM, Sir Ian. *The Pursuit of Leisure, and other essays*. Ernest Benn, 1929.

MILLAIS, J. G. *The Life and Letters of Sir John Millais*. Methuen, 1899.

NORTH, Marianne. *Recollections of a Happy Life*, ed. Mrs. J. A. Symonds. 2 vols. Macmillan, 1892.

NORWICH, John Julius, Reresby SITWELL, A. COSTA, *Mount Athos*. Hutchinson, 1966.

PROTHERO, Rowland E. *The Life and Correspondence of Arthur Penrhyn Stanley, D.D.* Murray, 1894.

QUENNELL, Peter. *The Singular Preference*. Collins, 1952.

SEDDON, J. P., *Memoirs and Letters of the late Thomas Seddon, Artist*. James Nisbet & Co., 1858.

SEWELL, Elizabeth. *The Field of Nonsense*. Chatto & Windus, 1952.

SHELLEY, Lady Frances. *Diary, 1787–1817*, ed. Richard Edgcumbe. Murray, 1912.

STRACHEY, Sir Edward. *Talk at a Country House*. William Blackwood, 1895.

TENNYSON, Charles. *Alfred Tennyson*. Macmillan, 1949.

TENNYSON, Hallam. *Alfred, Lord Tennyson, A Memoir*. Macmillan, 1897.

WOOLNER, Amy. *Thomas Woolner, R.A.* Chapman & Hall, 1917.

ZETLAND, The Marquess, *The Life of Lord Cromer*. Hodder & Stoughton, 1932.

ACKNOWLEDGMENTS

I would like to extend my warm personal thanks to: Mr Philip Hofer, Dr William Bond and Miss Eleanor Garvey of the Houghton Library, Harvard University, for their kindness and help before, during and after my stay at Harvard; Mr Angus Davidson both for his book, *Edward Lear, Landscape Painter and Nonsense Poet*, and for the help he has given me; Mr and Mrs Michell for the loan of their copy of Lear's letters to his sister Ann, and for family photographs and drawings; William Hornby for his endless trouble; Colonel and Miss Prescott for their hospitality and help; Mr Brian Reade for his help in selecting illustrations for this book; Mrs Burt; Lady Marjorie Gillies for the loan of books and family papers; Professor Richard Harrison; Mr William Carlton for details of the family of Jeremiah Lear of Batsworth Park; the late Dr Edelsten and Mrs Edelsten; Lord Strachie; Mr Lyonson and Mrs Michell at Knowsley; Mr Herbert Cahoon of the Pierpont Morgan Library, New York; Mr John Naimaster, Managing Director, The Fine Art Society, New Bond Street, and Mr Handasyde Buchanan who kindly read the proofs and made some helpful suggestions.

I would also like to thank: Sir Charles Tennyson; Miss Constance-Ann Parker of the Royal Academy Library; Mr Osbert Wyndham Hewett; Susan, Lady Tweedsmuir; Miss Elisabeth Davidson of the Arts Council; Mr Christopher Hollis; Mr Bakhurst, Secretary of the Stock Exchange, London, and Mr Thompson of the Public Assignees Office of the Stock Exchange; Dame Janet Vaughan, and Mrs Russell, Librarian of Somerville College, Oxford; Mr J. R. Cuthbertson, Manager of Drummonds Bank; F. T. Baker of the City of Lincoln Libraries, Museum and Art Gallery; the Rev. A. J. Adams, Vicar of Wanstead Parish Church; Lord Derby; Lord Cromer; Lord Stanley of Alderley; Lord Tennyson; Lord Northbrook; Mr Robert North; Mr Godfrey Lushington and Mrs Marie Fowler; Major G. G. W. Horton-Fawkes; Mr F. D. Martineau; Lady Mander; Colonel G. Phipps Hornby; Major Sir Richard Proby; Miss Ingrid Barr; Miss Rebecca Hornby; Miss Ann Horton; Mr Hugh Bedford; Mr Roger Musgrave; Mr. John Witt; Miss Elizabeth S. Henry, of the Worcester Art Museum, Worcester, Mass.; Messrs Walker Martineau; Mr Jack Baer; Mr Philip Spink; Messrs Thomas Agnew & Sons; Messrs Christie, Manson & Woods; and Messrs Sotheby & Co.

The staff of the following also kindly helped me: Somerset Record Office, Taunton; The Tennyson Research Centre, Lincoln; The John Rylands Library, Manchester; the Linnaean Society; The Zoological Society of London; the Chamberlain's Court, Guildhall; the Guildhall Library; the Department of Literary Enquiry, Principal Probate Registry, Somerset House; the Public Record Office; the Bodleian Library; Reigate Public Library; the Reading

Acknowledgments

Room of the British Museum; the Victoria and Albert Museum; and the New York Public Library.

For quotations from Queen Victoria's diary I am indebted to the gracious permission of Her Majesty the Queen.

For permission to quote from unpublished work or to reproduce drawings and paintings I would like to thank: Harvard College Library; Lord Strachie; Mr William Hornby; Colonel Prescott; Mr Michell; Sir Charles Tennyson; Mrs Cuthbert and Mrs Burt; Susan, Lady Tweedsmuir; Lord Aberdare; Trinity College Library, Cambridge; and the trustees of the following: the Pierpont Morgan Library, New York; the Henry E. Huntington Library and Art Gallery, San Marino, California; the National Library of Scotland; the John Rylands Library, Manchester.

For permission to quote from published works I wish to thank: John Murray, from *Edward Lear* by Angus Davidson; *The Diary of Frances, Lady Shelley*; *The Creevey Papers*; The British Council from *Tennyson* by F. L. Lucas; Macmillan from *Recollections of a Happy Life* by Marianne North; *Alfred Tennyson* by Sir Charles Tennyson; Chapman & Hall from *Thomas Woolner* by Amy Woolner; George Rainbird Limited, and Harper & Row, Publishers, Inc., from *Mount Athos* by John Julius Norwich, Reresby Sitwell and A. Costa; Mrs Edward Pickmann from *Roman Spring* by Mrs Winthrop Chanler; Oxford University Press from *Early Victorian England*, and Jane Austen, *Minor Works* (ed. R. W. Chapman); *The Observer* and Dr E. T. Hanrahan; Gerald Duckworth & Co. Ltd. from *Edward Lear's Parrots* by Brian Reade.

Finally, I would like to extend my particular personal thanks to: Jonathan Field; Mrs Caroline da Costa; Mrs Judi Morris; Mrs Shione Carden; Mrs Patsie Gritton; the Warden and staff of St Deiniol's Library, Hawarden; the staff of Oatlands Park Hotel, Weybridge; Miss Sheila Watson; Adrian House of Collins; and above and beyond all to my husband, Michael Noakes, both for his professional advice as a painter, and for his encouragement, enthusiasm and support without which I would neither have begun nor completed this book.

INDEX

Index

Index

Index

Index

Index

Index

Index

357

Index

Milan

Venice

Trieste

Spezia

Ravenna

San Remo

Florence

ITALY

Corsica

Abruzzi

Rome

Adriatic Sea

Sardinia

Monastir

Naples

Salo

Brindisi

Dukadhes

GREECE

Corfu

Calabria

Thermopyla

Messina

Ithaca

Marsala

Palermo

Reggio

Cephalonia

Patras

Mt. Etna

Argos

Zante

Syracuse

Bassa

Sicily

Gozo

Malta

M E D I T E R R

LIBY

0   100   200   300   400 M